# Depicting Deity

# Depicting Deity

## *A Metatheological Approach*

JONATHAN L. KVANVIG

# OXFORD
## UNIVERSITY PRESS

Great Clarendon Street, Oxford, OX2 6DP,
United Kingdom

Oxford University Press is a department of the University of Oxford.
It furthers the University's objective of excellence in research, scholarship,
and education by publishing worldwide. Oxford is a registered trade mark of
Oxford University Press in the UK and in certain other countries

© Jonathan L. Kvanvig 2021

The moral rights of the author have been asserted

First Edition published in 2021

Impression: 1

All rights reserved. No part of this publication may be reproduced, stored in
a retrieval system, or transmitted, in any form or by any means, without the
prior permission in writing of Oxford University Press, or as expressly permitted
by law, by licence or under terms agreed with the appropriate reprographics
rights organization. Enquiries concerning reproduction outside the scope of the
above should be sent to the Rights Department, Oxford University Press, at the
address above

You must not circulate this work in any other form
and you must impose this same condition on any acquirer

Published in the United States of America by Oxford University Press
198 Madison Avenue, New York, NY 10016, United States of America

British Library Cataloguing in Publication Data
Data available

Library of Congress Control Number: 2021939016

ISBN 978-0-19-289645-2

DOI: 10.1093/oso/9780192896452.001.0001

Printed and bound in the UK by
TJ Books Limited

Links to third party websites are provided by Oxford in good faith and
for information only. Oxford disclaims any responsibility for the materials
contained in any third party website referenced in this work.

# Preface

Theorizing about the nature of God is perhaps the riskiest of all intellectual endeavors. For, on the assumption that theism is true, the object of inquiry is most certainly as far from the reach of our comprehension as anything could be. Moreover, on the assumption that theism isn't true, the risk is that of tilting at windmills, engaging in such a waste of time and effort that even full enjoyment of such brings to mind images associated with the myth of Sisyphus.

The crucial question is whether there is a reason to engage, in spite of the risk. For some, such as I, there is hardly a choice: the project is inescapable. For others, the task will seem more optional, and my apology for it is conditionally this. If you find theism no longer a serious option, the task is not worthy of your pursuit. For the rest of us, no task could be more important, for it is intimately connected with questions about the good life considered in its totality, including matters concerning eternal destiny and the hope of salvation. So, even if we stumble blindly as we make our way, we still try because the issue matters.

Once we begin the project, issues of structural organization come first in trying to answer the question of what God is like. In this way, this issue is like other important philosophical questions, for we rarely have an idea of how to start thinking about them. Some approaches begin with a list of things thought to be defensible concerning the nature of God, perhaps accompanied by some indication of the source of epistemic propriety for items on the list, thereby beginning the task of constructing a full theology. The history of Christian thought is replete with examples of such, but these approaches bypass the more fundamental question which is the focus of this work. Moreover, by starting further down the road than with questions concerning the fundamental nature of God, they risk presupposing stances that do not withstand scrutiny and perhaps would never have been endorsed if considered directly. In addition, approaches that ignore the issue of fundamentality often switch from one set of assumptions to another without noticing the change in perspective that results, giving rise to a chance of incoherence and to an approach that is theoretically suspect. So here we will begin with the more basic question of where to begin thinking about God, where it is best to start the project of theology, in a way that offers some hope of a defensible theory. The task is thus metatheological:

an investigation into the kinds of approaches one might take in developing a theology.

We can get a better sense of what falls within the domain of metatheology by analogy with metaethics. As Geoff Sayre-McCord (2014) puts it, "Metaethics is the attempt to understand the metaphysical, epistemological, semantic, and psychological,[1] presuppositions and commitments of moral thought, talk, and practice." Metaethics is thus an attempt to address fundamental questions about the nature of morality, questions that arise in an important sense prior to the development and articulation of a moral theory itself. Such questions in the early part of the twentieth century were first addressed in semantic and psychological terms, looking for proper linguistic or conceptual analyses of moral thought and talk.[2] But the more metaphysical and epistemological underpinnings of morality were not being ignored in the process. Instead, the particular conception of philosophical methodology encoded in the linguistic turn made such linguistic and conceptual discussions the right way to address these questions. Philosophical investigation no longer supposes that metaphysical and epistemological discussions should proceed in terms of inquiry into the meaning of terms and concepts, and once we drop that assumption, we can get a clearer picture of the broad range of issues that fall within the scope of metaethics, and also are in a position to learn by analogy something concerning the domain of metatheology.

The relationship between ethical theory and metaethics is itself a controversial issue, with some claiming that the two need have nothing much to do with each other.[3] Such independence, however, is difficult to sustain. Instead, what is central to the distinction between ethics and metaethics is that the latter involves a stepping back or abstracting away from the dialogues, discussions, and disputes found in ethics to address more fundamental questions about the nature of morality.

Much the same is true for metatheology and the distinction between it and theology. It involves a stepping back or abstracting away from the discussions, dialogues, and disputes found in theological inquiry and asks fundamental questions about the nature of divinity and hence about how any approach to theological inquiry is to be grounded. The particular aspect of this enterprise that I pursue here is the metaphysical question of fundamentality: what is the

---

[1] I leave this fourth comma, unnecessary as it is, because it is in the original.
[2] The first use of the term 'meta-ethical' relevant to such investigations is in Edel (1942).
[3] See, for example, Stevenson (1937).

fundamental nature of God, and when theorizing about God (i.e., constructing a theology), where does the explanatory structure bottom out?

Other metaissues will be ignored here. In particular, the epistemological issues arising from apparently irresolvable disagreements about morality and religion we will bypass. These issues, to some, threaten the relevance of the notions of truth and justification for ethics and theology, but it is worth noting that going meta on such issues provides no safe haven, for going meta just lands one squarely within philosophy, a context noteworthy for the presence of irresolvable disagreements.

Another set of issues will be bypassed as well, those issues that concern the semantic and conceptual elements involved in religious thought and talk. If one's preferred philosophical methodology requires addressing metaphysical issues through semantic or conceptual lens—as already noted, a common assumption in the early part of the twentieth century—one could not engage the topic of interest here while bypassing the psychosemantical issues that have been central to much of metaethics. For reasons tracing historically to Kripke's seminal work in *Naming and Necessity*,[4] we have learned that issues of meaning and issues of metaphysics must be kept distinct, and our interest here in metaphysical matters thus can be direct, ignoring any circuitous path through the topics of meaning and cognitive significance.

Other issues in metaethics will have analogues in metatheology that we will come up at various points, though we will not be focusing directly on them. One example is about moral judgment itself, whether such things are intrinsically or extrinsically motivating. If, for example, I judge that child abuse is horrific (which I do) and am motivated to do what I can to prevent it (which I am), am I so motivated by the judgment itself, or only insofar as I desire or prefer that no such incidents occur? In the context of metatheology, a similar issue can arise, given a connection between something's being God and being an individual regarding whom worship is binding in some sense. So when Moses confronts the burning bush and judges that he is in the presence of God, his behavioral response may have involved an attitude of worship.[5] Here, too, we might ask whether a response of worship results from the judgment itself or indirectly through some desire or preference to show honor and reverence for God. Such issues will find a minor place in our discussion and so are a bit different from the ones mentioned above which will be ignored here. At the

---

[4] Kripke (1980).
[5] The text in Exodus 3 doesn't say this, but only reports that Moses hid his face, afraid to look. So it reports a fear response, and the response may have been nothing more than that. Perhaps, though, the hiding of the face was also an act of submission of the sort that is an aspect of worship.

same time, though, questions about the links between judgment and behavior are ancillary to our main metaphysical project.

In recent times, the dominant metatheology has been Perfect Being Theology (PBT), the position associated with Anselm and his strategy of conceiving of God in a way that might culminate in a successful ontological argument for God's existence. Though there are earlier endorsements of the idea of God's perfection in the Hebrew Bible, Plato, some of the Stoics, Augustine, and Boethius,[6] the metatheology of PBT finds its source in Anselm's identification of God as "that than which a greater cannot be thought."[7]

One can view this source as arising late enough in the history of Christian thought to find the dominance of this perspective perplexing. Ancient and venerable sources seem to start elsewhere, with a conception of God as the creator and sustainer of the universe, and the ubiquity of religious practices centering on the worship of God do not point in the first instance to PBT, even if they end up there. Moreover, there is a strong suspicion in the history of theology of the ontological argument, the central hope of PBT, in favor of cosmological and teleological arguments, leading one to wonder why the Anselmianism of PBT should be endorsed by those suspicious of its intended target. We thus find historical considerations for questioning the philosophical hegemony of PBT in recent history, including at least the past half-century.

If we begin to look for alternatives, the remarks in the last paragraph give us some ideas to pursue. Among the most obvious alternatives to PBT are conceptions of God which make use of one of the other two descriptions of God noted in the previous paragraph. In brief, I will label these approaches "Creator-Theology" and "Worship-Worthy Being-Theology" (or, for short, "Worship-Worthiness Theology"). Using abbreviation, we thus have three initial positions to consider: CT, PBT, and WWT. To assume one of these three standpoints is to assume that one of these three is fundamental to an adequate account of the nature of God, and that what is valuable in the other approaches can be derived from what is fundamental.

We thus have two central generic issues to comment on before proceeding, for this description adverts to the notion of fundamentality and to the idea of derivability. I will postpone a discussion of fundamentality to subsequent substantive chapters, but a word or two about the notion of derivation can be dealt with here. The notion of derivation lies at the intersection of logic and epistemology, where the notions of inferential support and implication

---

[6] For discussion and defense, see Leftow (2006) and Nagasawa (2017).
[7] Anselm (1965[1078]).

connect. Clarifying the notion of derivability thus requires addressing two distinct issues, one the holistic issue of the conditions under which a given belief or system of beliefs is supported, confirmed, or implicated by a given total system of information, and the other an atomistic issue about when one has a reason for a given claim, a basis for inferring it, or some degree of confirmation for it.[8] If we begin with the atomistic realm,[9] we find two important forms of derivability—monotonic and non-monotonic—but both are defeasible by further learning. Monotonic implications continue to hold no matter what additional information is added and thus are not subject to defeat by rebutters, where a rebutter is information that is evidence against the truth of the conclusion. Instead, monotonic reasoning is subject to defeat only by undercutters, where an undercutter challenges the supports relation between premises and conclusion. Non-monotonic derivability is subject to rebutting defeaters, leaving open the possibility that additional premises will undermine the confirmation relation between premises and conclusion (though not affecting the confirmation relation between the original premises alone and that conclusion).[10] The important point to note here is that when speaking of derivations for a given metatheology, we are not claiming that the arguments offered have to be deductively valid ones. Such a requirement is too restrictive, since it would limit the kind of derivability in question to the monotonic sort. What we seek is a way of supporting a given conclusion from an assumed starting point that will allow that metatheology to endorse that conclusion, provided the derivation remains undefeated. The standard description of such derivability uses the notion of *pro tanto* support for a given conclusion,[11] and I will follow this practice here, appealing to such language as a reminder that the language of derivability should not interpreted so restrictively that only a deductively valid argument can be adequate.

Returning to our main competitors, then, we have CT, PBT, and WWT to consider. Perhaps, though, these possibilities will not succeed, and so we need at least a placeholder for alternatives to these three. I will call this point

---

[8] For elaboration and defense, see Kvanvig (2019b).

[9] For a defense of the idea that such a start is the right approach, see Kvanvig (2019b) and Kvanvig (2021).

[10] For further explanation of these types of defeaters, see Kvanvig (2014, chapters 1 and 2). For early work on defeasibility in epistemology, see Chisholm (1948) and Chisholm (1957). For the distinction between rebutters and undercutters, see Pollock (1974) and Pollock (2001).

[11] In epistemology especially (though the practice has its source in Ross (1930)), *pro tanto* support is often indicated using the language of *prima facie* support. For the reasons given in Kagan (1989), the conflation is unfortunate. Anything *prima facie* is something that appears present at first glance, whereas a *pro tanto* reason doesn't disappear on closer inspection, but is determinative of rational status unless overridden in some way by further information, and the relation doesn't disappear when such further information undermines, but instead simply ceases to be determinative of rational status.

"metatheological anti-fundamentalism" (MAF). According to MAF, none of the three approaches can be successful in generating a defensible theology. MAF thus points to the need for something else, whether a different fundamental starting point or some agglomerative effort incorporating elements from more than one starting point. MAF thus includes a manifold of options, ranging from the most minimal versions, versions which simply conjoin two of the more basic approaches, to wildly extravagant claims that flatten the metaphysical territory completely, urging that no features of God are any more primitive, basic, or fundamental than any others.[12]

We can get to this way of thinking about the space of options through a variety of routes. We might approach the question of the nature of God epistemologically, wondering how we might find out that God exists and what such a journey would teach us about the nature of God. We might also approach the issue psychosemantically, asking what our conception of God involves or what part of our conception gives us the meaning of the term 'God' (and its translational equivalents in other languages).

As this investigation proceeds, it will become clear how and why I avoid these approaches in favor of a metaphysical strategy, asking what aspects of our conception of God could generate the best metaphysical account of the nature of God. The guiding principle will be to hew carefully in light of this metaphysical focus, in part because, as we shall see, the metatheological literature has rarely been careful in this respect. Others are free, of course, to approach the task of metatheology in whatever way they think is appropriate, but the justification for the metaphysical approach taken here is its fittingness for the task. The question of the nature of God is obviously a metaphysical, rather than an epistemological or semantic, question; so, the way to investigate it best is to treat the inquiry as metaphysical.

In part I of this work, then, I begin the project by first explaining the motivation and justification for focusing on these four proposals. I then offer a preliminary investigation into what I will call "the common ground" that needs to be respect by any metatheology, in terms of the standards or conditions of adequacy on which all proposals are to be evaluated. The discussion is preliminary and partial, since it is aimed only at the task of setting initial parameters that each approach needs (at least *pro tanto* to aspire to satisfy). After this backdrop is in place, we will be in a position to evaluate each position to see how it might be developed and what its strengths and weaknesses are.

---

[12] On the distinction between flat and non-flat ontologies, see Schaffer (2009).

The order I have chosen for Part II is to start with CT, move on to PBT, and then to WWT. I order things in this way for several reasons. First, I am sensitive to the possibility that the God of the philosophers might not be the God of any of the sacred writings in the Abrahamic tradition, and so I want to begin with a metatheology more attuned to religious traditions than Anselmianism is. CT provides such a metatheology, one that fits well with religions of the Abrahamic tradition but also with Hinduism and perhaps some versions of other religious traditions emanating from the *Vedas*.[13] Moreover, this more ancient tradition is typically misunderstood, since typical discussions treat its content in terms of what conception of God can be sustained by teleological and cosmological arguments for the existence of God. We will return to this point in detail later, but even given the brief discussion so far, suspicions should arise that such approaches confuse metaphysics and epistemology, and we will see that these suspicions are warranted. Finally, the order signals an argumentative arc, for in seeing where CT and PBT fall short, we will be in a better position to appreciate the least explored of the three, WWT. If the arguments are persuasive, the reader will come to view the last half-century of philosophical theology as misguided, seeing WWT as much more promising than PBT, with the only question being whether MAF has to be endorsed because WWT must be supplemented by CT to be adequate. As we will see, that is the ultimate conclusion.

---

[13] Since the focus of this work is on the nature of God and the metatheologies for generating theories about God, rather than on religion and religous traditions, I ignore here the hard questions of what religion is and what individuates one religion from another.

# Contents

## PART I. INTRODUCTION

1. The Major Positions — 3
   1.1 Introduction — 3
   1.2 Perfect Being Theology (PBT) — 6
   1.3 Creator Theology (CT) — 8
   1.4 Worship-Worthiness Theology (WWT) — 19
      1.4.1 Leftow's Derivation of Personhood — 21
      1.4.2 Leftow's Characterization of Worship — 25
      1.4.3 Worthiness and the Uniqueness Challenge — 27
      1.4.4 Fundamentality and Worship-Worthiness — 31
   1.5 Conclusion — 34

2. Categorizing Metatheologies — 35
   2.1 Introduction — 35
   2.2 The Wider Logical Space — 35
   2.3 Theologies and Metatheologies — 38
   2.4 Alternative Category Systems — 42
   2.5 Conclusion — 45

3. Initial Desiderata on Metatheology — 46
   3.1 Introduction — 46
   3.2 Semantics and Metaphysics — 47
   3.3 Monotheism and Personhood — 56
   3.4 The Question of Embodiment — 61
   3.5 Conclusion — 69

## PART II. THE SHARED GROUND

4. Creator Theology and the Shared Ground — 73
   4.1 Introduction — 73
   4.2 Monotheism — 73
   4.3 Personhood — 79
   4.4 Embodiment — 91
   4.5 Conclusion — 94

5. Shaky Ground for Anselmianism — 95
   5.1 Introduction — 95
   5.2 Creator Theology and Contingency — 95

| | | |
|---|---|---|
| 5.3 | The Metatheology of Perfection in Being | 99 |
| 5.4 | Creator Theology and the Problems of Contingency and Profligacy | 106 |
| 5.5 | Conclusion | 108 |

6. The Shared Ground Prospects for Worship-Worthiness Theology   109

| | | |
|---|---|---|
| 6.1 | Introduction | 109 |
| 6.2 | Monotheism | 109 |
| 6.3 | Personhood | 112 |
| 6.4 | Embodiment | 115 |
| 6.5 | Conclusion | 116 |

## PART III. TOWARD COMPETING STARTING POINTS

7. Creator Theology's Disadvantages   119

| | | |
|---|---|---|
| 7.1 | Introduction | 119 |
| 7.2 | From Creator Theology toward Worship-Worthiness | 119 |
| 7.3 | From Creator Theology toward Perfection | 130 |
| 7.4 | Conclusion | 142 |

8. Perfect Being Theology's Difficulties   143

| | | |
|---|---|---|
| 8.1 | Introduction | 143 |
| 8.2 | From Perfection in Being to Sourcehood | 143 |
| 8.3 | From Perfection in Being to Worship-Worthiness | 148 |
| 8.4 | Conclusion | 159 |

9. Worship-Worthiness and Its Drawbacks   161

| | | |
|---|---|---|
| 9.1 | Introduction | 161 |
| 9.2 | From a Worship-Worthy Being to a Perfect Being | 162 |
| 9.3 | From Worship-Worthiness to Sourcehood | 174 |
| 9.4 | Conclusion | 181 |

## PART IV. CONCLUDING PARAMETERS

10. Theological Systems and Their Derivations   185

| | | |
|---|---|---|
| 10.1 | Introduction | 185 |
| 10.2 | Summary | 185 |
| 10.3 | Theological systems | 188 |
| 10.4 | Issues of Derivability | 190 |
| 10.5 | Metatheological Resources | 193 |
| 10.6 | Conclusion | 197 |

11. Conclusion   199

*Bibliography*   205
*Index*   219

# PART I
# INTRODUCTION

# 1
# The Major Positions

## 1.1 Introduction

What is God like? How can we properly portray, interpret, represent, elucidate, characterize, or limn the divine nature? That is the central question of theology, and here I undertake to explore ways in which the project of theology might begin. The task I set is thus metatheological: an investigation into the kinds of approaches one might take in developing a theology, an investigation into the proper starting point for characterizing the nature of God.

It is worth noting that I rely on a bevy of verbs to describe the task, some more suggestive of invention on the part of the theologian and others more suggestive of discovery. No matter how confident one is about our capacity to uncover the fundamental nature of the universe, no one should have near so much confidence about our capacities in the realm of theology. From mysticism to apophaticism, we must heed warnings of our limitations in this area that go well beyond whatever attractions one has for skepticism more generally. In what follows, we will pursue vigorously the project identified, in a way that may strike some as presumptuous about these capacities. It is important, however, to distinguish the project envisioned from our reflective stance on appropriate levels of confidence regarding the conclusions reached. I thus begin with this cautionary word, to prevent the impression of such a presumption. We thus pursue the project as best we can, to see what results can be achieved, postponing reflection on our limitations so as not to let the inevitable but perhaps guarded pessimism be an excuse for lack of effort. The world already has more than enough dabblers and dilettantes.

Among the most promising beginnings for such a project are conceptions of God which begin from one of three initial assumptions. In brief, I label these three approaches "Creator Theology", "Perfect Being Theology", and "Worship-Worthiness Theology"; for short, CT, PBT, and WWT, respectively. To assume one of these three standpoints is to assume that one of these three is fundamental to an adequate account of the nature of God, and that what is valuable in the other approaches can be derived from what is fundamental.

An alternative to these three is metatheological anti-fundamentalism (MAF). According to MAF, none of the three approaches can be individually successful in generating a defensible theology. MAF thus maintains that a proper account of the nature of God cannot be derived from any one of the three approaches. Perhaps there is some further option to consider; perhaps what is needed is some combination of the three proposed or a combination of some subset of these three. Perhaps, even, there is no feature of God that is more basic or more fundamental than any other. This last category includes all of these options.

Our metatheology will focus first on the prospects for CT, PBT, WWT, positions described in more detail in §1.2. Such a focus is, however, in need of defense. Why these four, in the vast expanse of the logical space of metatheology? I turn to this issue in §1.3, followed in §1.4 by comparisons with other ways of carving up the logical space, category schemes, where I focus attention on the differences between metaphysical and epistemological approaches, favoring the former. Once completed, we will then be in a position to examine in detail in succeeding chapters the prospects for each of these approaches.

Before proceeding at any length, a qualifier is needed about these approaches, for none of them is a single, definable theory or approach, but rather a family or group of approaches sharing a common theme. We might say that each approach is a model that can be made more specific in a number of different ways. This point is most obvious concerning MAF, since the different possibilities that all deny the plausibility of the other three are manifold. But even for the three primary positions, there are variations to consider. I will signal these complexities as our discussion progresses, explaining the variety and tracing its implications. We will focus on the variations that have the greatest power to generate a complete theology, though wary as well that such versions also carry the greatest risk of being indefensible. For example, one version of PBT claims that God is a perfect being, but a stronger version claims that God is the most perfect possible being. The latter claim is stronger than the former, but because of this power, faces objections not encountered by the weaker claim. This risk is as it should be for our project, for the task of determining the theoretical power of a given starting point is epistemically prior to the question of all-things-considered defensibility of such an approach. For if a given starting point lacks the resources to generate even a moderately impressive theology, there is no special need to waste time asking and addressing the question of what else might be wrong with it.

One way in which an approach could founder further down the road is if its initial starting point cannot withstand scrutiny when it comes to the question of whether that description identifies an essential property of deity. So, for example, if God is actually a perfect being but could fail to be one, PBT is in trouble. Similarly, if God is actually worthy of worship, but only on the basis of contingencies that need not have occurred, WWT will be ultimately indefensible.[1] The justification for this concern is that we are trying to identify the nature of God, not merely some happenstance features, and natures are constituted by or involve essential rather than contingent features of a thing.

There is a way to sidestep this issue, by arguing that the distinction between essential and accidental properties is incoherent. I am skeptical of such an idea, but we need not be sidetracked by such arguments at present. For even if the distinction can't be maintained, there is some distinction in the neighborhood, where some features of a thing are appropriate for characterizing its nature while others are not. That is the lesson of Aristotle's example of understanding what it is to be human in terms of being a rational animal versus a featherless biped. Even if he was wrong about the essentiality of the former description, he wasn't wrong about the first being more appropriate than the second for characterizing the nature of humanity. In what follows, I will assume that the appropriates features to focus on need to be essential properties of deity, and the arguments will be structured around this assumption. I do so because attempted weakenings of the assumption have to introduce some measure that generates a priority ordering among possibilities, discounting some as being too far down to list to undermine an account of the nature of a thing or too high on the list to be tolerated. Articulating any such measure is fraught with difficulty: just look at the history of trying to say what the similarity measure involves for the semantics for counterfactuals.[2] It is a much simpler assumption to insist that no characterization of a nature is adequate unless that characterization is correct for any and every possible instance of that nature.

These points will play out in detail in further discussion, but the central point to re-emphasize before proceeding is that each metatheology is best understood as characterizing a family of theories—a model—rather than as a single theory. Each family will have stronger and weaker members, and membership in the subset of defensible versions of the model will have to explain exactly what makes the characteristics in question appropriate for

---

[1] Such contingent worthiness of worship is defended in Murphy (2017).
[2] For a taste of the complexities as well as some grounds for thinking that there is no one similarity measure up to the task, see Lewis (1979).

6 THE MAJOR POSITIONS

characterizing the nature of God. With these qualifications in mind, we can turn to the task of describing versions of each approach that show the greatest potential for generating a full and complete theology, or at least something approaching it. I turn first to PBT, followed by CT and WWT, respectively.

## 1.2 Perfect Being Theology (PBT)

We will move most quickly through the position of PBT, since it is the one that needs the least in terms of introduction and clarification. For, in philosophical contexts, it is the approach to our question that gives rise to "the God of the philosophers." The slogan for PBT is that in order for anything to be God, that thing must be maximally perfect or "that than which a greater cannot be thought." There are complications that need to be addressed arising from the differences between imaginability, conceivability, logical possibility, and metaphysical possibility, but we need not rule out any of these options at this point. For now, the more general descriptions suffice for identifying the basic metatheology, the approach to philosophical theology that has arguably dominant status in the field, at least since the rise of modal metaphysics after Kripke's seminal work in *Naming and Necessity*.[3] It is thus the staple of philosophical theology of philosophy in the analytic tradition.[4] It is sometimes

---

[3] Given first as lectures at Princeton in 1970, but not published till a decade later as Kripke (1980).

[4] I choose this phrase with care and in opposition to those who can't tell the difference between analytic philosophy and philosophy in the analytic tradition. The right story here, though I won't take the time to defend it, is that analytic philosophy died long ago. The time of its death is controversial, but its beginning is in the early twentieth-century rejection by G. E. Moore of the absolute idealism of Bradley (see especially Moore (1903a); here I oppose Dummett (1993, 1995), though I am not alone in doing so—his characterization of analytic philosophy has become the "whipping boy" of serious work on the history of analytic philosophy (see Preston (2005) for details), and his efforts to make Frege and Brentano into analytic philosophers is a bit too reminiscent of the gross exaggeration that even Plato was an analytic philosopher). Its death occurred at least by the time of the demise of Logical Empiricism and the work of Kripke that made the world safe for metaphysics again. But the wars against it were initially epistemological in the 1950s, with the metaphysicians coming to the battle a bit later: analytic philosophy, though not philosophy in the analytic tradition, was the target of the arguments in Chisholm (1948); Quine (1951); Goodman (1955), and Sellars (1956). (To my mind, the most deadly of the attacks was by Chisholm, even though the work by the grand coherentists is much better known.) By the early 1960s, even Carnap had surrendered, relying now on pragmatic settings for parameters on the notion of confirmation, thereby abandoning the analytic tenet of his earlier work, in search of a "logical and objective" notion of confirmation (see, e.g., Carnap (1962)). The arguments of modal metaphysicians, including Kripke but also Marcus (1961), brought the end of analytic philosophy. It was an era originating in the sense of its participants of something new and different, one that made philosophy of language and philosophy of logic central (though it is a vexed issue how and whether any doctrinal account can do justice to the era while still keeping in place the card-carrying credentials of all of the major figures of the era, including Moore, Russell, Wittgenstein (both early and late), Ryle, Ayer, Carnap, as well as the sub-movements of Logical Positivism, Logical Empiricism, and Ordinary Language Philosophy (all of which have their own vexations when it comes to doctrinal characterizations)), but which ended when the epistemology was untenable and the skepticism about

referred to as "Anselmianism," which I will do so on occasion as well, since the generic characterization of the view is itself Anselm's characterization.

One word of caution is in order about the view, however, for in Katherin Rogers (2000, p. 4) we find the claim that "If... the vast majority of philosophers who attempt to describe God take their own version of the divinity, whatever it may be, to be the best possible, then it could be argued that in a sense almost any philosopher who is talking about God is doing Perfect Being Theology." Her reason for making this claim is found in the following quote:

> To my knowlege it is the case that in all the debates between various conceptions of the nature of God, none of the participants argues for a God who they judge to be *less* than the best. For example, the process theologians who argue against the traditional view that God is eternal and immutable hold that it is neither possible nor desirable that God should be so transcendent. God is best in virtue of being engaged with the created universe and capable of becoming better than He is. *That* God is the best seems taken for granted. What that means is the subject of debate.   Rogers (2000, p. 2)

We must be careful here, though, for PBT is simply not as universal as these remarks might suggest. First, the idea that God is the most perfect being is not the same claim as that God is the greatest metaphysically possible being. The second claim is a modal claim but the first is not. Second, when the issue concerns what is fundamental, the mere fact that a theorist appeals to the idea of a perfect being doesn't show that such perfection in being is taken to be fundamental. It might be fundamental or it might be derived from some other starting point. So it is simply false that "almost any philosopher who is talking about God" is engaged in the project of PBT.[5]

So we must be careful to distinguish the following claims:

I. God's nature is not, fundamentally, that of being the most perfect possible being
II. God is not the most perfect possible being

---

metaphysical indefensible. Its lasting effect is the dominance of philosophy in the analytic tradition, an approach that shares much in common with the revolutionary period from the early twentieth century into the '50s and '60s, but with less anxiety about the threat of metaphysics to empiricism and without any demand for an epistemology depending on logic and meaning alone.

[5] I should also point out that the last sentence of the quote should be resisted. The metaphysical project about the nature of God is not a semantic project, and thus even if we are discussing the question of what it is to be the greatest possible being, we are not talking about what this claim means.

Rogers is correct to note that it is hard to find a philosophical theologian who denies the second claim, but it is the first claim that constitutes PBT. Moreover, the second claim can be false even though the first is true.

Regardless of the precise character of PBT endorsed, it presupposes an objective value theory on which we can identify which properties are great-making, one that does not identify such features in a way relative to any human interests, purposes, needs, intentions, or culture. That is a central difference between kinds and artifacts, as I'll label them. A table is what it is in virtue of its functional relationship to human interests and purposes; a tiger is not.[6] In this respect, the nature of God is characterizable in a way that is more analogous to that of tigers than tables; as I will put it, *deity* forms a kind rather than being artifactual.

Moreover, PBT is committed to there being some combinations of these great-making properties that are maximal; that is, it must deny that there is a never-ending sequence of greater and greater possible beings. I note in passing that PBT so characterized thus does not presuppose monotheism, since the possibility is left open at this stage of there being ties among great-making combinations of properties. This point is important, since the implication of monotheism is not one that should come too easily.

## 1.3 Creator Theology (CT)

Creator Theology, even though the most natural starting point for those for whom biblical literacy was formative, is not nearly as popular in philosophical theology as is Perfect Being Theology. Perhaps this situation is well deserved, but I will argue that it is not. I will show that if we proceed carefully in characterizing the view, the rather facile dismissiveness toward this position can easily be seen to arise from misunderstanding. In particular, I will argue that CT is fundamentally a metaphysical position about the nature of God, as are both PBT and WWT, and that the dismissive attitude toward it results from replacing a properly metaphysical understanding of the view with an epistemological caricature.

I have just claimed that there is a dismissiveness toward CT that is prevalent in philosophical theology and in philosophy of religion more generally, and the reader might want to know the basis for such a judgment. What I'm thinking of

---

[6] Of course, there are those who think otherwise on this point, but it would derail this project in philosophical theology to document the multiple muddles involved in denying what I claim in the text.

here is the general attitude toward thinking of God as a first cause or designer—the general conceptual domain for thinking about God in terms of being the creator or source of the universe—gives us an insipid characterization of God, in comparison with the high and exalted conception of God found when characterizing God as the most perfect possible being. If what we say about God from the perspective of CT derives from cosmological and teleological considerations alone, we find grounds for a limited deity only—one with, at best, impressive but not unlimited power, wisdom, knowledge, and love.

John Stuart Mill articulates just such a position in Mill (1874 [1957]). There are grounds, he holds, for positing a *demiourgos*, an artisan/craftsman for the universe, one of considerable power and knowledge as well as goodness. He notices, however, imperfections in the product, perhaps resulting from a design aimed at the preservation of individuals and species rather than at wellbeing. Such imperfections, Mill holds, provide evidence against any artisan or craftsman of unlimited knowledge, power, and goodness.[7]

Mill did not wish to leave us without hope, however, and he notes that the evidence available is compatible with an artisan/craftsman of limited knowledge and power but also possessing unlimited goodness. He notes that the beneficial effect of hope about such a possibility is "far from trifling" (p. 81). Such hope generates optimism that death is not the end, enhancing our nobler sentiments and efforts at character formation. It also supports a relation of fittingness between our standard of excellence in a person and the adequacy of the provisions needed for realization.

Perhaps this epistemically attenuated attachment to hope, optimism, and the happy thought of divine providence is a bit speculative. I won't pursue the point at any length, but it is a far cry from having epistemic support for these claims to note that these claims are compatible with the available evidence. Perhaps the idea is that the epistemic characterization of a theology of sourcehood or creatorship should be supplemented pragmatically, so that the resulting theology is not merely an epistemic implication of this starting point, but rather an implication that is part epistemic and part pragmatic. This difference will make no difference to the point I will press, which is that

---

[7] I ignore in the text the claim about an evidential connection, but note it here to make clear why it might be questioned. First, the lack of perfection in the expediencies of nature may be questioned, as in Morris (1984), discussed later. Second, even if the expediencies are imperfect, one might argue that this only undermines the claim that such imperfect expediencies are evidence for a perfect being, not that they are evidence against a perfect being. The difference between lack of evidence for and evidence against is a difficult but important issue, though one that we can safely ignore at this point, since the misconceptions about CT that matter don't touch on this issue.

substituting anything else for a metaphysical characterization of the starting point generates a caricature of CT.

The inadequacies of Mill's view are easy to see. As Thomas V. Morris notes,

> But the flaws of the argument should be evident on even a moment's reflection. First of all, efficiency is always relative to a goal or set of intentions. Before you can know whether a person is efficient in what he is doing, you must know what it is he intends to be doing, what his goals and values are governing the activity he is engaged in. In order to be able to derive from the story of evolution the conclusion that if there is a God in charge of the world, he is grossly inefficient, one would have to know all the divine goals and values which would be operative in the creation and governance of a world such as ours. Otherwise, it could well be that given what God's intentions are, he has been perfectly efficient in his control over our universe.
>
> Morris (1984, p. 179)

Morris notes here that Mill's focus on the imperfections of nature's contrivances presupposes an understanding of the artisan's goals, plans, and intentions in order for what is seen to count as an imperfection. Transposed into our context of trying to determine what is fundamental to the nature of God, such a presupposition would render the project circular. For if such a presupposition is present at the very beginnings of CT, then CT cannot be the starting point it pretends to be concerning the nature of God. Instead, it could only play a derivative role after these presupposed and thus more fundamental elements were already in place. Notice as well that this point is not dependent on the particular assessment of the evidence and its significance that defines Mill's account of what can be gleaned about the nature of God from a starting point that seems to endorse a version of CT. Even if he had shown a greater disposition to try to derive a theology more in line with classical theism, the same point could be made: that CT presupposes something more fundamental in order to get off the ground.

This way of thinking about CT deserved to be buried, not praised. Mill's discussion is a paradigm example of what happens when CT is thought of in epistemological rather than metaphysical terms. Since our project is metaphysical, and thus neither semantic nor epistemological, CT should not be characterized in terms of what can be supported by cosmological and teleological considerations. Instead, it should be characterized in metaphysical terms. The central feature involved is that of a creatorship or sourcehood, which I will characterize as follows: according to CT, God is fundamentally the asymmetrical source of all else. This account thus claims that the fundamental nature of God involves aseity and independence from all else.[8] The idea is to start with the characterization of God that is central to CT and see what can be learned about God from that fundamental starting point. The common mistake noted above is to conflate the metaphysical project with an epistemological one. The latter project has us focus on what we can learn about a creator through cosmological and teleological considerations; our project, however, involves the question of what can be derived from the assumption that God is, fundamentally, the asymmetrical source of all else.

Confusing or conflating the epistemological project with the metaphysical one is prevalent enough that further elaboration of the point is worth our time in hopes of avoiding this tendency. We can appreciate the distinction better by noting that Perfect Being Theology doesn't begin, either historically or theoretically, in dependence on the ontological argument. Instead, Perfect Being Theology begins from a fundamental conception of God as a perfect being, and develops a theory about God from that starting point. If theory construction goes as hoped for by defenders of the ontological argument, the theory includes God's necessary existence. This argument arises, however, quite a distance down the road of theory development. To use Plantinga (1974) as an examplar of this approach, the argument must be preceded by an account of great-making properties with intrinsic *maxima*, followed by a search to find a way of include something involving existence on that list. Perhaps it is possible existence, or existence-at-a-world. My preferred approach for explaining the argument is to talk about possible beings that have maximally fragile existence, where any change to a world in which they exist results in a world where they don't exist. The next step is to define durability in terms of the capacity to continue to exist despite changes, with maximal durability implying necessary existence. If all goes well here, we discover that God is not only an omni-being, but also necessarily existent if possible. Notice, however, the metaphysical nature of the project: we start with the perfect being characterization, and derive the ontological argument in the process of characterizing what maximal perfection involves. We don't start with an ontological argument and then try to figure out how exalted or limited a being might be who is necessary if possible.

---

[8] The view is also known as Divine Foundationalism (see Bohn (forthcoming)). I prefer avoiding this terminology for a couple reasons. First, the concept of a divine being and the concept of a deity are not the same, though I realize that there are uses of these terms that are intended to express the same concept. Angels, for example, are divine beings, but are not deities. Second, the term 'Foundationalism' has iconic status in epistemology, and it is confusing to use the same term for a wide variety of positions, as illustrated by the manifold uses of 'Realism'.

I want to insist that we follow the same plan when we characterize CT. We don't start with the question of what arguments can be generated for thinking that there is such a source or creator of all, but instead we begin with the basic conception noted above concerning the asymmetrical source of all else, deriving a theory, a theology, from the metaphysical starting point. Such a project is independent of the epistemological issue of whether and how one might come to know or have reason to believe that the being so described exists. So, what does CT look like, when we refuse to be distracted by the kinds of epistemological and pragmatic elements that lead philosophers such as Mill to a pessimistic assessment of CT?

Creator Theology involves the central claim that fundamental to the nature of God is the dependency of the cosmos on this independent and self-sufficient being, and I use the term "creator" here because of familiarity, even though it can mislead. Talk of a creator can convey the idea of a specific activity at some point in the past when things came into being, but we should not saddle CT with such a claim. Instead, we should think of the view in terms of sourcehood or ontological dependence as our starting point for explaining the nature of CT. The justification for this generalization of the idea of creation is that creation involves the sourcehood of all in God, and even if such dependence actually involved creation in time, we can abstract from the temporal idea to the more general idea of sourcehood, leaving open whether the sourcehood is that of creation in time or something more generic.

As described, this approach has the advantage of including atemporal perspectives about what the dependence in question might involve. The view also makes claims about the scope of such dependence, claiming that, in addition to characterizing God in terms of sourcehood, God is the source of all else. Moreover, if God is the source of all else, we can derive that God is ontologically unique, since nothing else, and no combination of things other than God, has or can have this property. God is thus independent in a way nothing else is. That idea is the idea of aseity, and on the basis of this reasoning, we can make clear exactly what CT involves by characterizing it as the approach that identifies the fundamental nature of God in terms of being the asymmetrical source of all else. That is, everything depends on God and God does not depend on anything at all. That is, God is not only the source of all else, but also God is not sourced in any of the things that fall within the scope of this quantifier. Such a stance thus characterizes God both in terms of sourcehood and aseity: God is different from everything else in virtue of their dependent status on God and God's independent status with respect to all else.

These points follow as well from more general conditions of adequacy on metaphysical explanation. First, metaphysical explanation is asymmetrical: if $x$ explains $y$, then $y$ doesn't explain $x$. So, if God is the source of all else, God is also the asymmetrical source of all else, since there is no thing or combination of things that fails to find its source in God. In addition, metaphysical explanation is irreflexivity of metaphysical explanation: nothing explains itself. This irreflexivity blocks the thought that CT might be open to the idea of God being self-sourced, thus disallowing a formulation of CT on which God is the source of all. We thus reaffirm our basic characterization of CT in terms of God's being the asymmetrical source of all else, thereby displaying the aseity of a being that everything else depends ontologically upon.

This characterization involves a quantifier, and a complete characterization of this starting point for CT requires addressing the scope of this quantifier in order to make clear what CT is claiming when it claims that God is the source of all else. A first issue concerning this quantifier is the difference between "flat" ontologies, such as defended in Quine (1948), with the governing motto being that to be is to be the value of a bound variable, and hierarchical ontologies, where many ordinary things (tables, chairs, mountains, etc.) are claimed not to exist on grounds that these things are not fundamental. Talk of such non-fundamental things is, on these ontologies, to be explained in terms of relations to what is fundamental, often through appeal to some grounding relation.[9] Exactly which entities are counted as fundamental varies by theorist, but the important point to note here is that CT is not to be understood as holding any brief on this issue. It can be combined with either approach to ontology, so no further commentary is needed here, with one exception. Talk of fundamentality and grounding can be taken to the extreme of affirming a version of Monism, according to which there is only one fundamental thing and any sensible talk of other things can be affirmed only in virtue of being grounded in this fundamental thing. Some versions of Monism are eliminativist about everything other than the One, and this version could be a version of CT only trivially. On such a version, the One is identified with God, and God is trivially the source of all else because nothing else falls under the scope of the quantifier.

For those bothered by this possibility, we could amend our account of CT to requiring the sourcing of something distinct from God. I will not do so here, and think it is unwise to do so. Suppose, perhaps *per impossibile*, that there

---

[9] See, for example, Schaffer (2009).

are possibilities in which God does not create and thus in which there is no concrete thing other than God. Such a possibility should not be incompatible with CT, since the heart of CT involves a conditional dependence relation between God and whatever else there is. CT thus maintains that what is ruled out is the idea of something existing independent of God, and that stance is encoded in our characterization of CT. As I see it, this is a virtue of the characterization.

There would still be an explanatory burden faced by a combination of CT with this sort of eliminativist Monism. One wonders how such an eliminative Monism can avoid the charge of fatalism, the view that implies that there is only one possible world. For it appears that if truth supervenes or depends on being[10] and there couldn't be more than the One, then it becomes mysterious, to say the least, how fatalism could be false. If this implication is disastrous for a view (and I take it to be, though won't argue for that claim here), eliminativist Monism has some explaining to do. Perhaps there is hope in the distinction between things and their aspects, so that even if there is only the One, the One could have various combinations of aspects, giving rise to a multiplicity of possibilities of just the sort needed to resist fatalism. This issue, however, isn't one for CT as such, but rather for the eliminativist Monism attached to it, and since this is a work in philosophical theology rather than basic ontology, I'll leave that problem to the side here, only noting its existence and the burden shouldered by endorsing this form of Monism.

The basic issue here is that of the relation of the theories of truth and being, and if we are wont to see truth and being as related in some fundamental metaphysical way—as we should—we must face as well the issues that arise for CT regarding the distinction between necessary and contingent truth. As described above, I was purposely vague enough about CT to allow the reader to focus on the realm of contingency when thinking about the idea of sourcing. As I put it, the entirety of the cosmos finds its source asymmetrically in God. Putting the point this way puts the focus on the cosmos, which is best viewed as a contingent thing or combination of things.[11] Yet, if truth and being are intertwined in some way, it appears that we can deduce the existence of a variety of necessary beings, given the necessities we find in logic and mathematics, and perhaps in vast swaths of philosophy as well, including

---

[10] For defense and explanation of this motto, originating in Bigelow (1988), see Lewis (1994) and Lewis (2001).

[11] For an alternative account on which everything is a necessary being, see Williamson (2013). For discussion and criticism, claiming that Williamson's necessitarianism is (as I would put it) just a version of Meinongianism in sheep's clothing, see Menzel (forthcoming).

metaphysics, epistemology, and the collection of arenas investigating normativity more generally.

The issues here are complex and give rise to a variety of possibilities for theory development under the general rubric of CT. It is not surprising to find historical precedent for embracing versions of nominalism to ward off concerns here. As I use the term here, nominalism retains the links between being and truth, but claims that the necessities in question arise from the realm of contingency alone. In good Aristotelian fashion, the instances of properties and relations are explanatorily prior to the properties and relations themselves, leaving open the possibility of delimiting one's ontology to just those things that are explanatorily basic. Such a view allows a combination of CT and nominalism to explain all such necessity as finding its source in God via the dependence of the entire cosmos on God. The only necessities that escape this explanatory rubric would be necessities about deity itself, and it is fairly easy to see how a defender of CT can unproblematically explain such necessary truths as dependent on being without having to introduce any necessary being into the ontology distinct from God.

An alternative to embracing nominalism here leads to what I see as the beautiful version of CT. This version of CT gives up on the need to defend nominalism from the objections of the realists,[12] and instead embraces a limited Platonism on which all necessities are either about God and sourced in deity itself, or are sourced in the operations of the Divine mind.[13] Technically, such a divine conceptualism need not be a version of Platonism, which I understand to be an ontological thesis committed to the existence of Platonic entities (such as propositions, properties, and relations) used to explain the panoply of necessary truths in logic, mathematics, and philosophy. In combination with particular versions of a hierarchical ontology, ones that refuse to reify aspects of things into things, including ideas in the mind of God, the ontology might contain only deity plus the cosmos if there is one. Such a non-Platonic conceptualism bears the burden of every ontology that wishes to avoid the Quinean dictum that to be is to be the value of a bound variable, for we certainly can quantify over the items that such hierarchical ontologies refuse to reify. Again, however, this issue is one in basic ontology rather than in philosophical theology, so we can note the option for defenders of CT without requiring that CT itself take a stand on these issues at this point in our investigation.

---

[12] An excellent account of these debates is in Loux (1978).
[13] The earliest clear expression of this view can be found in Augustine (1982 [396]).

To summarize about divine conceptualism, then, we have two versions of the beautiful view. One versions is Platonist, embracing the products of the Divine mind as full members of a complete ontology. The other version is deflationary, refusing to reify such aspects or offshoots of the Divine mind, hoping to limit the ontology to God and whatever contingent beings are sourced in God.

All such precisifications of CT have considerable explanatory work to do before laying claim to being a satisfactory version of CT, but our goal at this point doesn't founder because of it. For we aim to provide preliminary understanding of CT, together with some inkling of the variety of options to pursue in developing a complete version of this approach. We can thus notice the opacity and mystery of the claims being made above while avoiding the impetus to turn to full theory development. We will have the opportunity to travel that road in later chapters.

A further issue about the quantifier involved in our characterization of CT concerns whether it should be understood to be unrestricted or restricted quantification. The phenomenon of restricted quantification is well-known and linguistically well-behaved: one can correctly point out that there is nothing in the refrigerator, even though there is a working light bulb inside (not to mention air and shelves). So, one thought might be that we can get different versions of CT depending on what kind of restriction is being used in quantifying over all else.

This issue intersects with the ontology issue just discussed. If one sides with Quine, maintaining that to be is to be the value of a bound variable, it is clear that the quantifier needs to be understood as unrestricted, since leaving out some things when tracing sources to God would not be faithful to the underlying thought and motivation behind CT. Among hierarchialists, however, some treat certain objects as non-fundamental, but existing nonetheless. If such a view were combined with CT, the option is open to treat the quantifier as a restricted one, restricted to the domain of fundamental entities.

I will leave this an open issue at this point, though a couple of remarks about it are in order. First, I want to register a bit of disappointment with such views. If we move to restricted quantifiers, though, the view can begin to look a bit evasive. For example, suppose we endorse the claim that everything necessary is grounded in contingency (other than necessities about the realm of deity itself, which are grounded directly in God). (I'm not claiming this idea is plausible—it's not—but it remains a theoretical option for hierarchialists.) Then, with restricted quantification, one might demur on the demand for an explanation of necessity: no such need, it might be claimed, since CT is only a view about fundamental things.

As I said, I will treat this option as an available one for a defender of CT, even though it disappoints me. For notice that it treats the non-fundamental as indirectly sourced in God simply because it is grounded in something that is directly grounded in God. I find this commitment of the view troubling. To see why, suppose (perhaps *per impossibile*) that God sources all the fundamental contingent things but without realizing what non-fundamentals these basic things give rise to. On the view in question, there is no explanatory concern to be addressed here: the non-fundamentals are sourced in God, albeit indirectly.

Here an analogy in the domain of legal responsibility is helpful. Consider the rather bizarre case of *Palsgraff v. Long Island Railroad Co.* The causal chain runs as follows. A passenger in danger of missing his train leaps toward the train. Two railroad employees try to help, but in conflicting ways (one pushes, one pulls), resulting in the dropping of a suitcase. The suitcase contains fireworks, which go off, causing panic on the platform. In the panic, a set of scales are pushed onto Ms. Palsgraff, who sues the railroad for damages based on the injuries she suffered. The court rejected the claim, plausibly arguing that the lack of foreseeability on the part of the railroad exempted them from legal responsibility for the damages.

Something similar is present in the metatheological context, I suspect. Sourcehood in God should leave no room for the accidental and unintentional, on pain of an obvious inadequacy in one's theology. Beings who bumble their way to a complete cosmos are not good candidates for deity. This point points quite naturally to the virtues of PBT, but a defender of CT need not abandon ship on the basis of this point alone. For there may be a way for CT to argue that God is an agent, and then to embrace the lemma that follows from this point, that agential responsibility is explanatorily prior to responsibility that doesn't involve agents. If so, inquiry into the nature of agential responsibility can advert to the plausible lessons from exotic legal cases, to wit, that awareness and intentionality are central components of agential responsibility.

Further discussion of these issues is certainly needed, and we can leave these issues open at this point, even given the discomfort appropriately experienced with versions of CT that indirect sourcing is fully adequate without further qualification or emendation. The appropriate stance to take, then, is that there is some preference for understanding the quantifier in the slogan "the source of all else" as involving unrestricted quantification. This prefernce is not an inviolable requirement for CT, so long as the restriction on the quantifier maps cleanly onto the ontological distinction between what is fundamental and what is not, and the concerns arising from our discussion of agential responsibility can be adequately addressed in some way or other.

18   THE MAJOR POSITIONS

When first considering CT, it is natural to wonder how the view stands with respect to the possibility of polytheism. Consider, for example, versions of Hinduism that seem to involve such multiplicity (e.g., Brahma, Shiva, Vishnu), but only one creator God (e.g., Brahma).[14] What does CT imply about such perspectives?

CT, strictly speaking, is incompatible with such polytheism. We will pursue this issue further in succeeding chapters, but it will be useful here to note that if there are multiple deities and only one of them is the creator, that shows that CT is not the appropriate metatheology for understanding the nature of deity. Instead, there is some other feature of the multiplicity in virtue of which it is correct to count each member of the multiplicity as God. Such versions of polytheism must look to another metatheology for inspiration.

All hope is not lost for CT here, however, for it is easy to confuse the idea of multiple deities with the idea of multiplicity with the realm of the divine. A defender of CT has as a conceptual resource the distinction between God and the gods, where the latter is understood in terms of the concept of a divine being, rather than that of a deity. Moreover, there is a clear need for a distinction between the concept of a deity and the concept of a divine being, especially when considering religious perspectives that countenance the idea of things in the created order becoming gods. Such language motivates just the kind of maneuver that CT will need if it is to have an adequate response to certain versions of polytheism, for the idea of created things becoming gods should not be understood to imply polytheism, all by itself. A bit more subtlety connecting ordinary language with philosophical theory is needed, and once in place, eliminating CT from the competition on the basis of such considerations would be premature.

One final issue to note here is the question of the modal strength of the connection between being such a source and being God. Since the metatheological project is that of identifying what is fundamental to the nature of God, we cannot restrict metatheologies to contingent connections between God and what the metatheology claims is fundamental. At least, we cannot do so without considerable spadework in basic metaphysics to explain how to talk sensibly about fundamental natures without endorsing the necessity of what we conclude. So, in each case, we take the fundamentality point to imply that what is claimed to be fundamental is an essential property of God,

---

[14] I note that there may be no such version of Hinduism, but only the appearance of such. For it is possible that, wherever multiplicity is described, it is a multiplicity only at the level of appearance and not at the level of reality.

one that metaphysically cannot be absent and yet God exist.[15] Such a position does not require that God is a metaphysically necessary being, though some metatheologies claim to be able to demonstrate this conclusion (think here of PBT and the ontological argument), but that conclusion is something to be shown rather than something internal to the beginning point for each metatheology.

## 1.4 Worship-Worthiness Theology (WWT)

Perhaps the least explored approach is that of WWT, which claims that what is fundamental concerning the nature of God is that God is worthy of worship. Part of the reason, I am convinced, is that there is very little clarity on the structural issues we are here addressing. It is not because the connection between worship and deity has gone unnoticed, but even when it is noticed, it is brought up to be dismissed in favor of other ideas. Consider, for example, what Ninian Smart says about the relationship: He writes,

> One hypothesis is that typically what is worshipped is a god or God. The hypothesis of course raises the question of criteria—what counts as a god or God? It would not of course do to suppose that a god is a being who is worshipped (though this is tempting), for then the hypothesis collapses into an analytic truth.    Smart (1972, p. 3)

Smart notes that it is tempting to identify deities with objects of worship, but in the context of his discussion, he worries that the hypothesis at the beginning of the quote then becomes an analytic claim. This concern is a confusion, since there is no reason to assume that an account of the nature of God has to be true in virtue of the meanings of the terms. But my interest in the quote is not in the confusion between analyticity and necessity that it displays, but the temptation Smart notes. The remark is a bit incautious, since it fails to account for the possibility of an unworshipped deity, but the emendation needed to avoid this result is obvious. Perhaps a deity is an appropriate object of worship. Smart's temptation would still remain under this modification, I suspect.

---

[15] Here I will ignore positions that claim there aren't and couldn't be any such essential properties. If that view is correct, modification of our project would be required, but in that direction lie dragons. The argument against essentialism is Quine (1953b), but that argument is clearly fallacious, as is argued by, e.g., Plantinga (1974). The argument, in essence, commits a scope fallacy. How to proceed responsibly under the assumption that some other, better argument might be forthcoming, is, I submit, beyond any sensible requirement.

In order to pursue this idea further, we need clear understandings of the nature of worship itself and what kind of worthiness is envisioned. I begin with the issue of the nature of worship.

One task for any metatheology is to see what that approach can tell us about the nature of God if adopted, and though there is little literature on the issue of the nature of worship, Brian Leftow has claimed that the nature of worship involves elements that require that God is a person. If correct, his view would be helpful in a couple respects: first, it would show something of the theoretical power of WWT to be able to derive from it that God is a person, and second, we would learn something about the nature of worship from an argument that derives personhood from the nature of worship itself. Here is what Leftow claims about worship:

> I make only two claims about what worship is, both obvious given actual religious practice. One is that worship is a form of address: when we worship, we *say things to* what we worship.... The point of the practice is for these words to be heard and understood. The other is that worship always involves praising, at some point. Practice makes this clear, but it's even part of the word's etymology: it is from the Anglo-Saxon worth-ship, the proclaiming of worth. So if something is to deserve worship, it must deserve praise, at least in some respect.   Leftow (2016, p. 71)

Leftow intends to use these features of worship to show that God must be a person. Notice that the second point won't by itself sustain such an inference: praising a thing isn't inappropriate merely because the thing in question is not a person. We praise animals, we praise the government (though hardly ever), we praise universities and corporations and beautiful gardens. None of this is inappropriate, so the second point can't get us to the conclusion that worship implies personhood.

The first point shows more promise, however, and it is the point Leftow relies on. If worship is a form of address, it answers to the general normative features that govern communication. Leftow focuses on linguistic communication, but the point can be made without limiting communication to speech acts: one can communicate by a downcasting of the eyes in addition to saying something. What is important, according to Leftow, is that such communicative acts can't be forms of address unless the practice involves, in some way or other, the idea that the information communicated be heard and understood.

Those attracted to this account will want to amend it slightly, however, for Leftow holds that worship involves *saying things*, and that claim is more restrictive than is needed. Instead, this approach need only claim that worship may involve communicative acts, but need not involve speech at all. Even so, if worship involves such communicative acts, such actions involve intentions or aims or plans or goals for a message to be received by a hearer, and hearers are persons, given our minimal understanding of a person as involving mind and will.[16]

### 1.4.1 Leftow's Derivation of Personhood

A first complication for Leftow's derivation of personhood from the concept of worship arises when we attend to the kinds of things toward which worship is directed. As Smart notices, some people worship money and others their stomachs Smart (1972, p. 3); lovers are sometimes said to worship the ground their beloved walks on; and idols are worshiped, as are heroes, sacred cows, saints, and religious relics.

There is a line of defense for Leftow's derivation to be considered, before one rejects the argument on the basis of these simple examples. The line of defense argues that the apparent counterexamples are examples in which the language of worship is used metaphorically, and hence no counterexample to claims about what worship literally involves.

It is probably true that the language of worship is being used metaphorically in some of the examples above, especially if we combine the examples with Leftow's claim that worship entails personhood, since taking the examples literally would require positing some act of deification on the part of worshipers. But when we say that some worship money or their stomachs, we imply no such deification. Moreover, even apart from the point about deification, these examples seem best understood to involve a metaphorical use of 'worship'. The same is true about lovers worshiping the ground their beloved walks on, a claim somewhere in the conceptual neighborhood that is the overlap of synecdoche and metonymy. So, perhaps what looked like counterexamples to Leftow's claims about worship turn out to be no such thing, once we attend carefully to the literal/metaphorical distinction.

Resistance to my inclinations here will come from religious concerns, with the idea being that mere metaphorical truth isn't serious enough to capture the seriousness of important sacred texts. Consider, for example, Jesus's remark

---

[16] As will be obvious to those well versed in the work of H. P. Grice, the basic idea here is found in Grice's theory of communication articulated in Grice (1968).

that you cannot serve two masters, so you must choose between God and mammon. And when St. Paul counsels followers of Jesus "to offer your bodies as a living sacrifice ... this is your true and proper worship," much Christian devotional thought takes flight from this passage to the conclusion that, for a Christian, all of one's life should be an act of worship. The idea, I think, is to take the Pauline remark literally and derive from it a devotional thought, which is metaphorical, but serious, important, and true nonetheless.

Once we see things in this light, the objection from important religious texts loses much of its force. For we should resist the temptation to draw the literal/metaphorical distinction on the basis of whether or not the point being made is serious: some of the most important ideas in life we find hard to put into language except through the use of metaphors.

Returning then to Leftow's argument, the appeal to metaphor can help avoid some of the obvious counterexamples to his derivation of personhood from worship, and there is no ground for rejecting the appeal to metaphor simply because of the importance of certain remarks about worship that would thus need to be treated metaphorically. To sustain this response to the examples, it would be nice to find support from a careful articulation of how to determine whether a bit of language is to be understood as a figure of speech of some sort or is to be taken as literal.[17] Drawing the distinction is, however, a perplexing matter.[18] There are clear cases where a non-literal meaning is obvious (e.g., "Juliet is the sun"), but that doesn't make the distinction itself easy to describe. Especially noteworthy in this regard is the explosion of interdisciplinary work on metaphor that resists the traditional view that metaphor is a special rhetorical tool that allows language users to rise, at least momentarily, out of the mundane world of literal meaning, represented well in Gibbs (2008).

One finds several strands in the literature when attempting to characterize the distinction in question. Sometimes accounts advert to the concept of what is conventional: literal meaning is conventional, non-literal non-conventional. Others focus on context-independence for literal meaning. Still others focus on the semantics/pragmatics distinction: semantics is the domain of the literal and pragmatics the non-literal. That viewpoint has the undesirable

---

[17] I ignore in the text the complicating factor that one has to regiment the use of 'literal' a bit when using it for theoretical purposes, as we are here. Witness the following passage from Frances Brooke's 1769 novel *The History of Emily Montague*: "He is a fortunate man to be introduced to such a party of fine women at his arrival; it is literally *to feed among the lilies*." If we prefer to think of such uses as non-literal uses of 'literal', we should say that such non-literal uses are not new. We should also note that such uses introduce an important circularity worry in trying to articulate the thesis that certain uses are literal while others are non-literal. Perhaps we should pound the table as we insist that something is *really* literal.

[18] See, e.g., Lakoff (1993).

consequence of ruling out *a priori* the Lakoff thesis that many terms in natural language have a semantic value that involves metaphor (see Lakoff (1993)). Perhaps some would relish that thought, but that result strikes me as excessive.

Given the plurality of approaches here, and the fact that none of them clearly show which uses of 'worship' will count as metaphorical, there is no decisive argument from this direction for the carving that I find most plausible. The idea of worshiping one's stomach, for example, is so obviously metaphorical that I don't think it takes much of an argument to sustain the conclusion, but it is worth noting the initial hesitance we experience when first hearing such a claim. We look for contextual clues to ascertain what is meant, finding them in the gustatory behavior of the people being described. The same is true, I believe, of the claim that all of life is an act of worship, and the related idea that no one can fail to be a worshiper, the only choice being the object of worship.[19] If we don't confuse literality with the seriousness and importance of the point being made, we should respond more to the tell-tale signs of conceptual creep involved in such hyperbole. Moreover, especially in Christian contexts, the danger of unnoticed hyperbole is enormous, given a background presupposition shared by many that the language of the serious and important ought to be literal language (e.g., serious and important truth is a matter for the language of science and math). For, to the extent that we can find the language of Jesus in the Synoptics, Jesus loves to use hyperbole and other figures of speech, in a way that is masterfully effective. The resulting points hit their target so forcefully that they generated plots for his execution, and the points made form the core of what he proclaimed to be good news regarding the Kingdom of God. That makes the language among the most important in human history, but we ought to be able to retain that perspective on the language and still be able to distinguish the figures of speech from the literal in the message being presented.

This conclusion is good news for Leftow, for talk of worshiping one's stomach or mammon is sufficient to undermine his position if such language is best understood literally. For such worship is not a form of address at all, but rather a structuring of personal priorities that make food or money trump all (or nearly all) other concerns.[20] But if we have a more nuanced and sensitive attitude toward the literal/non-literal distinction, we can grant the non-literal

---

[19] For an account of worship that makes such claims, see Smith (2013).
[20] It may be worth pointing out to those who maintain that everyone worships something that if the idea is a generalization of the point in the text, then the universality point itself is a form of hyperbole. Some people simply lack the needed structuring of priorities to make any of them count as a trump card. They just meander from momentary priorities to other momentary priorities, with no pattern or coherence to the sequencing; and then they die.

truth, and importance, of such language without making the unwarranted maneuver of rejecting Leftow's account on the basis of such truths.

This appeal to metaphorical truth, however, has its limits, for it is not a plausible response to other apparent counterexamples involving the worship of inanimate things, such a religious relics or nature and its objects. It is easy to take derisive attitudes toward such behavior, as we find in this passage from Isaiah:

> The man shapes iron into a cutting tool and does his work over the coals, fashioning it with hammers and working it with his strong arm. He also gets hungry and his strength fails; he drinks no water and becomes weary. Another shapes wood, he extends a measuring line; he outlines it with red chalk. He works it with planes and outlines it with a compass, and makes it like the form of a man, like the beauty of man, so that it may sit in a house. Surely he cuts cedars for himself, and takes a cypress or an oak and raises it for himself among the trees of the forest. He plants a fir, and the rain makes it grow. Then it becomes something for a man to burn, so he takes one of them and warms himself; he also makes a fire to bake bread. He also makes a god and worships it; he makes it a graven image and falls down before it. Half of it he burns in the fire; over this half he eats meat as he roasts a roast and is satisfied. He also warms himself and says, "Aha! I am warm, I have seen the fire." But the rest of it he makes into a god, his graven image. He falls down before it and worships; he also prays to it and says, "Deliver me, for you are my god."
>
> They do not know, nor do they understand, for He has smeared over their eyes so that they cannot see and their hearts so that they cannot comprehend. No one recalls, nor is there knowledge or understanding to say, "I have burned half of it in the fire and also have baked bread over its coals. I roast meat and eat it. Then I make the rest of it into an abomination, I fall down before a block of wood!" He feeds on ashes; a deceived heart has turned him aside. And he cannot deliver himself, nor say, "Is there not a lie in my right hand."   Isaiah 44:12–20 (New American Standard Version)

The prophet notes the offensiveness of the idolatry but focuses on the absurdity of fashioning an object with one's own hands and then deigning to worship the object. It is not impossible to do such a thing, but rather only a sign of the folly of which the human race is capable.

What are the implications here for Leftow's argument that worship can only be directed toward persons? First, these examples show that worship need not be directed at persons, but there is a complicating factor, once we attend to the human capacity for reification, personification, and deification. Some people speak to their vehicles, others to their plants. Such behavior is not impossible, even if slightly amusing. We make sense of such behavior in terms of the personification capacities to treat something that isn't a person as if it were one. The same can be said about the worship of graven images and objects in nature.

If we understood Leftow's argument to insist that worship can only be directed at persons, the argument fails. But if we take the argument to be aimed at the conclusion that worship must treat the object of worship in personal terms, then we can conceive the argument as one aimed at showing that the fittingness of worship only appears when the object of worship is actually a person. Leftow's argument for this claim is thus the communicative theory of worship, according to which the heart of worship involves acts of communication that are generate such fittingness only when sender and receiver share certain intentional traits.

I do not think that we should endorse this position yet, however, for I do not think it quite grasps the nature of worship. When properly understood, I'll argue, we will end up endorsing Leftow's conclusions, but we'll also have a better understanding of the nature of worship, something essential as we proceed with our investigation of the promise of WWT as a metatheology.

### 1.4.2 Leftow's Characterization of Worship

Leftow's account of worship involves two elements, one that worship always involves praise and the second that worship is a communicative act of some sort. Leftow appeals to the etymology of 'worship' to sustain the first point, involving the affirmation or pointing out of worth.

For both points, I think we would do well to attend more to the ideas of submission and surrender, of subservience and obeisance, that seem to me to form the core of the notion of worship. It is for this reason that the behavior of bowing down and prostrating oneself is so intimately connected with worship, since these are the bodily postures that are easily understood as expressions of the attitudes in question.

We see such elements on full display in the Hebrew language that is translated using the Anglo-Saxon term 'worship'. The most common term in the Hebrew Bible that is translated as 'worship' is (when transliterated) "shâchâh", which has a literal meaning of depressing or prostrating oneself. This term is translated as "worship" typically when the object in question is God, and in terms of bowing down, doing obeisance, showing reverence, crouching, falling down, humbly beseeching, or making to stoop, sometimes in relation to God (as in Ps. 72:11) but more often in relation to other entities (as in Isaiah 45:14, where kings bown down to Israel).

Moreover, religious expressions are best understood as normal and expected developments from such attitudes. Communal worship practices develop as corporate and institutionalized ways of expressing shared intentions of this sort, though of course it is easy for the practices to continue even as the attitudes dissipate and disappear. These attitudes, however, remain as the core element of worship, even if simulacra are possible or even widespread.

It is in light of this understanding of worship and imitations of it that I think we are to understand Jesus's remark about worship, in his conversation with the Samaritan woman when she asks whether worship should be done in Samaria or in Jerusalem. Jesus's answer is worth quoting in full:

> Woman, believe me, the hour is coming when neither on this mountain nor in Jerusalem will you worship the Father. You worship what you do not know; we worship what we know, for salvation is from the Jews. But the hour is coming, and is now here, when the true worshipers will worship the Father in spirit and truth, for the Father is seeking such people to worship him. God is spirit, and those who worship him must worship in spirit and truth.
> (John 4:21–4, English Standard Version)

Perhaps Jesus's answer about worshiping in spirit and truth is another example of the rhetorical strategy of antimeria and hendyadis, where one part of speech is turned into another in order to enhance rhetorical force. This rhetorical device is on display when Jesus says, "I am the way, the truth, and the life" (John 14:6), transforming the less forceful claim "I am the true and living way" into a claim with greater rhetorical force. If so, Jesus claims that the appropriate kind of worship is "truly spiritual worship," an enhanced and special kind in comparison to other kinds familiar in ordinary life. Most especially, such true worship would provide a natural contrast to a preoccupation with where various corporate rites and rituals are conducted.

In defending the idea that the heart of worship involves notions of surrender and submission, we need not undermine Leftow's claim that worship is a communicative act and thus appropriately directed only at persons. As already noted, the central point for Leftow is not that worship of nature and other non-persons is impossible, but rather that it only occurs (non-metaphorically) when it involves the kind of personification involved in communicative efforts with such things. This reliance on an appeal to metaphor is crucial, since it is easy to find attitudes in the general vicinity of worship that are nonetheless distinct from worship, but which lend themselves to the language of worship used metaphorically. One can experience awe and reverence concerning nature, one can have great admiration for its beauty, one may even feel at home in nature and having a feeling of dependency on it and experience gratitude for the array of experiences and emotions it evokes. Such experiences and attitudes can be part of worship but need not be; as Leftow (2016, pp. 74–5) points out, Platonic mathematicians can instance all of these attitudes regarding the mathematical realm but are not worshiping that realm and do not take themselves to be worshiping it. And if we choose to metaphorically describe these attitudes toward nature as demonstrating a kind worship, there is no need for philosophical remonstrance: sleeping metaphorical dogs can be let lie, too.

Once we get to the point where the gestures and attitudes central to worship, properly understood, involve communicative acts, we have the material Leftow relies on to show that worship is truly deserved only by persons. That point leads us to the second crucial component of WWT, the notion of the worthiness of worship, as opposed to its nature. I turn to this issue next.

### 1.4.3 Worthiness and the Uniqueness Challenge

Regarding the question of worthiness of worship, we face two central questions. The first concerns the relationship between the theory of value and the theory of obligation, for we need to know whether there is a demand for worship for certain kinds of beings. The second concerns the question of uniqueness, for there is a tendency among some to think that nothing other than God can be worthy of worship. If so, our task will be easier, but I will begin by registering dissent on this point.

The line of thought I will oppose is found in religions of the Abrahamic tradition, according to which worship belongs exclusively to God. Consider, for example, biblical narratives where angels rebuke humans who prostrate themselves in worship in the presence of the angels. The narratives caution against such, on grounds that the angels aren't God. Most clear on this score is Revelation 22:9 where an angel, in King James language, says, "See thou do it not." And a reason is given: "for I am thy fellowservant." An additional example is found in one of the temptations of Christ, where Jesus is encouraged to worship Satan. Jesus's response is clear and direct: "You shall worship the Lord your God, and serve Him only." For another, Paul characterizes the deceived in Romans 1:25 in terms of worshiping and serving the creature rather than the creator.

Even so, we might suspect that a more nuanced position might be able to accommodate such passages, a position on which there is a special kind of worship involved. On this position, worship itself is something that is allowed for things in the created order, in the same way that praise, awe, reverence, admiration, and adoration can be appropriate for these things as well. In addition, we need to acknowledge that the Scriptural record is ambiguous about whether things other than God can be worshiped, for there are Old Testament passages where the angel of the Lord appears, or "commander of the army of the Lord" appears, and these beings are apparently worshiped without rebuke.

Such passages raise important exegetical problems, and one way of reconciling these passages with prohibitions about worshiping angels is to note that in some such passages, the being in question is identified by the narrator as the angel of the Lord but by the end of the passage, the character in the narrative is also identified as God. See, for example, Genesis 16, where the angel of the Lord appears to Hagar, but Hagar reports that it was God who spoke to her. If an angel appears and is taken to be God, or if God appears in the form of an angel, there would be little problem in reconciling a prohibition of such worship with actual cases of unreprimanded worship of angels.[21] In addition, some narratives slip easily between language about the angel of God and God himself, as in Genesis 31:11–13, where "the angel of God" says to Jacob, "I am the God of Bethel, where you anointed a pillar and . . . made a vow to me." Again, in the story of the burning bush in Exodus 3, it is the angel of the Lord who appears to Moses as a flame of fire, and then it is God who speaks out of the bush; and it is the angel of the Lord who, after preventing Abraham from killing Isaac, says that Abraham has not spared his only son "for My sake."

---

[21] I do not say here what the reconciliation will look like, for some suggested reconciliations are problematic. For example, distinguishing subjective and objectives oughts is a possible approach, claiming that objectively one ought not worship the being in question but subjectively one ought to do so. I would reject this path of reconciliation on more general philosophical grounds, on the basis of arguments given in Kvanvig (2014, chapter 3). My claim in the text is only that there is an acceptable reconciliation to be found.

Trinitarian Christians often embrace such passages, seeing in them both an identity and a difference between God and the angel of the Lord, positing that the latter is the second person of the Trinity.[22]

Other explanations can be and have been offered. One especially promising idea is that of interpolation theory,[23] according to which the reference to an angel is a later insertion into the text, once a more transcendent notion of God was being emphasized.

In addition, a further point suggests some discomfort with the uniqueness claim. Once we attend to the obvious possibility that philosophical presuppositions affect translation, it is worth noting the predilection to translate "shâchâh" in terms of worship when directed at God, but in other terms when directed toward other things. Perhaps this translational choice signals a desire to make the record cohere better with explicit prohibitions about worshiping beings other than God, putting the translational choice at the bidding of the theology in a way that is problematic.

For those seeking theoretical resolution, there is an easier path. One need not deny that things other than God are worshiped, nor that things other than God are legitimately worshiped. Such language can be thought of as generically in terms of the standards of morality, but the prohibitions about worshiping things other than God need not be treated in this way. Instead, it is a commonplace in religion to find duties imposed that are specifically religious in nature, generating a class of religious obligations that go beyond those of morality itself. So there is no need to shrink from the uniqueness claim, if it is treated in terms of a religious requirement rather than a general moral one.

The implication here, then, is that a defender of WWT needs to identify a special kind of worship that belongs only to God, rather than relying on some general requirement that nothing but God can truly be said to deserve worship. We can address this issue by using the language of supremacy, either modifying the kind of worship in question or the kind of worthiness in question. On the former approach, God is worthy of supreme worship, the deepest and most intense kind of worship. On the issue of worthiness,

---

[22] A view that can be found, for example, in Justin Martyr. See Garrett (2008, p. 224, n. 28). And not just Justin Martyr:

> The second view is that the Angel of Jehovah is a self-representation of Jehovah, the second person of the Godhead.... This view was held by most of the Greek Fathers, by Justin Martyr, Irenaeus, Tertullian, Cyprian, and Eusebius. The Lutheran theologians, as one might expect, were decidedly in favor of this explanation, and in modern times it has found further staunch defenders in Hengstenberg, Keil, Langue, Nitsch, Beck, Haevernick, Ebrard, Wordsworth, Candlish, and others. (Kretzmann, 1922, pp. 33–34)

[23] See Meier (1999).

whatever the kind of worship in question, such worship can be accompanied by a worthiness that runs anywhere from minimal worthiness to maximal, but in the case of whatever worship is appropriate for God, the worthiness must itself be supreme. The supremacy here has a special feature, for it must be strong enough so that it becomes mandatory that such worship be given.[24] It is not merely a good thing to worship God, but instead the worthiness to be worshipped is so exalted that failure to do so is indefensible.

As described, then, there is no need to endorse only one of the two features just noted. So, in what follows, I will interpret the Worthiness-of-Worship motto as short for the idea that what is fundamental to the nature of God is that God is maximally worthy of the most supreme worship, in a way that makes such worship mandatory. From this perspective, one can understand Jesus's remark about truly spiritual worship as contrasting with mere bodily motions that are described in the language of bowing down, prostrating oneself, and dropping the eyes in obeisance to a superior. Instead the kind of supreme worship indicated is worship that engages the spirit, the mind, will, emotions, and intellect, and it is only such worship that can count as supreme worship and be the kind of worship that is due God and of which God is maximally worthy.

We thus skirt the issue of whether worship belongs only to God by identifying the kind of worship that uniquely belongs to God. We do so using the language of supremacy, interpreting the Worthiness-of-Worship motto as short for the idea that what is fundamental to the nature of God is that God is maximally worthy of the most supreme worship, and distinctively so.

It is worth emphasizing one feature of this understanding. As characterized here, even though the language of worth and worthiness is value-theoretic, it has whatever the needed value-theoretic features are to generate an obligation for worship. The kind of worship that belongs to God is not only something good to participate in, but an ideal and most appropriate response on the part of human beings. It is thus not only a position about the nature of God that speaks of the value of God and the value of a certain kind of response to God, but it also speaks of something stronger, more demanding, more binding, regarding the relationship between humans and God. It is thus not to be located only within the theory of value alone but also the theory of obligation:

---

[24] In Kantian terms, the duty is imperfect, as with charity: it must be done in some times and places, where appropriate, but need not be done at all times and all places. Using the formulation of Tom Hill, perfect duties have the form "One must never (or always) $\Phi$ to the fullest extent possible in $C$", whereas imperfect duties only requires that "One must sometimes and to some extent $\Phi$ in $C$." See Hill (1971).

it is not only good, but right, to relate to God in the way that is central to WWT.[25]

### 1.4.4 Fundamentality and Worship-Worthiness

It is fair to say that it is hard to find any historical defenders of WWT, and it is also hard to find any extended discussion of the nature of worship itself[26] or of the qualifications necessary for being worthy of worship (in the sense that defines WWT).[27] The discussion that can be found focuses on the question of what might ground an obligation to worship, and this approach raises the question in our context invites us to wonder about the connections between fundamentality and grounding in contemporary metaphysics: what are each of these, and how do they relate to each other?[28]

If fundamentality and grounding come to the same thing, so that being fundamental is just the same thing as being ungrounded, then we have no issue to address here, for it would follow from the fundamentality of worship-worthiness that this property has no ground. This identity claim, however, is not plausible. As Timothy Williamson's epistemology reveals, it is possible for knowledge to be indefinable and thereby fundamental to both epistemological theory and the philosophy of mind, even if belief and truth and perhaps other properties function as both necessary conditions for knowledge and grounds of it.[29] So let us assume that fundamentality and grounding are distinct. If we then suppose that certain of God's properties are fundamental, that claim does not require that the properties in question are ungrounded. It could be that a property is fundamental to a thing, and yet that thing couldn't have the property without having other properties, properties that count as the ground of the fundamental property. Of course, if the grounding properties

---

[25] In Murphy (2017, ch. 7) we find an argument that an Anselmian being might not be worthy of allegiance. The Anselmian being becomes worthy of allegiance, according to Murphy, by adopting a permissible, but not required, contingent ethics. It is thus this contingent fact together with the perfections of an Anselmian being that make God worthy of worship and allegiance. This view raises concerns that WWT must address, since it isn't easy to see how worthiness of worship could be fundamental to God if allegiance were only contingent. We will discuss this issue at some length in Chapter 8, §8.3.

[26] An exception here is Smart (1972).

[27] Recent and relevant literature includes Smart (1972); Bayne and Nagasawa (2006, 2007); Cray (2011); Gwiazda (2011); Smuts (2012).

[28] For a taste of the complications involved, see the seminal articles Fine (2001); Rosen (2009); Schaffer (2009) as well as Bennett (2011); Wilson (2014); Kriegel (2015); Tahko (2015); Bernstein (2016); Lipman (2016); Raven (2016); Schaffer (2016) and Mehta (2017).

[29] For details, see Williamson (2000).

are not only necessary for the fundamental property but also sufficient for it, there is some explaining to do in order to preserve the fundamentality claim. What might such an explanation look like? It is not clear what it could look like, but that lack of clarity may be present precisely because the notion of grounding isn't clear enough to give guidance here. After all, the notion of grounding is, at bottom, metaphorical, so until we are given a careful elucidation of this relation, we aren't in a position to determine exactly when metaphysical relations of necessity and sufficiency combine with grounding so as to imply fundamentality.

These points are important here, because a natural way to investigate what can be derived from the starting point of WWT is to ask what grounds the property of being worship-worthy. Doing so causes no initial worries about WWT, since a property can be fundamental to a thing and still be grounded in other features of that thing. When grounded in this way, the proposal about what is fundamental partakes of theoretical fecundity, for if property P is grounded in property Q, then we can derive the presence of Q from the proposal that P is grounded in this way. Thus, the idea that worthiness of worship must be grounded in certain specific features features of God, rather than implying that such worthiness cannot be fundamental, provides resources for theory development within a WWT metatheology. For example, suppose it could be shown that being maximally deserving of the most exalted worship couldn't obtain without the object of worship being a person with a mind and will. If so, and if such grounding is compatible with the claim about fundamentality that defines WWT, then WWT has resources for showing that a being worthy of worship will also be a person. What might have seemed a serious difficulty is perhaps instead a godsend.

We can enhance our understanding and appreciation of this point by considering a further arena in which the grounding worry can arise. Consider how we can think of the three metatheologies here as instancing a descriptive approach (CT), an evaluative approach (PBT), and a normative approach (WWT) to theology. The worry is now perhaps obvious: how could the normative itself be fundamental? Normative and evaluative features, it is often thought, supervene on the descriptive: no change at the non-descriptive level without a change at the descriptive level. Moreover, it is natural to glide easily between the language of a supervenience base and that of a ground, allowing us to say as well: no change to what is grounded without a change to the ground itself. Once we think in these terms, we can then raise the worry above as a concern about how the normative could possibly be more fundamental than the descriptive and evaluative?

It is worth noting in passing at least how this same objection can be brought to bear on PBT. For there is no good reason to think a fundamentally normative metatheology will fail in the face of this objection without also having to conclude that a fundamentally evaluative metatheology would suffer a similar fate. And yet I have found no one who voices the idea that PBT is flawed because of its attempt to start with the evaluative and derive attributes of God from that starting point. Of course, it is always possible that sanguinity here is a theoretical blindspot that only gets removed once WWT enters the competition, but the point remains that any defect from which WWT suffers in this regard is a shared defect with PBT.

I suspect, though, that the more defensible story is something like what I proposed above. On that story, even if WWT is a purely normative approach, identifying the properties that ground this normativity will help to fill out this metatheology rather than undermine it. Moreover, WWT might not count as a purely normative approach. Some non-descriptive language is "'thin" and other such language is "thick".[30] The thin language is that of good and bad, right and wrong; the thicker language can take many forms, but includes language concerning bravery, courage, open-mindedness, and other virtue-theoretic terminology. It may also include language about what is just and fair, though I suspect that such language has been on a diet lately and has been thinning considerably because of it. The relevance of the distinction between the thick and the thin here is that even though worthiness of worship is understood to entail that failing to worship is wrong, the property of being maximally worthy of the most supreme worship is not merely the thin property of obligation to worship. To say that God is worship-worthy is thus to say something much more substantive and laden with non-normative and non-evaluative dimensions than merely to say that it is bad or wrong not to worship God.

As a result, the generic objection to WWT arising from the language of grounding or supervenience simply has too many assumptions built into it to be plausible. This point should not be understood to imply that the objection can't be recast in ways that might still prove difficult for WWT to handle in the course of attempting to develop a full theology from this initial starting point. My point at this stage is only to note that it is mistaken to think that such considerations undermine WWT before theory development can even start. Warning signs are one thing, refutations another.

---

[30] The language comes from Williams (1985), for whom thick concepts apply correctly because of the way the world is, but also "if a concept of this kind applies, this often provides someone with a reason for action" (p. 140).

## 1.5 Conclusion

We thus have three main proposals to consider, plus a catch-all fourth possibility that denies that any one characteristic of God is fundamental to the divine nature. These proposals arise quite naturally when considering the history of thought about God. It is worth noting, however, that we often make progress in philosophy by attending to the range of logical possibilities instead of to the range of historical precedents. We turn to this issue in the next chapter, investigating the issue of how plausible it might be to focus on the three described in this chapter.

# 2
# Categorizing Metatheologies

## 2.1 Introduction

When we abstract from the historical precedents that we find in any area of theoretical inquiry, we ask whether there are types of theoretical possibilities to which the relevant history blinds us. Such a perspective is a needed one, even though it is easy to become overwhelmed by a feeling that we are traveling with hardly any light for our path. The journey is important, though, if only to remind us of the contingent and accidental ways in which certain options are foisted on our attentional gaze, in ways that can blind us to better options.

In this chapter, then, we abstract away from the historical options that first present themselves when asking the question about the fundamental nature of God. As we will see, an approach that focuses on these three cannot be completely free of the concern that is a bit myopic, but the worry is one that is mitigated to a considerable degree in the process of addressing the more abstract issues. We begin, then, by asking about the wider space in which these historical options arise.

## 2.2 The Wider Logical Space

The approaches I am focusing on are representatives in a category scheme derived from the twentieth-century concern that led to the rise of metaethics, a concern over what to make of the different kinds of declarative sentences in natural language. Some such sentences are straightforwardly descriptive ("$2 + 2 = 4$", "The cat is on the mat", "Water is a compound of hydrogen and oxgen in a 2:1 ratio," etc.), while others are evaluative ("Ice cream is the best dessert," "Wisdom is more precious than rubies," "One truffle is good, two are better, but an entire plate is too much," etc.), and still others are normative ("No one should use tobacco products," "Stealing is wrong," "Drinking and driving is forbidden," etc.).

We need not assume that this category scheme is precise enough so that every declarative sentence falls neatly into just one of these categories. For example, consider the claim that it is perverse always to prefer solitude to good company, and focus, not on whether the sentence is true, but whether it is an evaluative or a normative claim. The answer I think is not clear, but for our purposes this lack of precision is not troubling. What is important is the way in which these three categories might be plausibly taken to exhaust the options for the kinds of simple declarative sentences, where we understand the differences between declaratives and other types of sentences to be a central way of separating sentences that can be true or false from those that cannot.[1]

I have no proof of the exhaustiveness of these categories, but our Humean heritage, culminating in Logical Positivism and Logical Empiricism, should incline us toward this conclusion. That heritage takes the kinds of descriptive claims we find in factual discourse for granted. We can start with a list that includes all kinds of inquiry, including the physical sciences, the natural sciences, and both philosophy and theology. One might have reservations about some of these, as befits the Humean heritage, but the category thereby shrinks rather than expands. What remains is the stuff of morality, and here we divide that subject matter into the theory of value and the theory of obligation; or, using the language above, the evaluative and the normative. Of course, both these categories are larger than their morality component, for there are normative and evaluative judgments in many spheres outside of morality: the practical, the epistemic, the aesthetic, the political, etc. So in addressing the question of how to characterize claims within the theories of value and obligation, we include not only morality but all types of claims that fall within these areas.

One central metaethical concern since G. E. Moore has been the relationship between these categories, and whether there can be a theoretical explanation of the evaluative and the normative in terms of the descriptive. Moore was certain such an explanation could not succeed,[2] a conclusion that didn't trouble him, but which troubles those with Humean sensibilities significantly.[3] Moore's arguments led to perplexity by some about whether declarative sentences are

---

[1] A slight complication arises here if we think of alternatives to declaratives in terms of interrogatives, imperatives, and exclamations. It is clear that questions and commands are not alethically evaluable, but exclamations are a bit more complicated. "It is really cold today!" seems to be an exclamation (after all, it ends with an exclamation mark!), but seems also capable of being either true or false. Other exclamations aren't complete sentences, so are not alethically evaluable for that reason. Exclamations thus complicate the story of how to separate declaratives from other syntactic forms, but it is enough for our purposes to note that declaratives are distinctive in terms of being alethically evaluable, even if that feature is not sufficient for distinguishing declaratives from some exclamations.

[2] Details can be found in Moore (1903b), especially material on the Naturalistic Fallacy and the Open Question Argument. The standard view on these matters is that Moore's refutation of Naturalism fails, but there is no need here to pursue that issue.

[3] See, for example, Mackie (1977).

evaluative or normative are really truth-apt at all, and perhaps not cognitively significant either.

If we agree that this category scheme is exhaustive, and that each of the categories is sufficiently different from the others that paradigm examples of claims that belong in each (and not in the others) are easy to find, we are in a position to characterize the four approaches on which this work will focus. For the first three fall into each of these categories in paradigmatic ways. For a purely descriptive approach, we get Creator Theology (CT), which claims that God is fundamentally the creator or source of everything else. For an evaluative approach, we get Perfect Being Theology (PBT), according to which God is the best, or most perfect, being. Finally, for a normative approach, we get Worship-Worthy Being Theology (WWT), which claims that God is pre-eminently worthy of the most exalted worship in such a way that such worship is demanded of us. Metatheological Anti-Fundamentalism (MAF) is thus the mutt of the group, insisting that some mixing of elements will be required to identify the right starting point for developing an adequate theology.

Part of the explanation for referring to these approaches as metatheological is the nice analogy with the background that leads to metaethical inquiry in the twentieth century. One approach claims that theological judgments are fundamentally descriptive; another approach claims that such judgments are fundamentally evaluative; and a third claims that these judgments are fundamentally normative. The final approach opts for multiplicity, classifying theological judgments as some mixture of the three, leaving quite a number of options to be considered in the family of MAF. We should note, however, that the analogy is quite limited, for many, perhaps even most, of the concerns of metaethics find no place in our metatheology (especially, concerns about the semantic content of ethical judgments). There will be links, however, depending on what metaethical perspective one thinks is correct. For example, if one is convinced that only descriptive claims are truth-apt and that some other account has to be given of evaluative and normative claims or judgments, one will be inclined toward anti-realist and non-cognitivist understandings of theological discourse if one is attracted to either PBT or WWT. Here, however, we shelve the issue of the connections between metaethics and metatheology to concentrate on more basic issues involving the latter, attending to the wisdom of noting that sufficient to the day are the difficulties thereof.

Once we conceive of the four main competitors in the way described, we can see why there is good reason for such a focus in our inquiry. For, while it is true that the possibilities are manifold in each category, it is also true that each of the possibilities we are focusing on here are presumptive favorites in each category. If one thinks that theology is fundamentally normative, it is difficult to think of how it could be so unless through some link to the notion of a kind of worship that is mandatory. If one thinks that language about God is fundamentally evaluative, it is hard to see how it could be laudatory enough to be appropriate to deity without involving notions of perfection. And if one thinks that the nature of God is fundamentally descriptive, it is hard to see where to look for the right descriptions apart from identifying them in terms of creation itself and the ultimate source of all there is. So, I focus on these four here on the basis of such presumptive plausibility, granting all the while that there are possibilities ignored in the process, possibilities that may turn out to be better than any alternative considered here.

## 2.3 Theologies and Metatheologies

As just noted, this account of the category scheme for metatheology leaves open the question of whether there are other plausible examples of descriptive, evaluative, or normative foci when it comes to the starting point for theological investigation. I have no argument that there are not other alternatives, and perhaps some that will turn out to be more promising than those I have chosen. Perhaps more important than the unknowns in each category, however, is the temptation to muddy the categorical waters from which we are starting. One way to do so is to pick a theologian and attempt to retrodict a metatheological starting point to fit the theology endorsed. Perhaps for Ritschl, it is fundamental that God is love; for Royce, that God is omniscient; for Thomists, that God is pure act. One might then posit a metatheology to fit the theology. In the simplest case, the metatheology simply mirrors the theology, giving us metatheological options on which God is fundamentally loving or omniscience or pure act.

I resist such retrodiction, since it confuses theory with metatheory. What is fundamental within a particular theory is one thing and what to say at the level of metatheory another. Presumably, any decent theory will be amenable to formalization of some sort, with an axiomatic presentation the gold standard. Such a presentation will have basic axioms and thus some understanding of what is fundamental to that theory. But the philosophy of theology should not be confused with the theology or theologies themselves.

A couple examples will help to see this point. The first is the relationship between ethical theory and metaethics. While it is probably a mistake to think that there are no connections between these areas of inquiry, it would also be a mistake to confuse the two. As described earlier, metaethics involves a reflective stepping back from the domain of morality, including the theories of it that might be proposed, to address more abstract issues involved in that domain and theories of it. To offer an carefully crafted moral theory and claim that its structural features address and answer the questions of metaethics would be a mistake.

Another example arises in the study of logic. Here, too, it is a mistake to conflate the subject matter with the philosophy of it, to conflate theory and metatheory. Suppose we are developing a logic and begin by presenting a language a proof theory for it. The proof theory itself might be a natural deduction system or it might be an axiomatic system. But it would be a mistake to think that the arguments and reasoning involving in the construction and defense of the system in question were characterizable simply in terms of the system in question. For example, if the proof theory is intuitionistic, it remains an open question whether the arguments and reasoning involving in generating and defending that system are intuitionistic, classical, or whether it is a category mistake of some sort to use these object-level descriptions when talking about the what is going on at the metalevel.[4]

The difficult question is how to determine the defining characteristics of the metalevel. With the study of logic, this issue is easier to address when we have a formal language or collections of formal languages that we are reasoning about. When it comes to morality and religion, to ethics and theology, things are not quite as straightforward. There are, in the study of ethics, clear example of metaethical questions that are clearly different from the questions involved in moral theory itself. The question of the precise semantic content of ethical judgments is one particular example. We don't need a precise account of the distinction between theory and metatheory to acknowledge the difference, and

---

[4] Classicists in logic affirm, and intuitionists deny: excluded middle, the law of bivalence, double negation, and *reductio ad absurdum* (the version in which one subtracts a negation sign from an assumption after deriving a contradiction). The study of logic is one thing, the philosophy of logic another.

Defenders of Classical Logic include Frege, Russell, and Quine, among others. See Frege (1879, 1893–1903); Russell (1903, 1919); Quine (1950, 1953a, 1970). Intuitionistic logic derives from L. E. J. Brouwer's intuitionistic mathematics, with formal systems provided by Arend Heyting, Gerhard Gentzen, and Stephen Cole Kleene. A primary defender and articulator of the view is one of the greatest philosophers of logic of the twentieth century, Michael Dummett. See Brouwer (1907); Heyting (1956); Kleene (1965); Gentzen (1969); Dummett (1978, 1991).

One might claim that any difference between object-level theory and metalevel reasoning is grounds for a charge of *petitio principii* against the theorist, but it is worth noting that there can't be a substantive philosophy of logic if the assumption is that no theory development is philosophically adequate unless the metalevel reasoning satisfies exactly the standards of the proof theory thus developed and defended. Every defense of a logic would be as epistemically circular as every other, with only conceptual incoherence a ground for rejecting a logic.

once we do, we can see that using the terminology relevant for the object-level theory to describe a stance at the metalevel should yield suspicion.

My recommendation, then, is to find a category scheme into which various metatheoretical possibilities fall, and argue for the plausibility of one such option in a way that at least initially brackets the question of what the resulting theology will end up being. If we do so, using the Thomistic example, it is easy to see why a metatheology that begins from the standpoint of describing God in terms of pure act would be a philosophical headscratcher. What in the world could such a claim mean? Once we have the complete theology in front of us, we can (I think) make sense of the claim, but that substitutes theology for metatheology, just as an endorsement of utilitarianism followed by a reading off of its metaethical implications substitutes ethical theory for metaethics. The plan here is to take metatheology more seriously than that, and the result is that alternatives to the big four that I'm focusing on need to be proposed, clarified, and defended prior to and independent of any complete theology that includes or explains the claim in question.

Identifying plausible alternatives to the big four in the way just described is made more difficult because of the history of inquiry into the nature of God. Extant theologies have no clean line between the theology itself and the metatheology that generates it. Moreover, even though a theology is, in some sense, a theory about the nature of God, theologians do not generally have the aspirations that guide scientific and mathematical theories, where axiomatic systems take pride of place.[5] One can imagine a theology presented axiomatically, however, and such a theology could easily count as a theory on which being the creator, or being a perfect being, or being worthy of worship was theoretically fundamental. One can also imagine a theory on which all three had the same axiomatic status. Such a theology would be metatheologically suggestive, but also inconclusive. For there is no *a priori* reason prohibiting a theology that made being worthy of worship axiomatic in combination with a metatheology that endorses a different account of what is fundamental regarding the nature of God.

These points help us understand why thinking of God as pure act is not a serious metatheological competitor to the big four on which I focus here. My take on this approach is to note that the conclusion that God is pure act is something derived rather than a point from which inquiry begins. The

---

[5] For those who prefer to give pride of place to model-theoretic approaches to theories, instead of the syntactic idea of an axiomatic system as in the text, the same lesson holds. Theology rarely approaches theory development and defense in ways that conform to our best practices in science and mathematics.

derivation, as I see the basic nature of Thomistic theology, begins with the generic content of Creator Theology, that God is the asymmetric source of all else. One sign of this characteristic is the centrality of causal, teleological, and cosmological considerations in the arguments for the existence of God. The question is then what follows from this starting point, and a Thomistic theology begins to take shape through derivations from this starting point of a number of central metaphysical properties: aseity, transcendence, immutability, impassability, etc.[6] The account of these metaphysical attributes culminates with the doctrine of divine simplicity, which is at the core of the reasoning that gets us to the conclusion that God is pure act. Then, once we have the complete story in front of us, we can ask how it can be organized for presentation in the most elegant way possible, and here it may be attractive to start from the axiom that God is pure act. Notice, however, the derivations needed to get the pure act conception of God. We don't start inquiry from that point, but rather start elsewhere, perhaps with CT, in order to generate a theology that has the pure act understanding of God as axiomatic.

The claim here is not that it is impossible for there to be a metatheology beginning from the starting point which understands God in terms of pure act, but rather that in fact the approach that understands God in this way is as inadequate at the metatheoretical level as is a metatheoretical starting point that identifies gold in terms of atomic number 79. Moreover, this example of a theology derived from a quite different metatheology shows that there are no obvious or direct connections between what is fundamental to the metatheology and what is fundamental to the theology that is derived from that metatheology. So, the theology might claim that love is fundamental to the nature of God, and yet be derived from any of the big four metatheologies. In fact, a theology might claim that worship-worthiness is fundamental to the nature of God, but be derived from one of the other metatheologies. As far as I can tell, there are no limits here, and the only way to find out what is fundamental at each level is to look at the theology and how it is developed, since just looking at the theology and what is fundamental to it won't tell one what is metatheologically fundamental.

To summarize, then, I have claimed that there is a useful category scheme about simple declarative sentences that organizes them into the descriptive,

---

[6] I idealize here a bit, for theological development is rarely as pristine as one might like. So, the derivations often appeal to grounds from Scripture and tradition that haven't themselves been derived from CT, and such reasoning is metatheologically problematic for defenders of CT. For defenders of MAF, of course, multiplicity of original axioms is cherished, but given the characterization above of MAF, not just any multiplicity is acceptable. Appeals to Scripture and tradition would thus have to justified in terms of what MAF deems fundamental in order to preserve metatheoretical coherence.

the evaluative, and the normative, and that the initially plausible version of each give us CT, PBT, and WWT, respectively. Even in the absence of a proof that this scheme exhausts logical space, it is plausible to see it as doing so, and even though we have no guarantee that the best version in each category is the one identified, the historical record of thinking about God makes it attractive to focus on these three. That leaves only the fourth option to defend, and it arises precisely in response to the assumptions of the other three approaches, claiming the reality in question and the best way to theorize about that reality is going to be much more complicated than the simplifiying and reductive tendencies on display in the other approaches.

This approach to metatheology, involving the categories just noted, is unique in the history of thinking about theology. It will be useful to compare it to more common approaches, explaining how the present approach differs and the advantages such differences yield. I turn to this topic in the next section.

## 2.4 Alternative Category Systems

One quite common alternative to the category scheme described above is one that employs a distinction between general revelation and special revelation (GR/SR). On this scheme, there are potentially two sources of information about God, one independent of God's self-disclosure, available from an investigation of nature alone, and the other from direct divine communication. I will note, in passing, that this distinction is in need of precisification, but we need not be detained by that issue here, for we need no such precision to explain the differences between the present approach and GR/SR.

The first thing to note about the GR/SR approach is its fundamentally epistemological orientation. It considers the questions of theology by asking where our evidence regarding the nature of God comes from. Even if we grant that this approach is the best one to take, given such an orientation, there is the question of whether adopting such an orientation is required. An epistemological orientation is certainly appropriate for some projects, but is just as clearly not required or best for all. For our question, the question of the nature of God, a circuitous detour is needed to approach this issue from an epistemological direction. Our question is a metaphysical one, not an epistemological one, so there is no need to route our discussion through an epistemological lens.

An analogy might help cement this point. When we investigate the nature of the external world, there is no need to begin from an epistemological perspective that asks and addresses skeptical concerns about whether we can know of the existence of anything outside our minds. The epistemological project is a fine project in some contexts, but is a needless detour when we ask about the fundamental nature of the external world. For that issue, we should be investigating whether the world is fundamentally a matter of substance and attribute, or whether processes are fundamental; whether being or becoming is more basic; and whether the external world is fundamentally non-mental, or whether is mind-dependent through and through.

In the process of addressing any question about the nature of any particular thing or kind of thing, the questions of epistemology are bound to arise at some point, but a better approach for developing a theory about the nature of God—a theology—begins by acknowledging the metaphysical, not epistemological, nature of the project. In short, an inquiry into the question of the nature of $X$ is not best interpreted as an inquiry into the question of how we can know what $X$ is like or what are our sources of information about $X$.

It is rather remarkable how often this point goes unrecognized in metaphysical textbooks. When addressing metaphysical questions about the nature of the self, the mind, and the external world, typically no detour through skeptical concerns is found. But when turning to the issue of the nature of God, the focus generally turns to the standard arguments for the existence of God.[7] We would be perplexed by a similar epistemological focus when investigating the nature of mind or the self or the external world. My recommendation is to be equally perplexed by recommendations for taking an epistemological approach to the topic of the nature of God.

The same point is equally telling against approaches that begin by distinguishing between *a priori* and *a posteriori* sources of information about God (PR/PO).[8] If our question is about the nature of a given thing, our metatheory should consider various possible metaphysical starting points, and the PR/PO distinction is an epistemological distinction, not a metaphysical one.

In both alternatives to our metatheology focusing on fundamentality, we begin with an epistemological question. In the case of GR/SR, we ask where the source of our information comes from, Reason or Word. In the case of PR/PO, we ask whether the information we seek is derived from experience itself or independent of experience. While both questions are important ones

---

[7] For a typical example of this phenomenon, see Conee and Sider (2005), an otherwise excellent resource for teaching metaphysics (as well as superb on the argument for the existence of God).

[8] For such an approach, see Morris (1987b).

to ask and answer, they are not the first ones to ask when inquiring about the nature of a given thing.

There is, however, one standpoint from which such a metaphysical project must be rejected. If one is a thorough-going skeptic about the possibility of knowledge or justification or reasonability based on human reason, one might resist the metaphysical approach endorsed here in favor of retrenchment about our aspirations for understanding, a retrenchment that honors our limitations. In theology, we might describe such an approach as "Barthian," reflecting Barth's antipathy toward any defense of the gospel on the basis of human reason.[9]

Extreme skepticism, whether adopted generally or in specific domains such a theology, unfortunately has the power of stopping all inquiry, in favor of tracing the limits of our powers of discernment, and thereby substituting epistemological inquiry for targeted inquiry into some aspect of reality. Such a Barthian pessimism is thus an instance of a more general Pyrrhonian skepticism, and it is worth noting the intellectually stultifying implications of such a position. For if such a Barthian skepticism is endorsed, it must also be endorsed regarding our interpretations of the texts from which Barthian dogmatics is generated. Once one denigrates human reason across the board, that conclusion turns back on itself, undermining any plausibility or basis for endorsement one might propose. It is a rather amazing thing to watch when theoreticians propose such standpoints and then also show a capacity to ignore the obvious self-undermining character of the proposals.

Here, though, we won't pursue either the phenomenon of self-refuting positions, and I will also table the more general issue of what to say in response to skepticisms carefully crafted to avoid self-refutation, in favor of pursuing the targeted inquiry into the nature of God. At some point, of course, a full understanding of reality requires addressing skeptical concerns, but what I will resist here is giving in to such skepticism to the point where no inquiry can begin without a prior response to skepticism. I grant that such skeptics will want an epistemological starting point in place of the metaphysical one

---

[9] "Gospel does not enter into competition with the many attempts to disclose within the known world some more or less unknown and higher forms of existence.... The Gospel is not a truth among other truths. Rather, it sets a question-mark against all truths. The Gospel is not the door but the hinge. The man who apprehends its meaning is removed from all strife, because he is engaged in a strife with the whole, even with existence itself. Anxiety concerning the victory of the Gospel—that is, Christian Apologetics—is meaningless, because the Gospel is the victory by which the world is overcome.... [The Gospel] does not require representatives with a sense of responsibility, for it is as responsible for those who proclaim it as it is for those to whom it is proclaimed. It is the advocate of both.... God does not need us. Indeed, if He were not God, He would be ashamed of us. We, at any rate, cannot be ashamed of Him" Barth (1968, p. 35).

I propose here, but I do not grant that such replacement is mandatory or advantageous.

We thus have an explanation for focusing on the big four metatheologies here: theologies of sourcehood, perfection in being, and worship-worthiness, in addition to the option of multiplicity at the initial level that is characteristic of Metatheological Anti-Fundamentalism. These four are frontrunners in a category scheme that exhausts the metatheological options for accurately characterizing the object of theological inquiry. Thus even though we have no compelling argument that one of these four must be best, we have good reason for pursuing an investigation into the prospects of these four. For those wishing to propose alternatives to these four, I look forward to seeing what such alternatives might be and what there prospects are, in spite of thinking the chances of serious competition here are slim. It is time to become better acquainted with each position.

## 2.5 Conclusion

We have seen in this chapter an explanation and justification for focusing on four metatheologies, with primary investigation devoted to three proposals regarding what is fundamental about God for purposes of theological investigation. Our next task is to determine what standards these approaches should be measured by, and we turn to this issue in the next chapter.

# 3
# Initial Desiderata on Metatheology

## 3.1 Introduction

Once we have our metatheology in place, we have starting points and can begin the process of determining what derivations can be sustained by each starting point. Scoring each approach is partly a matter of determining what can be shown and what can't be, but there is a prior issue to consider and discuss before looking at the derivational power of each starting point. For what we want to know is the significance of failures to derive standard claims about the nature of God, and also how to score derivational successes when it comes to matters of dispute between various theologies, both the intra-religious variety as well as the inter-religious variety.

We thus need some discussion of desiderata to be used in rating each approach before attempting to assess the derivational arsenal of each approach. A word of caution about expectations is in order at the outset, though, for one might hope to generate a scoresheet that could be applied mechanically to each metatheology, thereby determining a winner. Or, to vary the metaphor, one might wish for a pocket calculator that takes as inputs either derivational successes or derivational failures and calculates a final score for each approach. As attractive as such hopes might be, it is not difficult to see that they are misplaced. First and foremost, we will not be able to generate any list of features of the divine by which to generate such scorekeeping. For we do not enter the project of theology with any such list in hand. Instead, we grope in the dark for what can be gleaned from each starting point, and assess each competitor in terms of what is generated by other competitors. As is typical of philosophical methodology, there is some preference to be shown for the more obvious over the less obvious, and for starting points that can generate the greatest amount of overall coherence and comprehensiveness in explaining and accommodating the more obvious over the less. The process is nothing like what a simple algorithm might generate, but instead often involves trade-offs between theoretical power and particular judgments about what is obvious, a process described by Rawls, in a different context, as aimed at reflective equilibrium.[1] When done properly, however, it results in the kind of rationality and justification for a theory brought about by coherence between the general principles of the theory and particular judgments about what is obvious and what is not.

We will thus approach the issue of desiderata on a metatheology, not in search of some simple algorithm to decide between competing metatheologies, but rather in search of something more like rules of thumb to rely on when starting our inquiry. We start from this imprecise launching pad, expecting that the rules of thumb will become precisified in the process of assessing our metatheologies, generating an interplay between these initial stabs at criteria of adequacy and assessment of metatheologies that will mirror the search for reflective equilibrium described in the last paragraph. So, we should think of this initial discussion as aimed at elucidating what looks fairly obvious as beginning points, though with no assumption made here that what looks obvious at the start is something that cannot be refined or even abandoned as inquiry progresses. Initial rules of thumb are necessary for our inquiry even though any assumption of inviolability for such rules would signal a failure to appreciate the significance of our fallibility in all areas of inquiry.

## 3.2 Semantics and Metaphysics

We can begin by noting that all three major positions ascribe supremacy in the possession of some property to God: God is not only perfect, but the most perfect possible being; God is not only worthy of worship, but is supremely worthy of the highest worship; and God is not only a creator or source of things, but is the asymmetrical source of all else.

These vague notions of supremacy and exaltedness involved in even the most undeveloped theologies may lead us to wonder about their source. This same issue arises for any inquiry into the nature of anything. Perhaps we want to learn about gold, for example: where do we begin? We advert here to descriptive content: the yellow stuff that we glean from rock formations, that dents easily, etc. But we don't assume that these features are essential properties of gold, but are instead the ways in which we go about identifying the stuff we want to investigate, and the ways we rely on for identifying things must, it would seem, be part of the ordinary meanings of the terms we use to pick out

---

[1] See Rawls (1971, ch. 1). For general discussion of this approach to philosophical methodology, see Kvanvig (1989b).

the items toward which our theoretical activity is directed. Even for those of us most intent to keep epistemology and semantics distinct from each other and from metaphysics, this initial vague and amorphous melding of the three subdisciplines of philosophy seems unavoidable.

If we begin from such a starting point, we might then elicit these notions of supremacy and exaltedness from our language concerning deity, perhaps from concepts of deity where the terms function as titles, or perhaps through the kinds of constraints we are familiar with concerning ordinary proper names.[2] Our starting point might seem to be endangered by a feature of the apophatic tradition that emphasizes God's transcendence, inaccessibility to finite minds, and ineffability, but this concern has to be carefully formulated to avoid easy refutation. No such claims can get to the table for debate without first linking semantics and ontology in some way that, provided theism is true, allows successful reference to God so that God's inaccessibility can be articulated. The extreme version of apophaticism that emphasizes transcendence, inaccessability, and ineffability to such an extent that all links between the metaphysics, epistemology, and semantics of talk about God are removed results in a view on which our theological language has mere syntactic structure with no semantic interpretation possible. It would be as if we introduce a new name into our language: 'We-Au-An' is a name, we say. We then begin to say things about We-Au-An: We-Au-An is like nothing we've ever enountered. Is this claim true? Obviously it cannot be if no semantic content can be identified for this name. To the extent that apophaticism can be sensibly articulated, it must treat the term 'God' in a way different from what we have stipulated about 'We-Au-An', for the claim that God is like no other is so central to apophaticism that the position ceases to have any content at all if it cannot endorse that claim.

So, it would seem best to understand our initial assumption regarding the source of the ideas of supremacy and exaltedness by which we initiate our inquiry into the nature of God by linking this assumption with the understanding we have achieved regarding ordinary proper names. If we think of ordinary names as arising from contexts of reference-dubbing,[3] contexts in which the capacity to refer to the object being named is present independently of and prior to the introduction of the name, we might generate an explanation of this language of supremacy and exaltedness from such a starting point.

---

[2] For an excellent investigation of the semantic issues concerning names of God, see Speaks (2019, esp. chs. 7–8).

[3] I borrow this terminology from Speaks (2019).

How would such an explanation go? Here we need no particular story, but only vague possibilities to allow us to move forward with our investigation. One idea I find particularly attractive adverts to the ways in which nearly any experience or event can be taken in enchanted ways, evocative of the presence of a being yet-to-be-named. In the background of such dubbing contexts are constraints on successful naming practices, and the background in question plausibly involves presuppositions concerning the supremacy and exaltedness of anything that can be appropriately called "God". It is easy to see why the experienced enchantedness would evoke notions of supremacy and exaltedness in comparison with any and every ordinary experience, since the to-be-named is something over and above the ordinary realm of experience.

Part of the attraction for this approach can be found in the pervasiveness of animistic tendencies toward personification and deification of everything in nature. Regardless of the details, however, this possibility of the experience of enchantment gives us one possible way of linking our metaphysical inquiry into the nature of God with appropriate semantic and epistemological sourcing from which to glean the language of supremacy and exaltedness from which we begin.

The contours of this story, however, have met with resistance recently, and it is worth considering the objection to see why it need not derail our direction before proceeding further. The objection comes from Jeff Speaks's recent book arguing against Perfect Being Theology (PBT), and in the process he argues against the idea of 'God' being an ordinary name, in concert with certain versions of PBT that drive their metaphysics about God off of a semantic thesis about the meaning of 'God'. Speaks writes,

> ... [T]here seem to be certain descriptions of the world which are coherent, but would be incoherent if 'God' were an ordinary name. Here is an example of the sort of thing I have in mind:
>
> > *God exists and created the world and everything in it. But God stayed remote from God's creation, and in particular never directly encountered any human being. No one has ever in any sense perceived God, or communicated with God.*
>
> It seems to me that this is a perfectly coherent view; it is not far off of the view which some classical deists seem to have had. Further, it seems to me, someone might hold this view while being a perfectly competent user of the name 'God.'

But this is difficult to understand if 'God' really is dubbing-introduced. For if 'God' is dubbing-introduced, then introducers of the name must have had some prior way of making singular reference to the bearer of the name. And if God stays remote from creation, and never encounters any human being via perception or communication, how could introducers of the name have secured such original reference, if not indirectly via description?"

Speaks (2018, pp. 165–6)

Speaks's argument, that 'God' should not be thought of as an ordinary name, accommodates the account of the nature of God in Mark Johnston's (2009) work *Saving God*, an account that requires that 'God' is not an ordinary name, but one attached to descriptive content. Part of my reason for resisting the impulse to drive a metaphysics from a semantics concerning the terms involved can be illustrated by considering Johnston's claims about God and 'God', and it will help to see the nature of our metaphysical project by looking at what happens when it becomes refracted through such a semantical lens.

We get a sense of Johnston's approach from this passage:

Suppose you look into your heart and see that there is *a god*, that is, an object of conventional prayer and worship, which you do believe in. How does that show that you believe in God? No amount of inspecting your own psychological state can itself determine whether you believe in God, as opposed to *a god*.    Johnston (2009, p. 2)

The central idea here, that one can identify an entity as God and yet be mistaken, is surely correct. Yet lurking here is a bit of a mystery as well, once we conjoin this passage with Johnston's later claim about the semantical content of 'God'. The quoted passage might be adverting to the distinction between actual and fictional deities, but it could also be relying on a henotheistic point involving allegiance to one God over other gods, but as Johnston's thought develops, we learn that the intended distinction involves the semantical claim that the meaning of the term 'God' is constrained semantically by the description "the Highest One", requiring that 'God' be a descriptive rather than an ordinary name. It thus has to have a semantic content that is tied to the description in a way that ordinary names are not tied to the descriptions that come to mind when we think about the individuals referred to by those names (Johnston, 2009, pp. 7ff.)).

This elucidation of the quoted passage raises a concern about the progression of descriptions of deity in the quoted passage. The passage begins with a conception of deity in terms of objects "of conventional prayer and worship," and if that description is the starting point for elucidating the nature of deity, it is most naturally thought of as a form of worship-worthiness metatheology, among the approaches we identified in Chapter 1. If so, however, the semantic thesis comes too late in the game to drive the metaphysics. If we already have an identification of deity with worship-worthiness, we can't then defend a semantic thesis involving the phrase "the Highest One" without saying something helpful to the perplexed reader who can't see what to make of the disparate semantic and metaphysical starting points.

The disparity can be resolved as follows. One can endorse the semantic thesis about 'God' and then, by some argumentative route, get to a conclusion about the appropriateness of prayer and worship directed toward such a being. After doing so, one could also point out our fallibility, so that what is being worshiped turns out not to the Highest One, and thus not God.

Some mystery remains, however, for this resolution awaits some further explanation of the argumentative route from perfection to prayer and worship. Without such an explanation, the passage simply pulls us in different metatheological directions. Moreover, once we introduce the distinction between *big-G God* and *little-g god*, characterizing the former as a descriptive name, we appear to have already moved into the land of monotheism without any entitlement for doing so. Once within the borders of monotheism, taking 'God' to be a descriptive name, it is not hard to see how the constraining description "the Highest One" is faithful to a broad range of monotheisms. But a thoroughly metaphysical project such as the present one takes as one of its problematics the truth of monotheism itself.

One further disadvantage of driving one's metaphysics concerning the nature of God off of a semantics for the term 'God' affects Johnston's general line of argument. The starting point of Johnston's project begins from the meaning of 'God' most at home in the monotheistic religions of the Abrahamic tradition, linking this starting point with the concept of idolatry, in hopes of generating an adequate argument for a panentheistic conclusion. For example, consider this passage:

> The inner truth of the ban on idolatry is best understood as a requirement that our worship be directed at the Highest One, and only to the Highest One.... We also know that if there is a Highest One, it deserves our fealty, not arbitrarily, but because of its perfections. We need not know what those

perfections are; ... but we do know that there can be none more perfect than the Highest One. Otherwise, that Other One would be the one to turn to for salvation.   Johnston (2009, p. 95)

From the perspective of this project, these remarks are a bewildering motley of talk of worthiness of worship, hope of salvation, and perfections of God, with little help in seeing how the derivations are supposed to work. Though it may be easy to see how to tie the notion of idolatry to some hope of salvation, there is nothing in either the notions of perfection or worthiness of worship that yields any obvious basis for generating a hope of salvation—finding such a link requires serious argumentative efforts that are not present in this passage. If one's project is a metatheological one, all this has to be sorted out properly. Finally, it is worth noting that a properly conducted metatheological inquiry can start from the claim that God is the most perfect possible being without relying on some contestable semantic claim about the meaning of the term 'God'. A defense of the semantic claim might give a quick route to PBT, as it would if one could defend the semantic thesis that 'God' means "the most perfect possible being", but getting there in this way is certainly not required. Moreover, the semantic claim is a distraction, since if PBT followed semantically, we'd could still think that the language of supremacy and exaltedness that is appropriate to deity would be best investigated by introducing some other term into our language. Meaning might constrain metaphysics to prevent using language already in place from being metaphysically abused, but there is no semantic story to tell as to why language shouldn't evolve in ways that reflect our enhanced understanding, both scientifically and metaphysically, of reality.

Johnston's discussion thus provides a cautionary tale about semantical appeals in service of metaphysics, and we can see a link between what Johnston claims and the deistic hypothesis presented by Speaks, quoted above. That passage calls into question my assumption that the term 'God' should be understood as an ordinary name arising from reference-dubbing scenarios involving ideas of supremacy and exaltedness on the basis of a deistic hypothesis, a suggestion that must be rejected by Johnston in order to justify the semantics used to drive metaphysical inquiry. We can see Speaks's argument as a gracious effort to be able to find some truth in the semantical claim that the meaning of the term 'God' is to be understood to involve the description "the greatest possible being" or "the Highest One". The truth would thus be that the name 'God' has a semantic content involving the description, and is thus not an ordinary name, because the possibility of the deistic scenario reveals that the term 'God' is meaningful in a way not generated by reference-dubbing contexts where we have in place some other way of identifying the entity in question.

This defense of Johnston's semantic claim is not successful, however, for it conflicts with standard accounts of divine conservation which mesh nicely with accounts of creation presupposed in the deistic story itself. The continued existence of the created order is as much in need of explanation as is the point of origin, where the latter idea is a presupposition of the deistic story itself.[4] The problem is that the deistic hypothesis fails to notice the other aspect to be explained, an *explanans* that once explained imputes a ubiquity of divine intimacy with creation, which can then provide the needed backdrop for divine names to arise as ordinary names. It is this ubiquity and intimacy with the natural order that forms the context for finding enchantment anywhere and everywhere, and noted above, in a way leading quite straightforwardly to the ideas of supremacy and exaltedness that are common to all the metatheologies we are considering. So, I don't think the deistic hypothesis Speaks mentions provides a decisive reason to abandon the semantic speculation above that the term 'God' (in at least one of its uses) is best understood as an ordinary proper name. The argument works only if the deistic hypothesis is coherent, and the link between creation and conservation suggests that it is not. In such a case, deists would just be another example of people holding metaphysically impossible beliefs.

My aim here, however, is not to defend any particular semantical treatment of theological language, nor to propose any particular link between semantics and metaphysics, but rather to explain why such commitments will not arise here. My remarks about possible approaches and possible links are thus offered as hints or suggestions rather than lemmas needed in order to proceed with our evaluation of various metatheologies. So I offer the suggestion above as one that I find intuitively attractive and as an example of the sort of story one might try to develop if engaged in the project of trying to link a semantics for theological language with the metaphysics of such.

I thus resist a conception of philosophy conforming to Richard Rorty's memorable language of "the linguistic turn."[5] Such a methodology, I maintain, is driven by anxiety about whether philosophy has anything substantive to contribute to the intellectual life of the mind, and it is a methodology that is indefensible apart from metaphilosophical assumptions about what is required

---

[4] This line of thought, linking creation and conservation, is explored and explained more fully in Kvanvig and McCann (1988); McCann and Kvanvig (1991); Kvanvig (2009a, 2017b).
[5] See Rorty (1968).

to make such a contribution. Interestingly enough, those metaphilosophical assumptions involve violations of the very turn they insist on, as amply demonstrated by the history of attempts to formulate a defensible version of the verifiability criterion of meaningfulness.[6] Moreover, as an approach to the nature of things, such a semantic focus is astonishing, to say the least. Who would have thought that, somehow, the meanings of our terms carry such secrets?[7]

None of this should be thought to imply that there is no connection at all between language and the world (what a bizarre idea that is!) nor that semantics and ontology are not linked in important ways. What it does imply, however, is that semantic stories about what is needed for successful introduction of names for God are not needed for metatheological purposes nor are such stories convincing enough to drive the metaphysical machinery. If such stories play a role at all, it is something much more general and amorphous: whatever is needed semantically for identifying the object of inquiry in a way that allows for significant theoretical change to occur concerning the object of inquiry without any need for positing semantic ambiguity. Once we have these rudimentary linguistic needs satisfied, we focus on the object of reference, rather than the vehicle by which reference is achieved.

This stance is beneficial to the metatheologies discussed in this work, for it would be an additional burden on each of them to have to defend, not only their metaphysical account concerning the nature of God, but a semantic thesis tying their preferred starting point to some descriptive content of divine names. The semantic and epistemological background, however, imposes a defeasible constraint on a metatheology, for if a metatheology can't be reconciled with any story about the semantic and epistemological source for the ideas of the supremacy and exaltedness for God, we have reasons for judging that metatheology to be inadequate. As far as I can tell, though, there is no such tension here, though perhaps nothing clear and precise enough to command our assent either.

Once we move past this discussion aimed at severing any strong link between semantics and metaphysics when it comes to inquiry concerning the nature of God, a central issue will be the extent to which each starting points of the major metatheologies we will consider can derive the starting points of alternative metatheologies. For it is a mark in favor of a metatheology

---

[6] For a nice cataloguing of the hazards here, see Hempel (1950).
[7] For expanded discussion and articulation of the underlying metaphilosophy related to this rejection of the linguistic turn, see Kvanvig (2018, ch. 1).

if it can derive the starting points of other promising metatheologies, even though only a defeasible one. So, for example, if Creator Theology (CT) can demonstrate that God is worthy of worship, that is an advantage for CT, and moreso if Worship-Worthiness Theology (WWT) cannot show that God is the creator of all. Disadvantages that arise from the inability to derive the starting points of other metatheologies are not as weighty, however, as failure to sustain the underlying presupposition of our language about God concerning God's supremacy and exaltedness. We need not try to quantify at this point the precise amounts of weightiness involved, but can leave that issue to be addressed once we find out where such failures occur. The point to note, though, is that it is one thing for a metatheology to fail to show that God is the greatest metaphysically possible being and quite a different, and worse, result to be able to show only that God is a pretty impressive being. Pretty impressive being theology is not much of a competitor here, and the explanation of its inadequacy is not merely that it is weaker than Perfect Being Theology, but rather that it provides no basis for explaining the supremacy and exaltedness of God.

Our initial desiderata thus give the starting points of each of the three major fundamentality metatheologies a privileged position in scorekeeping, though the primary disadvantage in light of this point is not failure to derive the starting points of other metatheologies but rather failure to provide a basis or ground for explaining the supremacy and exaltedness needed for deity. This point does not exhaust the common ground that can be found for evaluating metatheologies, for in the process of uncovering it, we have seen a variety of further notable possibilities. These possibilities include the question of monotheism, the personhood of God, and a further conditional issue: if God is a person, we will want to inquire whether an embodied one, a purely physical one, or a purely spiritual one. So, beyond the starting points of alternative metatheologies, our initial scorekeeping will need to attend to these issues as well.

These topics contrast with other claims about God that do not have such status. In order to see why, it is worth noting the priority that these possibilities have over other moral and metaphysical attributes that have been argued for in the history of theology. The personhood of God clearly takes priority over all moral attributes, since such attributes require God to be a person. Moral features include being morally good, morally upright, having moral freedom, being full of grace and forgiveness, displaying the virtues of justice, wisdom, temperance, faithfulness, etc. I use the language of personhood to indicate that status needed in order to be a moral agent, which includes mind and will. In the category of the mental, what is essential is the intelligence needed for practical and theoretical reasoning and for judgment regarding that which is prior to reasoning. For the will, we make no commitment to anything beyond the capacity for choices underlying the capacity to act, leaving to the side (at least initially) what is required to have such capacities. These capacities or abilities are thus requisite for having any of the moral features in question, so their status as derivably meritorious depends on a privileged status of personhood.

Something similar is true for at least some of the metaphysical attributes. The metaphysical attributes include items such as metaphysical goodness (or greatness), simplicity, unboundedness either temporal or spatial, immutability, impassibility, simplicity, transcendence, and aseity, among others. Some of these rely on conclusions from the privileged issues noted above, for if God is not a person and also a purely physical thing, pantheism becomes attractive and it would then count against a metatheology that it could derive transcendence and aseity, for example.

We thus find that it is best to postpone discussion of metaphysical and moral attributes, and the significance of derivability and failures of derivability in these domains, until we have settled the prior issues involving the privileged attributes. We thus turn to these more basic issues in the next section, to assess what significance they have for the adequacy of a given metatheology.

## 3.3 Monotheism and Personhood

Of the two issues of monotheism and personhood, the easier one to deal with is the former. It is an advantage for a metatheology to be able to show that "the Lord our God is one." I do not claim that failure on this score cannot be explained away successfully, but I first want to present the straightforward case for monotheistic predilections.

The case arises once we consider what happens when multiplicity is posited. As soon as polytheism arises, something has to be said about who is in charge and what happens when there is conflict. Any understanding of God has to involve some notion of supremacy, on pain of generating ridiculous discussions of whether a subatomic particle might be God or whether the earthworm I'm watching being eaten by the robin in my backyard might be God. To identify something as God that is a lower power than something else is a philosophical non-starter.

In addition, one ought also to be careful to distinguish the realm of divinity from that of deity. One should not confuse what it takes to be a divine being from what it takes to be a deity, and once we honor the distinction, supremacy will enter into any clarification of the distinction.

Even so, monotheism is not entailed by these considerations. What follows is the weaker claim that if there is a supreme being, then nothing else can be a deity. The possibility left open is that there is no supreme being, but a group of beings, all divine beings, none of which holds supremacy over the others but all of which are supreme when compared with everything else. A metatheology that implies such a society of beings might be a defensible version of polytheism, but questions have to be answered before allowing such a position to pass scrutiny. In particular, such a position must have a response to the Problem of the Pantheon: the embarrassing predicament of endorsing a theology that makes the gods into the kind of group described in Greek mythology.[8] Multiplicity where the entire group is harmonious is one thing, but the cacaphony of the Pantheon reduces the exaltedness of deity to lamentable displays of the foibles and follies of human society. Talk about illicit anthropomorphism! The result here is a preference for metatheologies that can sustain monotheism, with a fallback possibility of providing some guarantee of harmoniousness among the multiplicities if monotheism is rejected.

Such a conclusion generates a provisional preference for monotheistic metatheologies, given the difficulties involved in ruling out the Problem of the Pantheon. For, if harmoniousness is posited, we would then need to ask whether this harmoniousness is itself explained by some further factors, whether it was merely a matter of good fortune, or whether it is itself a necessary feature of the beings in question to partake of such synchronization. No matter which of these answers is given, more questions arise, questions that are avoided for metatheologies capable of sustaining monotheism.

We then turn to the question of personhood. Is there anything about deity itself and the supremacy it involves that should lead us to anticipate a benefit for those metatheologies that can sustain an attribution of personhood to God? Here I will rest content with pointing to the argument I will develop in Chapter 4, in favor of personal conceptions of deity. That argument is developed in the context of CT metatheology, showing how creation by a personal being can be made sense of in a way that creation by an impersonal force cannot. This argument can be generalized to theologies that posit creation by a lesser being than God, by some demiurge, since such a demiurge still answers to a deity. The same argument for making sense of creation by a personal power can be applied here as well, to show that if creation is done only by a demiurge,

---

[8] As argued in Kvanvig (2021a) and explored in more detail in Chapter 4.

we can understand the relation between such a demiurge and God, under the assumption that God is a person (as well as the demiurge), but not under non-personal assumptions.

Here is a quick preview of the argument. The key issue concerns the principles that link the specific total state of the source with the precise effect. In the case of creation, the assumption that these principles are found in the mind and will of God yields an explanation of the nature and existence of the needed principles, an explanation that has no intuitive and obvious competitor for non-personal conceptions of God. The same issue of needed principles arises if one posits creation by a demiurge, under the authority of God, for either the demiurge is personal or not. If not personal, then the demiurge is merely a tool by which creation is fashioned by God, and so God is the creator rather than the demiurge. If personal, then we still need the linking principles just mentioned, and finding them in the mind or will of either God or the demiurge yields an attractive explanation that is not easily mimicked by appeal to impersonal forces.

The important point to note about this brief summary is the way in which the linkage between God and demiurge mirrors precisely the linkage between God and creation itself, on the assumption that God is the creator of all. So the two issues are solved by the same explanatory hypothesis, which gives a privileged status to metatheologies that can sustain the conclusion that God is a person.

This argument presupposes a distinction between God and creation, and one might reject that assumption. Consider Mark Johnston's reasons for demurring on the distinction:

> Suppose that there is something created by the Highest One, but nonetheless *distinct* from the Highest One, in that it is not some part, aspect, principle, or mode of the Highest One. Call this other thing "the separate creation." If there is such a separate creation, then we would expect the perfections of the Highest One to be to some extent reflected in that separate creation. Consider, then, the joint reality made up of the Highest One and the separate creation. It would seem that this joint reality might be a more appropriate object of worship than the subpart of the reality that is the Highest One. Or, at the very least, the joint reality would be an appropriate object of fealty that was not identical with the Highest One. But this is inherently at odds with our principle that the Highest One and only the Highest One deserves worship. So there is no separate creation. What is called creation is some part or aspect of principle or mode of the Highest One. That is why a worshipful attitude to

the whole of reality is not idolatrous. It is not worship of creatures as such; they are seen only as manifestations of the Highest One.

Johnston (2009, p. 95)

Johnston gives a sketch of an argument here that there cannot be a separate creation, and we cannot generate privileged status for the personhood of God on the basis of the above considerations if there is no separate creation. Johnston's argument focuses on the distinction between God and, perhaps, the mereological sum that includes both God and a separate creation, arguing that the latter would be higher than the Highest One, and hence there cannot be any such separate creation.

He then considers the obvious objection that nothing can be worthy of worship without being a person, and writes in response,

> ... [I]t might be that reality as a whole has no will to which we can declare fealty. But if the Highest One has a will, then surely creatures will be an expression of that will, and so the whole can be said to manifest a will to which one can declare fealty.  Johnston (2009, p. 96)

This argument and response are woefully weak.[9] Let's see why.[10] The argument here has the form of a *reductio* beginning from the assumption that there is both God and a separate creation. It then assumes that this separate creation is an object, or is fully constituted by objects, and endorses a metaphysical principle that allows mereological sums of objects to count as an object as well. Both of these claims are controversial, so Johnston is correct that the argument is "much too compressed" Johnston (2009, p. 96). Next, Johnston assigns values to the Highest One and to the combination of the Highest One plus the separate creation, arguing that if the separate creation is of positive value, then the combination of it and the Highest One will exceed the value of the Highest One alone. The problem here is that the value of the Highest One will presumably be infinite, and the value of a separate creation may also turn out to be infinite. Yet, adding anything finite to a Cantorian infinity yields that

---

[9] After listing some problems with the argument, Brian Leftow says, "You could drive a truck through the holes in Johnson's [sic] argument" Leftow (2016, p. 83). I concur, for reasons that overlap with the ones Leftow cites.

[10] In the text, I ignore a further issue because it is exceedingly minor, but will mention it here since observant readers will see the issue. We have already considered and rejected the idea that only God is worthy of worship, and Johnston's argument presumes otherwise. The issue is minor, however, since it is easy enough to amend his argument to accommodate the point: just talk instead of the most supreme worship and who or what could be supremely worthy of it.

same infinity, and adding the same Cantorian infinity to a Cantorian infinity yields that same infinity, since for any Cantorian infinity $\mathcal{N}, 2 \times \mathcal{N} = 1 \times \mathcal{N}$.

One might think that this is just a special case of the general problem for utility theory of what to do with infinite values, but that is not the case. The problem of infinite values for utility theory involves trying to explain how two worlds each with infinite value can nonetheless be ranked differently in our value theory. This problem arises from adding infinite sequences of finite values, and though the problem and its solution can be traced to Frank Ramsey, the best presentation of a solution to it can be found in Vallentyne and Kagan (1997).[11] In short, the solution is to consider loci of value for the two worlds, and then consider finite subsets of the totality of loci. If every finite subset favors one world over another, the first world is to be favored over the second even if they are both infinitely valuable.

Note, however, that this problem bears no probative relation to the problem facing Johnston's appraisal of the value of God and the mereological sum of God plus creation, since the summations being considered begin from infinite values rather than finite ones. As a result, it will take a quite inventive, and non-Cantorian, approach to value theory and the mathematics of infinite numbers to support the conclusion that a possible scenario containing only God (and whatever is necessary) is less valuable than a possible scenario containing God plus a separate creation.

In addition, the response to the objection—that the mereological sum is not a person and thus could not be an appropriate object of worship—is inadequate. The last part of the response gives away the farm: "so the whole can be said to manifest a will to which one can declare fealty." Forget the dodgy "can be said" (after all, what can't be said? or, is it, what is can defensibly be said? shouldn't we simply want what can correctly or truly be said?) and focus on the core claim: the whole manifests a will. Yes, it does, because, as assumed, God manifests a will. And if one declares fealty to something, it ought to be something with a will. But, even if the sum in question contains a part that manifests a will, it is a mistake to say that this fact licenses attributing a will to the sum itself. The sum is an abstract entity, and abstract entities don't have wills. Compare: the set of animals in this room is not warm-blooded, even though its members are. Or again: the mereological sum of my right index finger and my shoe is not made of flesh, but it does have a part that is.

The conclusion to draw, then, is that this argument gives us no reason to reject the above argument for attaching privileged status to personhood as well

---

[11] Similar ideas are found in Segerberg (1976) and Nelson (1991).

as monotheism. It is worth noting in passing that privileging personhood in this way is a viewpoint Johnston endorses, forming a basis for his rejection of pantheism in favor of a version of panentheism on which personal pronouns are appropriate for referring to the Highest One.[12] The relevance of the above argument is thus not one Johnston would wish to use to dispute privileging personhood when describing God, but rather a weapon that others might wish to brandish to undermine the argument I've given for privileging personhood. For that purpose, however, the argument is anemic, giving no cause at all for questioning the argument or its conclusion.

As before, I do not take these considerations to be indefeasible. The fact that a personal account of creation can be made sense of in a way that can't be duplicated by an impersonal account does not guarantee that the tables couldn't be turned by further discussion. What it creates, instead, is an advantage for metatheologies that can sustain the attribution of personhood to God, and creates an explanatory burden for those approaches that cannot sustain such an attribution.

We thus generate privileged status for metatheologies that can show that there is but one God and that God is a person. The remaining question, among possibly privileged status issues, is the question of embodiment.[13] It there a privileged position here as well, where the options are to think of God as being purely spiritual, purely physical, or being embodied (and thus neither of the first two options)? We turn to that issue in the next section.

## 3.4 The Question of Embodiment

The issue of embodiment involves several possibilities for the relationship between God and the realm of the physical. There is the identity claim, that God is identical with some physical entity, and the dualistic claim, that God has a body but is not identical with it. In the latter category is the special version dualism according to which the physical universe itself is God's body. Moreover, each option can be given two different formulations, one on which the relationship is essential and one on which the relationship is contingent. So, for example, if a theory claims that the physical universe is God's body,

---

[12] Consider again the "much too compressed" claim: "This, to be sure, is a much too compressed argument for the doctrine that the Highest One includes his creatures as manifestations, aspects, or modifications" (Johnston, 2009, p. 96). The use of the personal pronoun 'his' is striking here.

[13] Relevant literature on the relation between God and the world is too enormous to document here, but a useful sampling includes Jantzen (1984); Lipner (1984); Mawson (2006); Taliaferro (1987), and Wainwright (1974).

but only contingently so, that theory may claim that there are possible scenarios on which God has no body at all, or that there are possible scenarios on which God has a different body than our physical universe.

Given the privileged position accorded to metatheologies that can sustain the claim that God is a person, we can think of these positions as analogous to positions about the nature of human persons. If one is a Cartesian dualist, maintaining that it is possible for a human person to exist even though no bodies exist, one would presumably think that a divine person would have the same status. Such a position would imply, not that God has no body, but that having one (or not having *this* one) is not an essential property of deity.

When we are asking about shared ground for all metatheologies, however, we should not grant privileged status to any view that is derived merely by analogy from arguments and positions about human persons. First, there are no uncontroversial positions about human persons that could provide a solid enough basis for the analogy. Second, analogizing in this way counts as anthropomorphizing, and the issue of when anthropomorphizing is allowable and how much of it is allowable is not a settled enough issue for it to be used as a condition of adequacy, even a defeasible one, on a metatheology.

So if there is a privileged position here, it won't come simply from an account of the nature of human persons. If, however, there were an argument that rules out anything but physicalist conceptions of persons, such an argument could be used to show privileged status for the embodiment thesis, assuming that the ruling out didn't appeal to features of finitude to draw its conclusion. Looking at one such argument will put us in a better position to see why no such privileged status will be forthcoming at the outset from these kinds of arguments.

The argument I have in mind is a version of the pairing problem in Buckareff (2016) derived from Kim (2005). The core idea of the argument is to rule out the possibility of causes not located in space-time bringing about space-time effects, on the basis of our inability to pair causes and effects, something that can be done with ordinary causal processes such as the breaking of a window by a thrown rock.[14] Here is the argument:

Suppose that C and C* are two non-spatially located mental events. For *reductio*, assume that the occurrence at $t1$ of *either* C or C* (and not both)

---

[14] Well, perhaps things are not so simple even in the case of purely physical processes, unless we can rule out the metaphysical possibility of action at a distance. But I leave these complications for another time and place.

causes the occurrence at *t*2 of a (spatiotemporally located) bodily action, E.... So, assuming that E is not causally overdetermined, either C or C* causes E. Hence, it is only the occurrence of C or C* that causally explains E. However, we do not know whether C or C* explains E and we cannot know. This is because E cannot be paired with its cause. That is to say, there is no spatiotemporal causal nexus in the universe where C or C* is paired with E.... If there is no location in space-time where the causal relation obtains that would explain the occurrence of E, then neither C or C* could cause E. So *neither* C nor C* cause E.     Buckareff (2016, pp. 220–1)

Central to this argument is that since both C and C* are occurrent candidate events to cause E, but not overdetermine it, we look for some basis for linking one of them to E in a way that we do not find for the other. So the central idea is contained in the notion of pairing: if the events aren't spatiotemporal, no pairing is possible, and without such pairing, no explanatory connection of a causal sort can obtain.

The central issue facing this argument, however, is its failure to consider the kinds of pairings that can occur in an infinite mind between causes and effects. If we don't assume from the outset that the mental can't cause the physical, but instead wish to derive the impossibility from the pairing problem, then consider an infinite mind with maximally specific intentions, with the metaphysical power for the willing in question to guarantee the result as described in the intention. In such a case, there is a pairing in virtue of mental content, and it rules out the possibility assumed for *reductio* at the beginning of Buckareff's argument, for maximally specific intentions describe events that have only one possible realization.

Here we see the point of my earlier remark about the danger of drawing conclusions that follow only on the assumption of finitude. For, if the minds in question are finite, there is no reason to think that the intentions in question can be uniquely paired in the way they can for an infinite mind. The requirement of maximal specificity implies that matters will be settled for every proposition, given any such intention, thus individuating the effects completely. So even if there is a pairing problem that shows that mental causation is somehow philosophically perplexing for finite beings, that problem does not generalize to give a presumption in favor of any theological position on divine embodiment.

So, as things stand, I don't think there is any need to pursue further arguments for physicalism at this point in our inquiry, given the intricate complexities of the issues that need to be sorted out in order to determine whether purely spiritual beings are possible, and whether substance dualism of the sort that claims a possibility for a person to exist without a body can be maintained. The central point here is that these issues are best left to a later point of development within each metatheology, rather than standing outside all metatheologies, imposing a (defeasible) condition of adequacy on them. For there is no simple argument, of the kind just considered, that can be used to justify such an imposition.

These points make it quite difficult to see how any particular position will count as common ground for acceptable metatheologies, but there is one feature that might prove useful here. When we consider the question of embodiment, we are asking whether it is part of the nature of God to have a physical part or be a physical being. This element of our discussion can be troubling, since it is far from clear what it is for anything to be physical,[15] but here we embrace enough of common sense metaphysics to insist that, whatever it is to be physical, the universe is full of physical things and things with physical parts. Moreover, the presence of the physical, at the very least, brings to mind the capacity for, and realization of, decay, deterioration, and disintegration. In a word, the physical realm seems to be the realm of corruptibility, and that fact by itself might suggest a reason to oppose any embodiment thesis.

It is natural to assert a necessary connection between corruptibility and contingency, but we need not rely on that link here. One reason for not doing so is to leave room for necessitarian ontologies, of the sort defended in Williamson (2013). I don't find such a position attractive, since I see it as a fanciful version of possibilism,[16] the view that reality involves two kinds of things, some actual and some possible, and I'm with Bertrand Russell in favoring a more robust sense of reality.[17] But there is no reason to enter into such issues at this point, since corruptibility is clearly a deficiency that is inappropriate to ascribe to God.

If this feature is part of what it is to be physical, we have a straightforward argument for rejecting some links between God and the physical. For no adequate account of the nature of God can attribute to God the corruptibility of the physical universe. Some qualifications are necessary, however, for not

---

[15] The source of my perplexity here derives from the considerations found in van Fraassen (1996).
[16] As argued in Menzel (forthcoming).
[17] "In such theories, it seems to me, there is a failure for that feeling for reality which ought to be preserved even in the most abstract studies.... A robust sense of reality is very necessary in framing a correct analysis of propositions about unicorns, golden mountains, round squares and other such pseudo-objects" Russell (1919, pp. 172–3).

every claim of divine embodiment will succumb on this issue, even if it is correct to go from being physical to being corruptible. What is critical here is the connection between being embodied and being corruptible, and there are accounts of divine embodiment that bar any inference from the claim of physical embodiment to a conclusion about being corruptible, even if it is essential to physicality that it is corruptible. For example, suppose I wear a hat, and suppose it is essential to a thing's being a hat that it play a certain functional role involving head-covering. Even so, the hatted one is not thereby a thing that involves head-covering—the connection between the hat and the one wearing it is not the right sort of connection for concluding such a thing about the wearer, even though the connection is the right sort to sustain the claim that the person in question is a hatted one. Moreover, it is not the temporariness of being a hatted one that undermines the inference. My blood type is A-positive (I think!), but I am not A-positive (whatever that would mean) even though there won't be a moment at which I have a different blood type. The same point would apply if, contrary to expectation, we found someone who never went without a hat. What more is needed than permanence isn't completely clear, but something more is surely needed.

Recall, for example, the Platonic account of the relation between the soul and the body in the *Phaedo*. In that dialogue, Cebes proposes that the relation between soul and body may be like that between a tailor and the tailor's coat.[18] If divine embodiment were interpreted as weakly as this, whatever corruptibility we find in the created order would not require imputing corruptibility to God, since we don't impute properties of the tailor's coat to the tailor.

For some, this view of the relation between soul and body is not merely archaic, but incoherent. For, it might be claimed, there is no sense to be attached to the idea that a person has a body but none of the aspects of the body signal aspects of the person. If my coat is made of nylon, shorter than 54 inches, dirty from being dragged through the mud, none of these features of my coat reveal anything about what I'm made of, how tall I am, or whether I need a shower. But if my body is dirty, and if my body is 67 inches tall, then I am dirty and I am 67 inches tall. It thus might be claimed that there is no interesting conversation to have about the question of divine embodiment if inferences from aspects of the body to aspects of the person are never acceptable.

This issue plays out in the Indian philosopher from the eleventh century, Rāmānuja. His view is described by Surendranath Dasgupta (1940):

---

[18] *Phaedo* 87b–88c.

...Rāmānuja maintains that, as there is difference between the soul and the body of a person, and as the defects or deficiencies of the body do not affect the soul, so there is a marked difference between God, the Absolute controller, and His body, the individual souls and the world of matter, and the defects of the latter cannot therefore affect the nature of Brahman. Thus, though Brahman has a body, He is partless (*niravay ava*) and absolutely devoid of any *karma*; for in all His determining efforts He has no purpose to serve. He is, therefore, wholly unaffected by all faults and remains pure and perfect in Himself.... Dasgupta (1940, pp. 200–1)

Rāmānuja thus holds that God has a body, which is the universe of souls and matter, but that this body is not a part of God, so that the defects and deficiencies of the universe do not count as defects or deficiencies of God. It is clear, then, that Rāmānuja's view is that God is embodied, but that features of the body do not signal features of God.

That is precisely the view that some will see as incoherent. To make progress on the dispute, we need to distinguish several things. First, we need to distinguish talk of the soul and the body from talk of the person. One option is that the person is simply the soul, that the person is strictly identical to the soul. In such a case, the position that describes the body of a human person in terms of the same kind of relation as obtains between a tailor and the tailor's clothes is appropriate: the features of the clothes do not signal features of the tailor.[19]

If persons simply are souls, however, the question of embodiment tends toward philosophical insignificance. Here are two positions: souls are contingently embodied in the way people sometimes wear coats; souls aren't embodied at all because nothing about any body signals anything about the soul in just the way that nothing about a person's coat signals anything about the person wearing it. One might still insist that there is a difference between an embodied soul and a disembodied one, just as there is a difference between a donned coat and one hanging in the closet. But that is a relational difference concerning the coat itself and the one donning it rather than a non-relational feature of the one who dons the coat. There is a similar distinction between a

---

[19] In using the language of signalling here, I remain intentionally vague, out of an interest in not being derailed by side issues. It is worth noting what the side issue is here, however. For there are properties of the coat that are also properties of the tailor: both exist, both bear a special relation to the tailor that they bear to nothing else, etc. So when I say that the features of the coat do not signal features of the tailor, I advert to a special epistemic support connection, where the former provides conclusive evidence for the latter, assuming that such a relation does not obtain whenever the former entails the latter. How to characterize this epistemic relation so as to have this result is a complicated matter that would take us too far afield here, but see the literature on epistemic closure principles for further information. I summarize and interact with that literature in Kvanvig (2006, 2008a).

universe created by God and a universe not created by God, whether purely physical or some combination of immaterial souls and physical stuff, but the difference in question is a difference *about the universe itself*. So, if we suppose that God has created the universe, and then we ask whether this universe or any part of it also counts as God's body, and we are told that whatever we say here, we cannot go on to say that the the universe is part of God in the sense of licensing any inferences from features of the universe to features of God, then we know enough to conclude that adding an embodiment claim tells us nothing new about God. Instead, it only tells us something about the universe itself, that its existence derives from God.

Notice that if we refuse to identify persons with souls, this issue doesn't arise. If persons are composites of souls and bodies, as standard substance dualists claim, then the Platonic view that analogizes the relation between persons and bodies to that between tailors and their coats is illconceived. For tailors wearing coats are not composite entities with coats as constituents. There is an entity, perhaps, that is composed of the tailor and the coat, but it is a mereological sum of the two and thus not identical to either of its constituents. Instead, substance dualism renders the relation between persons and their bodies intimate enough that features of bodies often signal features of persons: if your hand is bleeding, you are bleeding; if your brain dies, then you have suffered brain death; if an explosion tears the legs from a soldier, the soldier has lost their legs; etc.

In short, the intimacy of the metaphysical connection between persons, souls, and bodies drives the epistemic significance of features of the body for features of the person. In order to block the signalling of the former for the latter, one has to adopt a view on which the body is not a part or constituent of the person, and if one adopts such a view concerning the nature of God, what remains is the interesting question of whether the universe and the objects in them owe their existence to God, but the question of whether the universe or anything in it counts as God's body has been answered in the negative.

This discussion leads us to the conclusion that a defense of divine embodiment has to identify God's body in such a way that features of the body count as features of God, in at least an important class of instances, and that the body in question would thereby need to be free of the corruptibility we experience regarding physical things within the universe. Once we get to this point, it becomes clear that failure to derive an embodiment thesis is no demerit for a metatheology but rather something to be avoided. For any such derivation would create an additional explanatory burden of trying to identify the physical thing that is God's body but not subject to corruption.

It may be worth noting that there are theological perspectives in the Christian doctrine of the resurrection of the body that would provide precedent for the idea of such incorruptibility, for a resurrected body is understood to be incorruptible.[20]

Such an appeal, however, will not block the concern about the connection between embodiment and corruptibility when we start pointing to the specific things and claiming that they constitute God's body, as we do when we point to the universe itself. There are two points to note here. The first involves a bit of metaphysics. Start by asking about the source of the incorruptibility of resurrected bodies. A natural answer here is that the bodies in question are incorruptible, not because of their intrinsic natures, but by an act of will on God's part. For if the bodies were incorruptible in the metaphysically necessary sense, problems arise in explaining how we could ever be identical with something with such a body. I am not metaphysically necessary and neither are you. So we'd each have a metaphysically necessary part—a part that once in place, cannot be removed or cease to be—but the part would have to be only contingently part of us. For if you have a part that is metaphysically necessary and from which you cannot be separated, then you are metaphysically necessary. Yet, a fundamental fact about metaphysical necessity is that it is not a part of the land of becoming: nothing comes to be metaphysically necessary nor comes to lose it either. And yet none of us are necessary beings.

So, the better route is to treat the incorruptibility of resurrected bodies as involving some kind of necessity deriving from the operations of the Divine will. Such an account can be coherent, but the kind of necessity then becomes something weaker than metaphysical necessity, and thus provides no good model for how God's body, should there be one, could be free of the kind of corruptibility that would be problematic in theology. For it cannot be a matter of God's will what is metaphysically incorruptible and what isn't, and anything less than metaphysical incorruptibility would still leave one with a weakened account of deity.

Second, even if this metaphysical problem could be solved so that metaphysically incorruptible physical things are not ruled out, the universe does not seem to be one of them. Hence, even if bodies need not be corruptible, pressure is created on any view endorsing divine embodiment to identify just which incorruptible thing it is that is God's body.

---

[20] See, e.g., I Corinthians 15:53: "For this corruptible must put on incorruption, and this mortal must put on immortality" (KJV).

We thus end up with what might appear to be a privileged status for the position that God is a purely spiritual being, though only if this claim is thought of as a negative rather than positive one, i.e., the privilege resides in positions that do not sustain the claim that God is embodied rather than that the privilege resides in positions from which one can derive that God is not embodied. The idea is that claiming that God is or has a body is not given preferential treatment here, so without some special reason for a metatheology to insist on it, that metatheology will not be committed to any embodiment thesis. If a metatheology goes further and derives a non-embodiment claim, that result may be a benefit, but failure to derive such a claim should not be taken to count against a metatheology. Consider an analogy. If you have a conception of the good life that resists the demand that a place worth living must have public parks, it need not be beneficial from your point of view for a locale to prohibit public parks rather than merely lacking such places. Your concern is simply to include on your list of choices places that have no public parks. You might not even be averse to picking a place and finding out it has public parks; you just don't want your choices restricted in that way. Just so here with the issue of divine embodiment. There is no good reason to insist on the derivability of some embodiment claim. Moreover, there are difficulties in trying to find a way of endorsing such a claim, and the combination of these two points yields a privileged status for the claim that God is a purely spiritual being.

It is important to qualify this point as before, noting that it holds under the dominion of defeasibility, just as with the privileged status for monotheism and personhood. These features, together with the vague requirements of supremacy and exaltedness, form the foundational desiderata for our study, with the latter features generating significance for the issue of which of our metatheologies can sustain the starting points of competing metatheologies.

## 3.5 Conclusion

We thus have a structure in place for the chapters to follow, beginning with foundational issues in Part II of this work, followed by the issue of the starting points of competing metatheologies in Part III, and closing with the question of the moral and metaphysical attributes that are common in the history of theology in Part IV. This latter topic raises issues about the significance of successes and failures regarding these attributes, but this significance issue is already present in noting the defeasible character of foundational issues.

We turn then to the main competitors to see what they have to offer, where my goal is to show the superiority of both CT and WWT to PBT, making the crucial issue that of determining whether WWT needs supplementation by CT in order to count as the preferred metatheology. First, though, we need to see how this issue comes to prominence by noting the advantages of CT and WWT over PBT.

# PART II
# THE SHARED GROUND

# 4
# Creator Theology and the Shared Ground

## 4.1 Introduction

The focus of this chapter is Creator Theology's (CT's) implications regarding the issues of monotheism, personhood, and embodiment. The plan is to use these primary elements as stage-setting, showing that CT has impressive advantages primarily over Perfect Being Theology (PBT) on these matters, but also over Worship Worthy Being Theology (WWT). Such a result is stage-setting for later chapters where the derivability of starting points of alternative metatheologies takes center stage, moving on to the final questions about other moral and metaphysical attributes that each metatheology can sustain. Here, though, the focus is on the initial three mentioned above. I take up the first of these in §4.2, turning to the issue of personhood in §4.3, and embodiment in §4.4. We begin, then, with the issue of monotheism.

## 4.2 Monotheism

On the capacity to preserve monotheism, CT has the most obvious advantage. For if God is the asymmetrical source of all else, monotheism follows immediately. First, it follows on standard Russellian treatment of definite descriptions that there is at most one such being.[1] I'll explain later why no derivation of monotheism should rely on this Russellian perspective, so our focus should be on a second point instead. For monotheism follows from CT even apart from this Russellian stance, since nothing but one being could stand in the relation of being the asymmetrical source of all else to everything else.

Consider an attempt to avoid this commitment to monotheism, using the suggestion that the gods are the asymmetrical source of all else. Here we have an example of plural quantification and there are two readings of the claim. One reading is distributive and the other collective. The distributive reading has the gods jointly responsible for everything by dividing

---

[1] See Russell (1905).

responsibility for things among the gods: each god is responsible for some of the things. The collective reading has the group of gods itself jointly responsible for all.

A helpful example of the difference between distributive and collective predication is this:

(Distributive)   Some students sat to eat.
(Collective)   Some students sat in a circle to eat.

In (Distributive), the predicate attaches to each of the students individually; in (Collective), it does not, but only characterizes the group as a whole. But then, on the distributive reading of "the gods are the asymmetrical source of all else", we see an immediate problem. For each of the gods would have to be the asymmetrical source of all the other gods, and this result is coherent only on the assumption that there are no other gods. The result is incoherent when there is more than one god precisely because sourcehood is an asymmetric relation: if $x$ is the source of $y$, then $y$ is not the source of $x$.

Some will want to take refuge here by appealing to restricted quantification, and when we can correctly note that there is nothing in the refrigerator even though it contains empty shelves. The idea would be to treat the quantifier 'all' as a restricted quantifier, including only the things that are not gods.

It is not difficult to see that such retrenchment is strained. There are contexts in which quantifiers are properly understood to be restricted, and other contexts in which they are not. In set theory, for example, if I report, "no set is a member of itself", the context makes clear that the quantifier is unrestricted. The same point holds for philosophical contexts as well. If you report that there can be no disembodied minds, it is obvious that the quantifier is properly understood to be fully general. So, the same should be said for the claim that the gods source everything else.

I note, though, that some restriction on the quantifier may be forced on CT if problems arise for the view when taken at face value, employing an unrestricted quantifier. But it is one things to revise a model in light of problems and quite another to pretend that the initial characterization of the model was amibiguous between restricted and unrestricted readings of the relevant quantifier. That is simply false: the context of discussion makes clear that an unrestricted reading is the appropriate one.

We are left, then, with the collective reading of the claim. The sourcing, on such a reading, is collective, and there is no imputation of sourcing to any of the gods individually. An advantage of this reading is that it allows an unrestricted reading of the quantifier 'all', for the sourcing applies to everything not a part of the sourcing group.

Yet, if the sourcing is collective in this way, we can ask whether the sourcing is agential or non-agential. For if the sourcing is non-agential, the view will have all the disadvantages of any view on which God is taken not to be a person. As hinted already, we will find these problems severe, so let's consider what happens if we take the sourcing by the collective to be agential.

Once the collectivity is taken to be the agential source of all else, however, we encounter further perplexiities. To get to this conclusion, we first need to understand the sourcing to be something like a case of collective action, as we find when members of a music group play particular notes in order to perform a piece of music. But collective action isn't enough here, for such action can be unintentional, as noted in Searle (1990). Yet, if the collective action has to be undergirded by shared intentions of some sort, we should find the agency present in the collective action to be at the level of the individual gods rather than at the collective level. The collectivity is agential only by courtesy; agency is really present just in the individuals rather than in the group.

So to make the collectivity agential, the view will need to treat such agency differently from how we understand collective action more generally. Yet, if we cannot appeal to collective action by way of explanation, it will become difficult to explain why the resulting view is polytheistic.

Consider, in this context, social Trinitarianism.[2] This view is held by its proponents to be a version of monotheism on which the one God is identified with a three-person plurality. I note the obvious here, to prevent any misunderstanding: claiming something doesn't make it so! But, for the moment, suppose the claim is correct. If so, then agential collective sourcing is compatible with monotheism. Moreover, to the extent that the collective sourcing needs to be understood to be agential, to that very extent we have grounds for positing sufficient unity in the collectivity to undergird attributions of identity.

To resist such a monotheistic result, the view would have to rely on the possibility of disunity in some contexts, so that some of the gods could be doing things that other of the gods are not. Yet, if there is such a possibility, there is also the possibility of conflict among the gods, and the Problem of the Pantheon arises. So avoiding monotheism by positing the possibility of disunity gives rise to further problems.

The remaining hope for avoiding monotheism is to argue that social Trinitarianism is not, in fact, a monotheistic position. Yet, as we have already seen, our best understanding of collective activity gives us reason, albeit

---

[2] See, for example, Moltmann (1981) and Volf (1998). For discussion of objections to the view and a defense of it against these objections, see Hasker (2010, 2011).

non-monotonic in character, for drawing the conclusion that collective action arises in virtue of shared intentions among the collectivity, thereby generating activity by the collectivity that is best understood to be non-agential, even though arising out of the individual agency of the members of the collectivity. Moreover, it is no response to a non-monotonic argument for X to point out that the premises might be true while X isn't!

The point is that we have found grounds for linking CT to monotheism, so long as we resist the temptation to hold that no grounds or reasons or arguments are good unless they are monotonic in character. Such is a fairly ubiquitous temptation among philosophers, but it is a temptation to be resisted. The link between CT and monotheism is thus not as conclusive as we might like, but Cartesian certainty is pretty much always a philosophical chimera.

The proper conclusion to draw here, then, is that even without reliance on a Russellian treatment of definite descriptions, CT is best understood in terms of a monotheistic understanding of this claim about sourcing. We achieve this result while also noting that all of our metatheologies generate recipes for how to revise the metatheology without abandoning it entirely, if the view turns out to be objectionable in some way or other. But such revision is something to be considered further down the road of theoretical development, not some accommodation we make from the beginning.

Both WWT and PBT have more difficulty here than does CT. Though there are attempts to show that there cannot be more than one omni-being,[3] the arguments generally fall short by failing to rule out the possibility of multiple beings in full modal accord in heart, mind, and will. Consider omnipotence, for example, and the claim that there can't be two omnipotent beings because when conflicts between the two arise, only one could be the winner, and only the winner could be omnipotent. This reasoning isn't compelling without an additional argument for the possibility of such a conflict, for if the two beings can't experience such a conflict of wills, the inference to the superiority of one over the other is undermined. In order to sustain the inference, we would then have to treat it as a piece of *per impossibile* reasoning, and, to understate the point, our understanding of such reasoning isn't understood well enough to view the argument that would result as adequate. As a result, it is difficult to see how a defender of PBT could derive monotheism from the claim that a perfect being must be an omni-being: even if this claim is true, there is no obvious way to show that there can be only one omni-being.

---

[3] See, for example, Baillie and Hagen (2008) and Frigerio and Florio (2015).

Moreover, the idea that there is a being that is supremely worthy of the highest and most exalted form of worship doesn't immediately imply that there is only one such being. The possibility of ties for this status is in need of argument, and nothing about such supremacy rules out a community of beings all equally deserving. Hence WWT is in no better position than PBT to sustain monotheistic commitments.

A qualification is necessary here, however, for both WWT and PBT can be stated using a definite description: God is either *the* being most worthy of the highest worship, or *the* most perfect being. Once the definite description is in place, both metatheologies could then resort to a Russellian treatment of definite descriptions noted earlier to sustain monotheistic commitments. When I first mentioned this way of sustaining monotheism, I expressed a bit of skepticism about it, and it is time to explain why this strategy for sustaining monotheism should be resisted.

First, a Russellian treatment of definite descriptions is not sacrosanct, for there are perfectly adequate uses of definite descriptions that create difficulties for this position. Socrates was the teacher of Plato, and Plato of Aristotle, but no one thinks that these philosophers had one and only one teacher. Or, again, I visit the dog park and correctly report to you that the dogs barked a lot. Notice two definite descriptions here. The first one doesn't uniquely designate, and the second doesn't designate at all (there is a dog park that I visited but there is no thing that is picked out by the phrase "the dogs"). One more case: I baked a cake and put it next to the coffee maker. Again, we have a perfectly acceptable syntactic construction involving a definite description ('the coffee maker'), but the description does not uniquely designate.

In the face of such examples, the best way to approach the Russellian treatment of definite descriptions is in terms of a regimentation of language, requiring that much of our ordinary use of definite descriptions be seen as elliptical or contextual in some way. Or perhaps definite descriptions are often ambiguous, as Keith Donnellan (1966) argued; or, again, perhaps an appeal to pragmatics rather than semantics is needed, as Saul Kripke (1977) claims. Perhaps the most compelling reason for dissociating the derivation of monotheism from Russellianism about definite descriptions, however, arises once we see the full implications of a distinction between semantics and pragmatics, of the sort deriving from the work of Paul Grice.[4] Once this distinction is place, it may be possible to explain the difference between definite and indefinite descriptions in pragmatic terms, as is argued in Ludlow

---

[4] See, e.g., Grice (1968).

and Segal (2004). If such an account can be defended, no semantic significance should be attached to the use of a definite description, and hence no entailment of monotheism from such a description would be defensible.

So a defense of Russellianism faces significant theoretical roadblocks. Perhaps an amended version of it can be defended, perhaps not. My point is that it doesn't matter. For the slogan form of each metatheology gives no license for treating them as free from the complications faced by the kinds of examples used above to show the need for refining the original Russellian story about definite descriptions. Moreover, once we treat the slogans as of a piece with claims about who was the teacher of Plato, the derivation of monotheism from the presence of a definite description is undermined. So even if Russellianism can be defended in some modified form, we shouldn't credit any of our three initial metatheologies with a successful derivation of monotheism from the fact that each can be characterized using a definite decription.

It is for this reason that it was important to show that CT is capable of generating an argument for monotheism without appeal to such Russellianism. For there is nothing requiring that we formulate our metatheologies using definite descriptions. Instead, we can characterize PBT as the claim that to be a deity, one must be unsurpassably great; we can characterize WWT as the claim that to be a deity, one must be supremely worthy of the highest worship; and CT can be formulated as the claim that to be a deity, one must asymmetrically source all else. When formulated in these more generic ways, monotheism has to be derived from the content of the description rather than from a Russellian treatment of definite descriptions. As a result, CT has an advantage over both PBT and WWT, since its description can generate a commitment to monotheism, in contrast to what can be said about PBT and WWT. So, to the extent that monotheism is the preferred option in metatheology, CT has an advantage.

What is less clear is whether this advantage remains undefeated when we consider possible ways in which monotheism is abandoned. Multiplicity comes in two forms, one with the kind of embarrassing interactions and conflicts common in the mythology of the Greek pantheon, and another form where the multiplicity in question must be in harmony. Once we have harmony as a requirement on multiplicity, we also get a kind of unity within the divine realm that is at least close to a social Trinitarian view common in recent Christian thought.[5] If such a social Trinitarianism is not a black mark against

---

[5] See, for example, Moltmann (1981) and Volf (1998). For discussion of objections to the view and a defense of it against these objections, see Hasker (2010, 2011).

a theology, then perhaps the failure by WWT and PBT to sustain monotheism is not a problem either, at least so long as they can sustain a derivation of the claim that the divine realm must be harmonious. At the very least, however, the failure is not debilitating to these views: we might wish for a stronger position, but we can't rule out either PBT or WWT on this ground alone.

It is worth taking a moment to comment in support of the need for harmony, if monotheism is going to be abandoned. I noted in passing the embarrassing interactions and conflicts within the Greek pantheon, defects in the conceptions of deity sufficient to rule them out from the land of plausible positions. Here I side with Socrates and Plato, with one additional remark. There can be drama in the supernatural realm, but it is precisely this kind of drama that should lead us to draw a distinction between deities and other divine beings. The angels can war among themselves, if that is one's preferred narrative; other divine beings might pursue an agenda against their divine enemies; but that's why they are to be counted as merely divine beings rather than deities. It is this point that lies behind the advantage generated for a metatheology when it can sustain monotheistic inclinations, even if this inclination is a defeasible one.

We thus have an initial advantage for CT over both PBT and WWT. If the latter two can explain away this advantage by securing the needed harmony in some other way, this advantage may diminish to the point of insignificance. We will see whether such a result is forthcoming in later chapters devoted to the prospects for PBT and WWT.

The next issue involves sorting beings into kinds and asking what kind of being a deity is. Though we might begin generically in terms of living and non-living, animate and inanimate, the crucial task is that of determining whether divinity is to be thought of in personal or non-personal terms. To the question of whether and how CT might sustain the viewpoint that God is a person, we turn in the next section.

## 4.3 Personhood

On this issue, WWT has an immediate advantage, since worship is intimately connected with the bodily posture of bowing down involving an attitude of surrender or subservience.[6] There are attitudes related to worship that can be taken toward inanimate objects, objects without intellect and will. For

---

[6] Thanks to Eleonore Stump for pushing me to recognize the centrality of this point to a proper understanding of worship.

example, one can praise a work of art, one can be in awe in the presence of a grand landscape, one can acknowledge dependence on the order of things, and one can even show reverence for the vastness of the universe. One can also value to the highest degree inanimate things. None of these attitudes or responses need rise to the level of worship, for they bear no intrinsic connection to the obeisance and bowing down that is central to the nature of worship. Worship involves taking an attitude of surrender or submission toward another, where the attitude is displayed in some way or other, a way that constitutes a communicative act. One is not merely prostrating oneself, if such the behavior be, one is also communicating surrender or submission in so doing. Such communicative acts make sense only when directed at persons—things characterized by mental powers involving, minimally, cognition and will. Such acts make sense only on the (Gricean) assumption that one's utterances are accompanied by an intention of some sort directed at an audience, where mind and will are constitutive of anything that can be an audience.

The significance of this point can be lost if we are not careful in making it. For we can, of course, talk to anything: we can curse at machines, talk to one's plants to help them grow, complain to the sky about the weather, etc. When engaged in such activities, however, we are engaging in a kind of communicative pretense that is easy to detect on introspection: we, for example, first personify and then cuss. Worship involves no such pretense.[7]

It is interesting to note that, at least in western thought, the desirable derivation of personhood from CT and PBT is generally elided quickly. If God is the creator of all, we quickly ask questions that presuppose personhood: how powerful and knowledgeable and good must one be in order to pull off such a enormous task? And when we begin by claiming that God is the most perfect possible being, we immediately imagine or investigate the idea that God must then be an omni-being, perfect in power, knowledge, and goodness. But neither of these destinations can be reached without first showing that both PBT and CT imply personhood.

Here, in my judgment, PBT suffers the more serious disability. To derive the conclusion that God is a person, on the assumption that God is the most perfect possible being, one will need to argue that being a person is a great-making property. The first obstacle here is one voiced nicely by Xenophanes: "But if horses or oxen or lions had hands or could draw with their hands and accomplish such works as men, horses would draw the figures of the

---

[7] For discussion of worship and a related but different criticism of ways for defenders of impersonal conceptions of deity to try to make such positions religiously significant, see Leftow (2016).

gods as similar to horses, and the oxen as similar to oxen..." (Lesher, 1992, Fragment 15). The issue of anthropomorphism in theology is pressing on many fronts, but is especially pressing when it comes to this initial stage of theorizing, when the personhood of God is under consideration. It is good for persons to be persons, but what we need to assess is whether, for any given thing whatsoever, it is better for that thing to be a person than not. Such a remark engenders puzzlement. My garage is a thing; is a garage the sort of thing that would be better if it were a person? Well, it wouldn't be a better garage! Still, the thought might be that it would be better even if not a better garage. An affirmative response to this suggestion is dumbfounding, I submit. For one thing, it will be hard to avoid the conclusion that no universe is better than one composed only of persons, and that claim is indefensible.

Perhaps my hesitance here is the result of mischaracterizing PBT. As I portray the commitment above, PBT claims that, for any given thing, it is better for that thing to be a person than not. Perhaps we should substitute existential quantification for universal, claiming instead that being a person is better for some things and great-making because of it. As should be obvious, however, this weakening can't work. Having a roof is good for a garage, a long neck for a giraffe, etc., but none of these properties are great-making in themselves. Substituting an existential quantifier for a universal one fails to honor this point.

This point is crucial for seeing the burden that PBT faces. For an attractive idea is to identify the omni-properties as great-making and then infer personhood from them. But first we need an account of great-making that makes omni-properties great-making. If we quantify over all things, we fail since it wouldn't be an improvement in a garage for it to acquire omniscience. If we quantify only over some things, then the omni-properties are great-making for some kinds of things, but then we need a separate argument that they are great-making for deities. Either way, there is no route from omni-properties to personhood, but rather the direction of derivation needs to go in reverse: first generate personhood, and then derive the omni-properties.

But perhaps the quantification over things is generating this problem for PBT, rather than just which quantifier is chosen. Perhaps, in requiring that being a person is a great-making property, PBT needn't gloss this claim in terms of quantification at all. The only clear requirement that PBT must endorse is that nothing can be the greatest possible being without being a person. If value commensurability holds across all beings, PBT must also claim that things that are persons have an advantage, even if defeasible, over things that are not persons. If value incommensurability sometimes occurs, the defeasible advantage need hold only among commensurables. The only commitment that is indefeasible is that the greatest possible being must be a person (under the assumptions made by standard PBT, that being an omni-being, or as close to it as is possible, is central to PBT).

Even under this more carefully articulated position, however, we should still find the link between personhood and great-making properties well short of obvious. Thus, even if it is hyperbole to call "befuddling" the claim that personhood follows from perfection, it is still a link that is seriously in need of argument. It is interesting to note that no such argument has been given by the major defenders of PBT.

Moreover, the property of being a person is ill-suited for being the kind of property that PBT focuses on in characterizing the nature of God. In the standard way of articulating that position, those properties are supposed to be great-making properties with an intrinsic *maxima*. Such properties, we might say, are analogue rather than digital properties. Being tall comes in degrees, but has no maximal value, so isn't one of the properties to consider when characterizing the most perfect possible being.[8] Moreover, being a being isn't a property that comes in degrees, so it, too, is not one of the properties to consider when characterizing the most perfect possible being. Note that if it were, the ontological argument would be superfluous for PBT: one would only need to note that it is certainly better to be than not to be (Hamlet be damned), and then one could derive in one step that the greatest possible being exists. Instead, defenders of PBT must show that there is an analog property involving existence (such as the property of durability of existence in the face of possible changes to the entire story of a given possible world), and then show that necessary existence is the maximal value for such a property.

Just so with the property of being a person. It does not come in degrees and hence is not an intuitive candidate for being a great-making property. If one adopts the standard methodology of deriving the nature of God from great-making properties, it looks as if one should treat personhood in a similar fashion to the way in which PBT treats existence itself. That is, it must be a derived property from some other great-making property. In the case of existence, that property may be something like durability of possible beings, but there is no direct analogy here for personhood.

One might claim here that there is such a strategy available: just use the properties that constitute being an omni-being, and then derive personhood from one or more of them. In particular, one might appeal to omniscience

---

[8] This point about the connection between degreed properties and the idea of intrinsic *maxima* is developed in Wierenga (1979).

and omnibenevolence for such a derivation. But this strategy returns us to the problem noted earlier. If PBT involves a claim about what makes a thing better than it would be otherwise, it isn't clear that knowledge, goodness, and power are great-making properties, full stop. It may be true that to be the greatest possible being, a being must be an omni-being, but that is not a claim that can be derived from the claim that omni-properties are properties that make anything better than it would be without them.

The familiar way of avoiding this issue is to try to find a hierarchy among kinds of beings, and rank these kinds in terms of greatness. Doing so typically results in animals being superior to inanimate things, intelligent life being superior to the life of plants, and persons being superior to other kinds of intelligent life. Such an approach, however, is especially vulnerable to the Xenophanian point about anthropomorphism noted earlier, and is also threatened by the general motivations for apophaticism that question the degree to which we can transfer reliable assessments of the natural order beyond that order to the supernatural realm. Finally, the ordering in the hierarchy can be reasonably questioned as well. We might wonder, for example, exactly why solar systems and galaxies aren't to be ranked higher on this order of impressiveness of being than human beings. To be clear here, I'm not claiming that human beings aren't that impressive, but there is surely an interesting case to consider here whether the vastness of the universe doesn't have the implied dwarfing of the significance of what we see on a local scale. PBT may be able to overcome these concerns, but my point is that there is an issue here, one not easily resolved, and part of this issue makes it difficult to rest easy with the claim that PBT has the power to show that God must be a person.

It is for these reasons that I claimed that PBT suffers a disadvantage. I also claimed that the disadvantage is worse for PBT than for CT, and that result requires showing that CT is able to derive the claim that God is a person. Let's see why.

Noting the negative first, the simplest link in CT is that between sourcehood and power, for it is of the nature of sources to have a productive capacity, and such a capacity involves some element of power. But knowledge and goodness do not follow from this link alone, since productive forces fall into two categories—production by agents and production by non-agents. Such a category scheme mirrors discussions about causation where we distinguish between event causation and agent causation. Once we have such a scheme in mind, it is easy to see why one might be skeptical of the capacity for CT to sustain the view that being a deity involves being a person.

What is needed here is an argument that when we are considering the all-inclusive sourcehood definitive of CT, agential sourcehood is required. While it is true that non-agential sourcehood is quite common (for example, asexual reproduction involves non-agential sourcehood), the claim would have to be that creation itself is different.

Here's one way to press the point. When it comes to production of Y from X, whether agential or not, we need an explanation of the link between the productive nature of X and the particular, specific character of Y which it generates. In ordinary causation, for example, the link here might be provided by laws of nature: the motion, trajectory, and velocity of the cue ball generates a particular motion, acceleration, and velocity of the ball that is struck in virtue of the laws that link the precise values of the former with the precise values of the latter. We can describe the explanatory relation between source and product as thus requiring, as Schaffer (2017) claims, an ordered triple <Source, Links, Product>, where the links appeal to laws of nature.

Consider, then, the metaphysical status of such laws of nature.[9] Fine-tuning and cosmological reasoning proceeds on the assumption that we can make sense of imaginary situations in which such laws do not hold. We ask what a universe would look like if the gravitational constant were different, if the speed of light were other than it is, if the weak and strong nuclear forces were changed. Such reasoning presupposes some notion of possibility, and though there are other options we will consider later, one quite natural option to turn to first is the notion of metaphysical necessity itself. On this option, the laws of nature are metaphysically contingent.

We will consider later what happens when we question this assumption, but we'll focus first on the strategy that embraces this assumption. In the all-inclusive context in which the asymmetrical source of all else is generating the specific result which is the actual cosmos, we encounter a missing link. We note the presence of a productive power, but we must also explain the link between such a display of power and the precise output that results. In ordinary cases, such an explanation appeals to laws of nature. But in the all-inclusive context under consideration, such an appeal is hopeless. First, the laws aren't themselves metaphysically necessary, and second, they are part of the "all else" that must sourced in God. So any such appeal generates vicious circularity immediately.

---

[9] For some literature, see Bird (2007b); Drewery (2005); Roberts (2010); Swoyer (1982); Sidelle (2002); Schaffer (2004); Wolff (2013).

To avoid this difficulty, we might supplement the appeal to contingent laws of nature with metaphysical laws that are not contingent but (metaphysically) necessary. What of the other possibility, where we grant that laws of nature are contingent and so posit metaphysical analogues of laws of nature to deal with the problem?[10] A first issue is, as we might put it, the argument from incredulity. Why think there are such metaphysical laws? The best argument for the existence of such principles is in Schaffer (2017), and it is what is usually called a "transcendental argument". The requisite laws, according to Schaffer, are characterizable only in functional terms concerning patterns from source to output. Schaffer uses this minimalist result to resist more substantive requirements on metaphysical laws that give rise to objections to the idea of such laws. Such further requirements might involve further metaphysical commitments to essences or grounding relations, for example. Even if we grant the need for some such laws, though, such a minimalism about these laws makes them impotent for the explanatory purposes of our present context. Mere source-output patterns of a metaphysically necessary sort won't generate the insight that ties good explanations with the notion of understanding and its distinctive "aha" moment when the connections in question are grasped.[11] This point is simply a metaphysical analogue of a standardly recognized inadequacy about Humean regularity accounts of explanation. Contingent regularities alone don't explain specific instances of them, and neither do metaphysical regularities if all we have to go on are functional input-output links between displays of power and specific outcomes. To hold otherwise is like offering $p$ as an argument for $q$ and addressing a question about how such an inference makes any sense at all by insisting that the latter is a metaphysically necessary consequence of the former. There simply has to be more to the explanatory story than that.

This point leads quite naturally to the other option avaible for non-personal versions of CT, the option of denying that laws of nature are themselves contingent. At the very least, embracing this option doesn't leave us in the dark as to what the metaphysically necessary laws are that are being used to link a display of power to a given precise result, for even if we only see through a glass darkly what the laws of nature are, good science is at least giving us some such glimpse that goes beyond a merely functional characterization of these links.

---

[10] The first part—that there have to be metaphysical laws—has been argued for in recent literature. See, e.g., Rosen (2006, 2017); Kment (2014); Wilsch (2015); Glazier (2016), and Schaffer (2017).

[11] For relevant literature on understanding and its connection with explanation, see Kvanvig (2003, 2009b,c,d); Kosso (2007); Pritchard (2009, 2010); Grimm (2010, 2011); Mizrahi (2012); Gardiner (2012); Khalifa (2012, 2013a,b); Strevens (2013); Baumberger (2014); Camp (2014); Rohwer (2014); Kelp (2015); Turri (2015); Wilkenfeld et al. (2016), and Baumberger et al. (2017).

I note first a mild cost for this view. The argument noted above for a contingent understanding of laws of nature appealed to various counterfactuals concerning basic laws and fundamental forces. If we reject the contingency of laws of nature, these counterfactuals have to be understood as counterpossibles. Even though counterpossible reasoning is far from well understood, some comfort might be found by noting that much metaphysical explanation relies on laws and generalizations that have to be metaphysically necessary to do the needed work, and that combining this account with plausible interventionist elements in the notion of explanation entails that the needed counterfactuals are in fact counterpossibles.[12] To illustrate schematically, suppose being an $F$ both necessitates and explains being a $G$, and further suppose the notion of explanation requires an appeal to what happens to the *explanans* when the *explanandum* is absent. In such a case, the link is necessary and the account of explain must thus involve an appeal to a counterpossibility.

So the first mild cost is the additional burden of trying to make sense of counterpossible reasoning. Yet, even if we can live with this cost, the deeper problem is that resisting contingentism alone is not enough. For consider the possibility of *alien* properties, individuals, and laws relating such aliens. To be alien in this way, these possibilities can obtain only in other worlds, and so don't threaten the necessity of the laws that relate the properties and individuals that actually exist. Alien laws are just as metaphysically necessary as are native laws, it's just that the individuals and properties whose behavior and interactions are governed by the laws are alien, obtaining only in non-actual scenarios.

So, embracing necessitarianism about laws of nature doesn't by itself give us a sufficient characterization of the link between source and output in the story of God's sourcing of all else. To characterize that link , the necessities in question have to quantify over all the things that are to be found in all of metaphysically possible space. For example, if laws relate properties, appeal to laws of nature being metaphysically necessary won't give an adequate account of the needed linking principles unless exactly the same properties exist in every world.

In short, there is more than necessitarianism about laws that has to be taken on board to resist agentialism. Suffice it to say that the cost of such necessitarianism is enormously high.[13] Better to allow the possibility of aliens, to allow

---

[12] As argued in Wilson (2016), which also notes the tempting line of reasoning from this point to skepticism about this combination of views. Though tempting, eliminating the distinction between useful and detrimental appeals to counterpossibles is, I would argue, a road to nowhere, but there is no need to pursue that issue here.

[13] The cost is high even without noting a further cost concerning the problem of evil. J. L. Mackie (1982) spends considerable time initially describing how pain and suffering lead to benefits later on,

that whatever laws of nature quantify over is the sort of thing that needn't be worldbound but needn't be necessary either. If so, whatever necessitarianism is left isn't a necessitarianism that will solve the first problem the non-agentialist faces, which is to explain the precise generating effects of the display of power from the source of these effects.

It is worth noting that things don't get better if we shift to a powers-based approach to properties, claiming that properties have an essence consisting of their potential causal interactions.[14] Combining such an ontology with an endorsement of physical intentionality of powers has been proposed as a way of generating a defensible version of pantheism in Pfeifer (1997, 2016) and Bauer (2019). The idea, I take it, is to let the physical intentionality of powers mimic the role of divine mental states on standard theistic accounts of creation, thereby yielding a satisfying an explanation of creation in purely impersonal terms. Such an account does not succeed, however, for even if the potential interactions are metaphysically necessary, such an account provides no obvious way to show that alien properties and powers, as described above, are impossible. Moreover, if it were developed in a way to derive such an impossibility, it would an appeal to powers that would threaten contingency itself, in just they way described earlier. So changing to a powers ontology will not salvage an attempt to avoid a personal deity by appeal to some form of necessitarianism.

Moreover, no matter whether one is a necessitarian about laws of nature or merely posits some metaphysical analogue of contingent laws of nature, there remains the second problem noted above for non-agential accounts. Note that the sourcehood in question is an asymmetrical sourcehood of all else, we'll need to source the principles themselves in God since they are not identical with God. On what I think of as the beautiful version of Classical Theism, contingent truth finds its source in God's will and non-contingent truth finds its source in the operations of the Divine mind.[15] If one wishes to present a non-agential version of CT, one will it hard to see how to mimic the advantages of this version of CT. Most serious here is the apparent threat of circularity: the needed metaphysical principles have to explain contingency arising from

---

but notes that such a connection is of no help in addressing the problem of evil, since the connections in question are not metaphysically necessary, but only causally necessary. On the necessitarianism in question, this reply will be mistaken, making it easier for theists to respond to the problem of evil, even without resorting to a distinction between the logical problem and the evidential problem. (For the latter distinction and its relevance, see Howard-Snyder (1996).)

[14] See, e.g., Heil (2003); Molnar (2003); Mumford (2004); Bird (2007a); Martin (2007), and Mumford and Anjum (2011).

[15] This view is traceable to Augustine (1982 [396]).

some source, but also have to be themselves explained in terms of the same source. We get the familiar options involved in regress arguments: no circles, no stopping, and no infinite regress.

We need to be cautious here, however, since regress arguments are always suspicious! Here, I note that the target shifts: it is initially the realm of contingency, but then the target becomes the metaphysical principles themselves. When the target of explanation shifts in this way, the regress charge becomes less concerning.

When we press further, though, we see that the resources for explanation are limited. We are imagining a source of power that is non-personal and comparing it with a personal version of the view. On the personal version, we get a bifurcation: we explain contingency in terms of the Divine will and necessity in terms of other mental powers. If we go non-personal, we find no resources for such bifurcation, and without such bifurcation, we find no adequate account of the realm of necessity.[16]

If we turn to agential sourcehood, however, we find better prospects. We find, on this approach, the missing links in the mind of God, specifically, in the divine intentions. Basic actions, "tryings", give us a model here. To accomplish our ends, we often perform such basic actions: to win the game, I have to make this free throw, so I try to do so. Laws of nature enter into the story of when I succeed, but the success conditions for tryings are found elsewhere. For tryings, the intentional element involved itself provides its own success conditions.

Even if this account of basic actions needs refinement or outright rejection when applied to us mere mortals, it provides a useful model for characterizing CT when the asymmetrical source of all else is conceived in personal terms. In such a case, God creates by a display of power, and what makes for the precise character of the resulting cosmos is the precise character of the intentional element involved in that display of power.

The point here is that agential versions of CT have an advantage deriving from the increased complexity and sophistication about sourcehood that results from the dual aspects of intelligence and will involved in such versions. To mimic such complexity and sophistication, non-agential versions would have to find a way to bifurcate sourcehood into two kinds of sourcings,

---

[16] The argument for this claim is simply the folly of non-bifurcated explanations of necessity such as we find in Cartesian voluntarism about necessary truths. For details of the argument, see Plantinga (1980). For discussion of Descartes' actual position and the scholarly controversy about exactly what that position is, see Frankfurt (1977); Curley (1984); Bennett (1994); van Cleve (1994) and Alanen (2008).

one the analogue of the Divine will on agential versions of CT and the other an analogue of the operations of the Divine mind. But non-agential approaches lack any motivation or resources for such a bifurcation, except for that of the dishonest evasion of positing such a bifurcation in order to escape refutation.

Lest I be misunderstood at this point, I am not claiming that agential CT is a coherent philosophical viewpoint. I am claiming that it has resources of the right sort for constructing the explanations needed in order to sustain the claim that God is the asymmetrical source of all else. After thorough examination, we may find that the explanation of necessity in terms of the operations of the Divine mind cannot be sustained, or that there are contingencies that cannot be accounted for in terms of the Divine will. If so, so much the worse for this version of CT, at least, and perhaps for all versions. My point, though, remains: agential versions can clear the first immediate hurdles facing CT, whereas non-agential versions have no theoretical resources for doing so. The place to start, then, is with agential versions of the view.

Starting here makes especially relevant various attempts to undermine the idea of a personal God. One line of thought in this direction of apophatic, but such a view has to show restraint in order to avoid self-refutation. Consider non-exhaustive but exclusive predicates $\sim P$ and $\sim Q$, where both unnegated predicates count as positive predicates (however the distinction between positive and negative is characterized). If we accept the full-blown apophatic doctrine that no positive predicate applies to God, and we accept excluded middle as well, we now must characterize God as an impossible being (since the negated predicates are incompatible). More circumspect negative theologies, of the sort Brian Davies attributes to Aquinas,[17] where we distinguish real from nominal understandings of God, arguing that talk of personhood for God is affirmed only in terms of linguistic understanding and not in terms of a real nature, are not so easily dismissed. Even so, the metaphysical background needed for sustaining the position identified is, to understate things, substantial. We need a metaphysics of form and matter, essence and existence, and an understanding of God in terms of pure act. Perhaps the entire package is defensible, but at our initial point in metatheology, it would be premature to abandon agential versions of CT on such a basis.

The same is true of other recent arguments aimed at showing that God is not a person. Both pantheistic and panentheistic distancing from a personal conception of God requires traveling down a quite long and tortured road of

[17] See Davies (2016).

philosophical dialectic to get to such a conclusion,[18] with too many substantive issues to be decided along the way to undermine an initial preference in favor of a personal conception of deity. Or again, consider arguments that make language prior to mind and insist on externalist and perhaps social conceptions of meaning to argue that the prerequisites for personhood can't be satisfied by deity.[19] I confess here that such ideas strike me as wrongheaded in the extreme: the story of the learning of a language is as embued with mentation as is the notion of behavior itself, and we are all quite familiar with the failure of behaviorism to identify the target of explanation without recourse to the language of the mind. I fully grant the strong epistemic possibility of having common sense corrected by empirical investigation of the sort we find in the sciences, but I'm enough of a Moorean to resist such reasoning for obviously false conclusions. Mentation is abundant throughout (much of) the animal kingdom, language is not. Such a stance, though, is secondary at this point in our investigation, since once again the path to denying the personhood of God involves fairly long and complicated path of philosophical reasoning that is best thought of as arising at a later stage of theological development than what is relevant to the initial stages.

There is more that could be said on this subject, but I will close off this discussion by repeating the two fundamental mysteries—perhaps better termed "disadvantages", "weaknesses", "liabilities", "burdens", or even "flaws"—of non-agential CT. The first is the mystery regarding the content of the metaphysical principles needed to link a source of power with the specific details that result from a given display of that power. The second mystery concerns the need to distinguish two kinds of non-agential displays of power, one a productive kind analogous to causation within the created order, and another non-causal but explanatory display of power to account for necessity itself. To call the latter a mere mystery is, perhaps, to flout intelligibility itself, for it is quite tempting here to insist that the notion of a non-productive, non-causal display of power is inconsistent. But I will stick with understating if such it be: there is at least a mystery here with no apparent way to remove it.

We thus have the promised derivation of personhood for CT, giving it something of an advantage over PBT, which can only derive personhood in a way that invites concerns about anthropomorphism. We turn then to the final issue among the primary elements involved in the common ground for assessing metatheologies, the issue of embodiment.

---

[18] For a good example of such an attempt, see Coleman (2019).
[19] See, e.g., Hewitt (2019).

## 4.4 Embodiment

Recall from the discussion in Chapter 3 that the privileged position is that God is a purely spiritual being, primarily on the basis of concerns about the connection between concreteness and corruptibility, though the preference for denials of embodiment was qualified. The qualification is that this position is not one concerning the derivability of this point, but instead a position about the failure to derive its denial. It is thus an advantage to a metatheology if it doesn't require the embodiment thesis, though there is no need or advantage to a metatheology for a derivation of the denial of the embodiment thesis, so long as there is no proof of the link between concreteness and corruptibility.

To see whether any of our primary metatheologies is at a disadvantage here, we need to inquire about essential and non-essential embodiment. For the former, we need to divide the cases into those in which God has some body or other and those in which God's body is not a contingent thing. For CT, such a lack of contingency would make God's body not depend for its existence on the will of God, but rather something the existence of which is explained in terms of the operations of the Divine mind. In such a case, God's body could not be a thing such as the universe itself or any physical part of it. One might think there might be some hope for embodiment theorists here by adopting a Williamsonian necessitarianism (as in Williamson (2013)), but such hope disappoints. For on such necessitarianism, everything possible is actual, but not everything actual is concrete. In short, Williamsonian necessitarianism replaces the distinction between possible and necessary objects with a distinction between concrete and abstract objects: where contingentists find non-existence, necessitarians find *abstracta*. If we combine such necessitarianism with CT, we would explain the difference between the concrete and the abstract in terms of the operations of the will of God, and it will be a contingent truth that certain objects partake of concreteness in a way that makes it possible for them to be part of the embodiment thesis. If so, however, appeal to necessitarianism won't give us the conclusion that the universe or some physical part of it could be God's body, for the universe and its physical parts are only contingently concrete, and if some object is necessarily God's body, it will have to be necessarily concrete. So, just as on more standard views about contingency, on Williamsonian necessitarianism, God's body would have to be explained in terms of the operations of the Divine mind rather than Divine will.

In thinking further about the option on which God's body is not a contingent thing, there is one further point to note. That point is that it is either a necessary truth that everything is some particular physical thing or other, or it isn't. If it is a necessary truth that everything is some particular physical thing, then the embodiment thesis would be true as well, and any assumption of the existence of any deity, under any description, would entail the embodiment thesis. So our issue becomes significant only under the assumption that it is not metaphysically necessary that everything is physical. What we are looking for is some special reason, unique to the idea of a (personal) deity that would require such.

As far as I can tell, the only reason that could be forthcoming would be if we had a reason for thinking that the only things that could fail to be bodies or be embodied would be *abstracta*, such as things needed for mathematics, science, and semantics. In such a case, the only metatheologies that would be in trouble would be those that have a starting point that entails directly that God cannot be embodied. None of the metatheologies we are considering have such a startling implication, so we can ignore this defense of the idea that any deity must be embodied.

We assume, then, that not everything concrete has to be physical, and ask whether CT generates an argument for thinking that God has a body, either essentially or accidentally. Furthermore, recall here that the argument would have to incorporate an additional feature, emphasized in our discussion of embodiment in the last chapter. That feature is that the kind of embodiment that will matter for our purposes is a kind that allows an inference from having a body with certain characteristics to having those characteristics themselves.[20] If being embodied involves only bearing some relation to a physical thing that doesn't imply anything about the being in question, there is nothing to consider further here. For whatever we say about God, it is clear that God bears some sort of relation to the physical universe. Concerns can arise about this relation only when the relation is the right kind to generate the inference from features of the physical thing to features of God.

The concern bears repeating. Whenever contingency is involved, there is a fragility of existence implied by it, and such fragility is an imperfection. If features of parts of God are also features of God, then such fragility would imply an imperfection in God as well. In such a case, both PBT and WWT would have a ready argument against embodiment. The grounds cited by PBT and WWT would advert to the defect itself to explain why God couldn't have a body of this sort.

---

[20] A point emphasized in Wainwright (1974).

The question is whether CT has resources to join the chorus, and at first glance it doesn't, since CT is not characterized initially in a way involving notions of perfection. Moreover, issue of embodiment is connected with parts over which one has control, and if God is the source, both initial and sustaining, of all things, then all things fall within the kind of direct control that we typically have over (some of) our own bodies. For these reasons, there is an enhanced risk here for CT that it will not be able to avoid claiming that deity must be embodied.

It is a risk only at this point, however, rather than a certainty. First, CT might be able to sustain the starting points of PBT or WWT and thus exploit the grounds coming from those metatheologies for resisting the concern about imperfections in God. Second, CT might try to find a way to block inferences from part to whole when the inference involves an imperfection. What exactly such a blocking device would look like would depend on what else we learn about God from CT. For example, perhaps CT is compatible with indeterminism, both in nature and in human choices. In such cases, imperfections traceable to indeterminacies might be imperfections in the created order that are not imperfections in God.

We need not pursue details concerning such possibilities in our initial considerations of each metatheology. As with all of our initial considerations, there remains the possibility that further inquiry will undermine initial judgments. What would be decisive at this point in counting against CT would be if we could establish that there is no possibility of keeping the defects of creation from counting as defects in God, but it is clear that we are not in such a position. It is worth reminding ourselves that central to any response to the problem of evil is some device or other to keep the imperfections in creation from licensing an inference about imperfections in God. Indeterminacies are one such device, but not the only one. To the extent that such possibilities exist, to that extent we have grounds for resisting the idea that imperfections in creation count as imperfections in God. Perhaps these devices are merely consistent with CT, but perhaps as well we might find grounds for expecting such imperfections that arise specifically from a CT starting point.

We thus have a two-tier story to consider for embodiment. The first tier is whether any of our metatheologies require an embodied deity, and on this issue, all of our metatheologies appear to lack any such implication. There is the possibility, however, that the embodiment thesis can be derived from other purely philosophical considerations, and so there is a second tier to consider as well. For that tier, it is an advantage to a metatheology to be able to show that any connection between embodiment and corruptibility or imperfection in

God can be avoided. On this issue, PBT and WWT have simple and direct ways to prevent any embodiment thesis from implying difficulties for their point, ways not obviously available to CT. This difference yields a slight disadvantage for CT in comparison to PBT and WWT, though a determination of the significance of this disadvantage will have to await conclusions to be reached in Part III of this work, where we consider how successful each metatheology is at sustaining the starting points of alternative metatheologies. If, for example, CT could sustain either the starting points of PBT or WWT, the disadvantage just noted for CT would disappear entirely. For now, however, it remains.

## 4.5 Conclusion

We may conclude then that the derivation of personhood available to CT gives it some advantage, even if minimal, over PBT. This is an advantage that WWT shares with CT, in comparison with PBT. But PBT has at least an initial advantage on the issue of embodiment, an advantage it shares with WWT, over CT. CT, however, also has an advantage over both PBT and WWT when it comes to the issue of monotheism.

Given this mixed scorecard, the prospects for CT to sustain the starting points of competing metatheologies becomes a central challenge for this metatheology. We will turn to that issue in Part III, but before doing so, we can complete our survey of the prospects for each of our initial metatheologies with respect to the common ground of uniqueness, personhood, and embodiment. The next two chapters close out this initial topic for PBT and WWT, respectively.

# 5
# Shaky Ground for Anselmianism

## 5.1 Introduction

In the last chapter, we got a glimpse of some difficulties faced by Perfect Being Theology (PBT). One issue is that of sustaining monotheism, and another is the issue of explaining the personhood of God. In this chapter, I want to press these points further, showing how they are related to an additional issue involving a proper understanding of contingency.

In §5.2, I'll outline the Creator Theology (CT) account of contingency and remind us of its parsimonious ontology of the divine. In §5.3, I'll give details about the structure of the theology generated by PBT, and how it culminates with an ontological argument. I'll then show, in §5.4, how and why this structure threatens ontological profligacy and, relatedly, invites suspicion about its understanding of contingency.

## 5.2 Creator Theology and Contingency

As noted in Chapter 1, we endorse a generic characterization of CT on which God is the source of all else and is ontologically independent of all else. In some narratives, as in Genesis, such sourcehood takes the form of creation at a certain point in history ("in the beginning God created"), though it is easy to imagine alternative possibilities of sourcehood that do not involve creation, such as Aristotle's eternal universe finding its source in an Unmoved Mover.

Theological development then proceeds by addressing how sourcehood and independence are to be understood. As noted in the last chapter, the view has a pristine and restrained ontology of the divine: there is only one asymmetrical source of all else. Moreover, this result is not achieved simply by relying on the idea that all definite descriptions imply uniqueness. Even if we had said that the nature of deity involves being an asymmetrical source of all else, the same result is sustained: there is a defeasible argument from CT to the conclusion that there can be only one such asymmetrical source.

Note this difference from what we get with Anselmian PBT, which originates from the phrase, "that than which a greater cannot be thought." There is nothing in this beginning point alone that yields monotheism. One could try for such a result by replacing this language with that of the greatest possible being, but that gets the monotheistic result on the cheap. What is theoretically desirable is to show that there can't be ties for being the greatest, and so the beginning point of PBT does not yield monotheism as directly as does CT.

Notice as well that in both cases, we could avoid any commitment to monotheism by resorting to logical plurals. Doing so would have us say that the gods, however many there may be, are either the asymmetrical source of all else or the greatest possible beings. Such polytheistic-friendly versions face difficult issues almost immediately. First, it is no virtue of a theory to be ontologically profligate, so an explanation would be needed why more than one deity is important to affirm. Second, complications arise in characterizing the community of deities itself. Are there conflicts? Are there differing roles played by each member? Are some in higher positions of authority than others? Such questions, depending on the answers, can quickly lead to the suspicion that what is being characterized is, at best, only a collection of divine beings rather than one of deities. And things can get worse, for if conflict can arise in the community, who emerges triumphant? If there is a winner, one would think that it is the winner who would be God, not the loser.

It is for such reasons that sustaining monotheism is part of the shared ground relative to which we assess the plausibility of various metatheologies. This privileged status is, as already noted, defeasible, and central to its defeasibility here are the different ways in which monotheism can be abandoned. Multiplicity comes in two forms, one with the kind of embarrassing interactions and conflicts common in the mythology of the Greek pantheon, and another form where the multiplicity in question must be in harmony. Once we have such essential harmony as a requirement on multiplicity, we also get a kind of unity within the divine realm that is at least close to a social Trinitarian view common in recent Christian thought.[1] If such a social Trinitarianism is not a black mark against a theology, then perhaps the failure by PBT to easily derive monotheism is not a problem either, at least so long as they can sustain a derivation of the claim that the divine realm must be harmonious.

Even so, the doctrine of the Trinity puts rather strict limits in place, and even a harmonious group of deities leads one to wonder how many is too many.

---

[1] See, for example, Moltmann (1981) and Volf (1998). For discussion of objections to the view and a defense of it against these objections, see Hasker (2010, 2011).

As we will see, it turns out to be very difficult for PBT to limit the numbers in any sensible way. To see why will take a bit of preparatory work, and we begin the task with a bit of rehearsal about the agential version of CT and its explanation of contingency.

Once theoretical development of CT begins, a primary question concerns the nature of sourcehood itself, and the first stage of inquiry examines whether such sourcehood should be understood as agential or non-agential. Given the results in Chapter 3 granting privileged status to approaches that can sustain the personhood of God, we saw in Chapter 4 that mysteries are best avoided by thinking about sourcehood in agential terms. If so, sourcehood involves dependence on the will and intellect of the creator, where mind and will are the minimal conditions for being an agent. The natural way to develop this view is to hold that contingent truths depend on the will of God and necessary truths finding their source in the operations of the Divine mind.[2] I call this view the "natural" one for the following reason. On any account of sourcehood, some things will be source in God's will, a will capable of turning in any of a variety of different directions. The question that remains is whether there are things not sourced in God's will, since even though there is quite a range of items falling within the category of stuff that could be otherwise, there is also the category of stuff that couldn't be otherwise. Is it, too, explained by the activity of the Divine will? The problem is that if it is, and God's will is malleable, then the stuff that couldn't be otherwise is also stuff that could be otherwise. So contingent truths can be traced to God's will, but necessary truths must find there source elsewhere, in the Divine mind. There are philosophical concerns at each stage of this account, but let's pass on these issues for now to see their implications.

The central implication of concern here is that the will of God, on this account, is utterly unconstrained, except insofar as its operation answers to the mind of God. Metaphysical necessities constrain what can be done, of course, but no constraints beyond these can be found when we are talking about the asymmetrical source of all else. Moreover, if metaphysical necessities are themselves explicable in terms of operations of the Divine mind, these constraints are internal rather than external constraints. The will of God is thus completely free of influence or direction from any outside forces, and thus creation itself is a free act of God. We thereby generate a pleasing account of contingency: anything that finds its source in the will of God comes indelibly

---

[2] Such a view can be traced to Augustine (1982 [396], pp. 79–81). For discussion of Augustine's legacy on this issue, see Adams (1987, pp. 79–83).

stamped with the mark of contingency. That is, not only are the things so sourced contingent, they could not fail to be so: there is no such possibility as merely contingent contingency; instead, it is essential to every possible contingent nature that it is contingent.

The same is not to be said about things that find their source in the operations of the Divine mind, for here we find the landscape of modality itself.[3] It, too, is marked indelibly: with respect to that which is explained solely in terms of the operations of the Divine mind, there is no such thing as contingent necessity.[4] Here, there is no potentiality in terms of the relevant operations that would result in the operations being one way but capable of another. The argument for this conclusion is simply the incoherence of Cartesian voluntarism regarding necessary truths.[5]

We thus have an account of a fundamental notion of necessity, and what remains is to characterize the variety of necessities distinct from the fundamental notion of metaphysical necessity. Things may not be as easy as they seem, but the intuitive idea is that metaphysical necessity is absolute and unconditional, and other necessities are relative to some more specific claims.[6] We can then understand logical necessity as absolute necessity relative to, perhaps, a set of axioms; accidental necessity (at a time) as absolute necessity relative to the past for that time; nomological necessity as absolute necessity as necessity relative to the laws of nature, etc.

---

[3] For discussion and details, see Morris and Menzel (1986) and Menzel (2016).

[4] Note, to be clear, that I do not say that there is no such thing as contingent necessity. The necessity of the past is one kind of contingent necessity. There may be other kinds as well: if laws of nature are themselves not metaphysically necessary, or if they are but are always and everywhere "oaken" rather than "iron" laws (as explicated in Armstrong (1983), where an oaken law is capable of suffering violations even though true because of its essential *ceteris paribus* clause), then nomic necessity—the kind of necessity that obtains in virtue of explanations in virtue of laws of nature—is also a kind of contingent necessity.

[5] For details of the argument, see Plantinga (1980). For discussion of Descartes's actual position and the scholarly controversy about exactly what that position is, see Frankfurt (1977); Curley (1984); Bennett (1994); van Cleve (1994) and Alanen (2008).

[6] This idea can be traced at least to Aquinas (1948 [1265–74], I.82.1):

> The word "necessity" is employed in many ways. For that which must be is necessary. Now that a thing must be may belong to it by an intrinsic principle—either material, as when we say that everything composed of contraries is of necessity corruptible—or formal, as when we say that it is necessary for the three angles of a triangle to be equal to two right angles. And this is "natural" and "absolute necessity." In another way, that a thing must be, belongs to it by reason of something extrinsic, which is either the end or the agent. On the part of the end, as when without it the end is not to be attained or so well attained: for instance, food is said to be necessary for life, and a horse is necessary for a journey. This is called "necessity of end," and sometimes also "utility." On the part of the agent, a thing must be, when someone is forced by some agent, so that he is not able to do the contrary. This is called "necessity of coercion."

In the text, I prefer to label the basic distinction in terms of absolute and relative necessity, rather than intrinsic and extrinsic. Moreover, no commitment needs to be made at this point as to the species within each genera.

Such a pleasing picture is not without its critics.[7] We need not pursue this issue at present, however, for our goal is not a full evaluation of the prospects for CT. Instead, we aim here to see the general contours of CT and its accounts of contingency and necessity, leaving for later any refinements that have to be made in light of difficulties faced by an appealing version of the view.

Central to this perspective is thus a two-part account of natures and their essential properties, so that both contingency and necessity are built into natures in virtue of their source in either the mind or will of God, and the resulting divine ontology is strictly monotheistic. Let's now turn to see how PBT can be and needs to be developed, returning to the question of contingency once we have a picture in mind of what the metatheology of PBT looks like.

## 5.3 The Metatheology of Perfection in Being

PBT begins by identifying God as a maximally perfect being. This metatheology can be developed in two ways, top-down or bottom-up. The latter is the more familiar form, with Plantinga (1974) as the best-known version of the view. On Plantinga's account we first identify great-making properties that have intrinsic *maxima* and then derive that God is an omni-being, perfect in power, knowledge, and goodness. Once this characterization is in place, the bottom-upper aims to get existence itself, or something involving it, included in or implied by the collection of great-making properties, so that necessary existence will follow. (My preferred way of expressing this idea is to talk about possible beings that have maximally fragile existence, where any change to a world in which they exist results in a world where they don't exist; then define durability as the capacity to continue to exist despite changes, with maximal durability implying necessary existence.) So God is not only an omni-being, but also necessary if possible.

If we then add the claim that it is possible for there to be a maximally great being, the ontological argument achieves lift-off. My goal here, though, is not to address whether that argument succeeds (or what the relevant notion of sucess is supposed to be), but rather to understand the structure of PBT. The crucial element of this structure is where the property of being necessary if

---

[7] See, e.g., Fine (2002), where it is argued that there are three fundamental and irreducible notions necessity: the metaphysical, the natural, and the normative. See also van Cleve (2018) for consideration of the idea that there are brute necessities, which may not need any explanation at all.

possible enters the story. The ontological argument depends on the claim that there is a possibly necessary being, and this property of being possibly necessary is derived from two other properties: the property of being possible and the property of being necessary if possible. This latter property is added to, or follows from, a collection of great-making properties that have intrinsic *maxima*, so the structure of PBT involves two collections plus a possibility claim. The first collection is the set of great-making properties that purportedly yields the omni-being conception of God, what Plantinga terms the collection of "maximal excellences," where a maximal excellence (ME) is the maximal form for a great-making property with an intrinsic maximum. Thus, where $P$ is a property and $ME_P$ says that $P$ is a maximal excellence, we get a collection C(ME) defined as follows:

C(ME): $\{P : ME_P\}$

The second stage involves adding to C(ME) the property of being necessary if possible, on grounds that durability of possible existence is itself a great-making property with an intrinsic maximum. That maximum is, of course, necessary possible existence, or the property of being necessary if possible. This collection defines the notion of maximal greatness: maximal greatness is C(ME) plus the property of being necessary if possible. So, where $p$ is a proposition:

C(MG): $\{P : ME_P\} \cup \{\lambda p(\Diamond p \rightarrow \Box p)\}$[8]

The final stage in the development of bottom-up PBT is to claim that the collection C(MG) is metaphysically coherent:

$\Diamond$PB: $\Diamond$(all the members of C(MG) are co-exemplified).

That is the basic structure of bottom-up PBT: C(ME), C(MG), and $\Diamond$PB. If successful, it generates an understanding of God in terms of an omni-being and demonstrates the existence of such a being through the ontological argument.

---

[8] Some details about the $\lambda$-calculus used here. '$\lambda$' is an abstraction operator on formulas. Intuitively, $\ulcorner[\lambda x_1, \ldots, x_n \Psi]\urcorner$ denotes the $n$-place relation that holds between objects $a_1, \ldots, a_n$ just in case $\Phi(x_i/a_i)$, for any formula $\Phi$. Note as well that the formula in the text treats (the proposition expressed by) a complete sentence as (expressed by) a zero-place predicate. Further details can be found in Menzel (1986).

The challenges to this bottom-up approach concern the coherence of both C(ME) and C(MG) and the possibility claim, ◇PB, itself. Perhaps the properties in C(MG) are not coherent, either internally, or with each other, or with certain known facts about the world. Moreover, even if C(MG) is logically consistent, ◇PB does not follow from that fact, since such consistency does not imply metaphysical possibility.

In response to the first concern, one might resort to a top-down strategy, where instead of building up a collection of maximal excellences by identifying the maximal value for each great-making property included in the collection, one instead starts with the most impressive and possible total collection of great-making properties.[9] Such a holistic strategy offers, first, a replacement for C(ME), one that guarantees metaphysical coherence among the members of the set. If C(ME) is itself metaphysically coherent, the top-down approach yields the same result as the bottom-up approach. But if C(ME) isn't coherent, all is not lost. Instead, the top-down approach simply generates a set as close to C(ME) as is coherent.[10] Call this set "C(ME)-lite". The advantage of this top-down holism are clear. If omniscience is incoherent, no problem: the holism then only requires that God be as knowledgeable as is compatible with all other individual great-making properties. If omnipotence conflicts with omnibenevolence, no problem either: just withdraw from the lofty peaks a bit, so that God is very powerful and very good. C(ME)-lite is very forgiving when it comes to the potential problems for bottom-up PBT.

As articulated in Nagasawa (2017), one then constructs "C(MG)-lite" from C(ME)-lite by joining together the latter with the property of being necessary if possible. One then replaces ◇PB with "◇PB-lite", the claim that the properties in C(MG)-lite are possibly co-exemplified, running the ontological argument on this premise instead. For that argument to succeed, once the possibility premise is defended, we need only the distinctive S5 claim that anything that is possibly necessary is necessary.[11]

The advantage of this top-down approach is that the notion of coherence invoked to construct C(ME)-lite is best thought of in terms of metaphysical coherence, and thus saying that C(ME)-lite is coherent is the same thing as saying that the co-exemplification of this set of properties is metaphysically possible. That makes it appear at first glance, at least, that we can easily derive ◇PB-lite from this coherence claim, but that appearance is misleading.

---

[9] This top-down strategy is defended in Nagasawa (2017).
[10] I ignore for the time being the issue of whether there is a unique such set.
[11] Well, we also need the T axiom that anything necessary is true, but I suspect it belabors too much to put this point in the text.

For ◇PB-lite isn't a claim about C(ME)-lite, but rather about C(MG)-lite. Furthermore, even if the members of C(ME)-lite can be co-exemplified, that provides no guarantee that the members of C(MG)-lite can be co-exemplified, for one of the same reasons that one might worry that the members of C(ME) might not be able to be co-exemplified: combining coherent properties doesn't always preserve coherence.

So, here's the argument for being a top-downer. C(ME) has no guarantee of coherence, whereas C(ME)-lite does, so there is one way for incoherence to obtain for C(MG) that can't obtain for C(MG)-lite. So, be a top-downer!

Advantages can dissipate quickly on closer inspection, and such is the case here. Notice the recipe to generate the above advantage for top-down PBT. The first step is to find a collection of properties that are guaranteed to be metaphysically coherent, and the second step is to hope the ship can still hold water when we add to this collection the further property of being necessary if possible.

Problems arise at precisely this second step once we note that what happens when we assume that the second set, C(MG)-lite is coherent if C(ME)-lite is. Adding that assumption bloats our ontology and threatens reasonable assumptions about contingency itself.

To see why, we will need a distinction between metaphysically coherent sets of properties from natures, so let's first explain that distinction. A nature is complete, whereas a set of properties need not be. The notion of completeness here is vexed, but if we adopt both bivalence and excluded middle, it is easy enough to characterize: a complete nature is something that can be exemplified, and includes, for every property $P$ except those properties that entail exemplification, either $P$ or its complement $\overline{P}$, that property exemplified by everything that lacks $P$. If either bivalence or excluded middle are abandoned, a different account of completeness will be required, but we need not pursue the details here, for all we need to note is than any actual being in any possible world has a completeness that is to be contrasted with the incompleteness of fictional entities. There is no fictional fact of the matter about whether Sherlock has a mole on his left calf; there is an actual fact of the matter for each of us whether we have such a mole.

I note that it is essential to the methodology of either version of PBT to move from properties that are (purportedly) individually coherent, to sets of compossible properties that are clearly less than complete natures, to the possible exemplification of such a set together with the additional coherent property of being necessary if possible. It is here, in the gap between collections of compossible properties and complete natures, that problems arise for PBT's understanding of contingency.

With this distinction in hand, turn to the issue of what happens when we assume that any compossible set of properties will remain compossible when the property of being necessary if possible is added to the original set. Take any nature and divide it into those properties that metaphysically guarantee contingency and those that don't. A plausible division here will have the intrinsic properties of any object in the group that doesn't guarantee contingency, so that the set of intrinsic qualities of my coffee cup don't tell us one way or another about the cup's contingency. This claim holds even though, I assume, the cup is both contingent and necessarily so, so that every well-formed formula entails that the cup is contingent. My point, though, is that not everything that entails a claim explains it, and the intrinsic qualities of the cup don't explain its contingency.

Next, note that any object that has all of the intrinsic qualities of my coffee cup will be indistinguishable from it. So now take this compossible set of intrinsic qualities and add to it the property of being necessary if possible. If this supplemented collection is also metaphysically coherent, we now get a stunning duplication in ontology: we have both my actual contingent coffee cup and its metaphysically necessary doppelgänger. For the intrinsic character of my coffee cup is clearly exemplifiable (because it is actually exemplified!), and possibility entails necessity for any compossible set of properties that includes being necessary if possible.

The same recipe can be followed for any contingent thing whatsoever. The moral of the story is that loose scruples on when the addition of the modal property preserves metaphysical coherence leads to the absurd conclusion that every contingent thing has its own necessary doppelgänger. This result combines a problem of ontological profligacy with a problem of contingency: we get too many things, and the additional things we get threaten our understanding of contingency. My coffee cup can be destroyed so that it ceases to exist. If being so requires that it have a necessary doppelgänger that can't be destroyed, I think I don't understand this notion of contingency. We must have gotten confused in the process of finding a need for such doppelgängers, and I certainly don't understand how this necessary thing can be the *doppelgänger* of my coffee cup, once the cup is destroyed and the necessary being now shares no properties with this cup.

Can defenders of PBT take refuge in the claim that the intrinsic qualities of my coffee cup actually do guarantee contingency? Well, perhaps if they had an argument for the claim. There is an attractive one available (though I will stop short of endorsing it here), but it undermines the methodology PBT needs. Here's the argument. If an object is contingent, it is necessarily so. So, when we strip natures of some of their properties, and end up with a coherent subset of properties, we can only get to the conclusion that this set is possibly exemplified by retaining in the set all the essential properties of possible exemplifiers. In the case of my coffee cup, we thus have no reason to think that stripping its nature of contingency leaves us with anything other than the empty set.

This argument is intriguing, but deadly to the methodology of PBT. For if the argument is endorsed, any property or set of properties includes contingency or necessity in the properties themselves, and in a way that can't be detected simply by looking at the identifying description of that property. The intrinsic properties of my coffee cup—being oval in shape, white in color, having a mass of 73 grams, etc.—carry no conceptual or analytic connection to being contingent. So a defender of PBT simply can't take collections of great-making properties—either the omniproperties themselves or coherent limitations of some or all of them—and be guaranteed to have a further coherent collection of properties when adding the property of being necessary if possible. The only way to have such a guarantee would be for these properties to be free of the contingency implication that is supposed to plague the intrinsic character of my coffee cup. But such a result upends the order of inquiry central to PBT: it puts the needed conclusion in place before the derivation can be completed.

Could a PBT-er take refuge in the idea that there simply aren't any contingent things at all?[12] No. On such an ontology, the distinction between necessary and contingent has to be replaced by something else, such as the distinction between being concrete and being merely abstract. So reality is still bifurcated in an important sense, and the property appended to coherent collections for purposes of the ontological argument will not be the property of being necessary if possible, but rather the property of being necessarily concrete if possibly abstract. All the same problems re-emerge, just under a different label.[13] So, let's abandon the idea of re-labeling and press on with the problem under the more usual language.

---

[12] For a defense of such an ontology, see Williamson (2013).
[13] For criticism of an ontology limited to necessary beings, see deRosset (2016) and Menzel (forthcoming).

Generating these problems of profligacy and contingency is straightforward. Both top-downers and bottom-uppers hold that the modal property of being necessary if possible can be coherently added to some metaphysically coherent collection of great-making properties. But the coherence of doing so stands in need of an account of when and where such appending preserves metaphysical coherence.

A defender of PBT can resist some of the above, at least. For the argument for the existence of necessary doppelgängers depends on generalizing the central move of PBT, and a defender of PBT can rightly point out that such a generalization was never part of PBT itself. That point is correct. But a related problem will still be present, and it results in the disappearance of the advantage noted above for top-down PBT over bottom-up PBT. Bottom-uppers restrict how the modal property of being necessary if possible gets into the story of the nature of God: it gets in only because there is a great-making property or set of properties that either includes this property or implies it. Top-downers don't get to limit great-making properties in this way, since they don't want C(ME)-lite to be hostage to the metaphysical coherence of the maximal properties involved in being an omni-being. So, top-downers have to countenance less than maximal great-making properties in their account of the nature of God, and so have to embrace a recipe for constructing C(ME)-lite and C(MG)-lite that doesn't restrict membership to maximal great-making properties.

This feature of top-down PBT engenders profligacy concerns not generated by the recipe endorsed by bottom-uppers. Notice that C(ME)-lite is trivially coherent, in virtue of the recipe for its construction. Moreover, if $p$ is logically stronger than $q$ (i.e., if $p$ entails $q$ but not vice versa), then if $p\&r$ is metaphysically possible, then so is $q\&r$. Hence, if C(MG)-lite is coherent, any further weakening of C(ME)-lite will also cohere metaphysically with the property of being necessary if possible, so long as C(MG)-lite does. There are indefinitely many such weakenings, and thus the coherence of C(MG)-lite provide guarantees of the coherence of all the lower-calorie lites to come. Bottom-uppers can now rejoice, because their recipe only allows the conjoining of properties that are both maximal and great-making; top-downers have to allow conjoining of less than maximal but still great-making properties. They thereby generate a divine embarrassment of riches. Not one divine being at most, but as many as one wants to count, one for every combination of great-making properties that is weaker than C(ME)-lite. It is an inconvenient profligacy in ontology akin to the Greek pantheon. Add the further property of behaving in ways befitting a soap opera and there you are.

Bottom-uppers can insist that we not tread this path, that we shouldn't append the modal property to any and every metaphysically coherent collection, but must generate inclusion of this modal property into a set by a well-constructed recipe that forces its inclusion. Such a restriction, if defensible, will keep the problems of profligacy and contingency at bay, and in this way the earlier advantage touted by top-downers ends up dissipating once we notice this advantage of the bottom-up approach. There is thus at least an interesting dispute about which version of PBT to embrace, but one not to pursue at present, for things get worse for both versions.

## 5.4 Creator Theology and the Problems of Contingency and Profligacy

Things get worse precisely because no version of PBT can offer an explanation as to why the property of being necessary if possible must be combined only with some metaphysically coherent collections of properties and not others. Restrictions are needed to avoid the problems noted above, but it is one thing to insert restrictions to avoid a problem, and quite another to have an independent explanation of exactly why such restrictions are appropriate. It is the lesson of a *reductio*: when disaster follows, you have to give up something. To retain PBT, you have to restrict. But there is a further option: give up PBT itself or modify it in some way. To retain PBT in its present form, one thus needs a reason for requiring the restriction needed to avoid the difficulties noted, one that explains why such a restriction is needed in a way that doesn't simply point to the difficulties that arise apart from such a restriction. The problem is that of determining to which coherent combinations of properties we can coherently append the property of being necessary if possible. The solution to that problem will imply or depend on an independent account of which combinations of properties must be contingent and which must be necessary. Only such an account can give us way of determining when adding the property of being necessary if possible will result in a metaphysically coherent combination or a metaphysically impossible one. PBT has no theoretical resources to generate such an answer, so its only recourse is to restrict merely on grounds of needing to avoid the disaster.

Here CT, at least in its classical formulation, has a story to tell. Recall that CT is the claim that the starting point for developing an adequate theology is the claim that God is the asymmetrical source of all else. The first task for the classical view, after noting that there can be only one asymmetrical source of all else, is to show why such sourcehood requires that God is a person. We saw the argument for this claim in the past chapter, so I won't repeat the argument here; but it is crucial for the classical formulation of CT to affirm the personhood of God, since that version of CT finds the source of contingent truth in the will of God and the source of necessary truth in the operations of the Divine mind. Moreover, defenders of CT can insist that being the source of a thing isn't a matter of finding a compossible set of properties and co-exemplifying them, since that account will encounter the problem of incomplete objects noted above. Instead, God's responsibility for the existence of things involves instantiating natures, where a nature is complete except for the singularity, the haecceity, involved in its exemplification. So, smaller collections of properties are capable of co-exemplification only when part of some complete nature or other. Finally, it is an essential property of every nature that it finds its source either in the will of God or the operations of the Divine mind. Contingent things are thus necessarily contingent, just as possibly necessary things are actually necessary. So, since all natures depending on God's will are, of necessity, contingent,[14] we have a recipe for determining to which coherent collections of properties we can coherently append the property of being necessary if possible: only to collections that are part of a nature that finds its source in the operations of the Divine mind.

I hasten to point out that I am not claiming that this position is ultimately defensible or even coherent. Especially, there is a serious need to articulate what is involved in explaining necessity in terms of the operations of the Divine mind.[15] This version of CT is, in this respect, in precisely the same situation as, for example, bottom-up PBT: there is the position as articulated, and there is a need for a defense of the position's coherence and plausibility. All I am claiming here is that there is a standard formulation of CT that has little difficulty addressing the two problems that I claim plague PBT.

Defenders of CT can thus be rightfully suspicious of the major premise of the ontological argument, when presented without some accompanying account of contingency to make clear whether the appending of the property of being necessary if possible is mere chicanery. (It is probably worth noting in passing that the CT account provides no help in defending the premise in question, since the natures to which the modal property can be appropriately appended

---

[14] This point is not obvious and might be rejected. Perhaps there are beings that can't exist except by God's act of will, but such an act of will has to occur. To reject this idea, we need an understanding of the will that involves freedom of the sort that this hypothesis violated. I believe there is such an argument, related to van Inwagen's Consequence Argument from van Inwagen (1983), but it would take us too far afield to pursue those issues here, so I will merely note the concern and ignore it in what follows.

[15] For a hint at how such a position might be developed, see Morris and Menzel (1986).

are precisely those that were already assumed to be necessary beings.) A CT-er can have substantive reasons for limiting the range of natures to which one can coherently append the property of being necessary if possible, and substantive reasons for rejecting such an appendage to any nature not needed to account for some aspect of necessity itself. Such reasons may themselves be overridden or defeated by further considerations that go beyond present needs for further discussion, but it is one thing to have no story to tell, and it is another thing to have a defeasible one.

In contrast, not even bottom-up PBT is in such a position. It might insist on only conjoining the property of being necessary if possible only to other great-making properties with an intrinsic *maxima*. If pressed as to why such conjoining can't be done in other contexts, all that can be done is to cite the *reductio* resulting from the problems of contingency and profligacy. Doing so leaves one in any uneasy state, wondering what it is about the idea of maximal excellence that makes it a legitimate exemption here. Without such an explanation, the vestigial remains of the problems of contingency and profligacy plague even bottom-up versions of PBT.

## 5.5 Conclusion

Every version of PBT thus suffers at least mildly either from the problem of contingency or profligacy, or both. CT suffers from neither. It thus has at least one significant theoretical advantage over PBT, at least when PBT is saddled with the burden of trying to include the property of being necessary if possible in its account of the nature of God. Whether or not this advantage ends up carrying the day in metatheology, it is too early to draw conclusions.

Notice as well that none of the issues identified here as plaguing PBT seem to have any implications for Worship-Worthiness Theology (WWT). The lack of relevance arises most obviously because WWT is not constructed with hopes of generating an argument for the existence of God, and one might thus entertain the thought that WWT is going to fare much better in comparison with CT than does PBT on the issues of uniqueness, personhood, and embodiment. We consider this possibility in the next chapter.

# 6
# The Shared Ground Prospects for Worship-Worthiness Theology

## 6.1 Introduction

As noted already, the least explored metatheology among our competitors is one that begins from the idea that God is supremely worthy of the highest worship. We began our investigation of competing metatheologies by establishing a priority for the shared ground concerning monotheism, personhood, and embodiment. So our task in this chapter is to consider Worship-Worthiness Theology's (WWT's) standing with respect to each of these issues, discussing each in turn. As we will see, WWT shares some deficiencies with PBT in comparison with CT, but, more surprisingly, it has advantages over Perfect Being Theology (PBT) in other areas. This conclusion inclines one to wonder whether PBT will ultimately be the worst of our three main metatheologies, but we won't be in a position to assess such a claim until considerably further along in our investigation. So, to begin the task of this chapter, we turn first to the issue of monotheism.

## 6.2 Monotheism

As we saw in Chapter 4, WWT shares a disability on this issue with PBT. On the face of it, there is no particular reason why multiple beings could not all be supremely worthy of the most exalted worship, just as there is no obvious reason why there could not be multiple beings regarding which there could be none greater. All that would be required is that they be tied on whatever the relevant scale is for determining supremacy of worthiness and worship, in the case of WWT, or perfection of being, in the case of PBT.

To avoid this result, both PBT and WWT would need to find some further characteristic of God that can be sustained by their approach and which rules out multiple deities. For PBT, the best hope is for some omni-property such as omnipotence or the related property of omnipresence. The idea is that you can't have two omnipotent beings, because in a situation of conflict, only one could prevail. A moment's reflection shows that such an idea can't work. There would need to be some reason for thinking that situations of conflict must be possible, but there seems to be no incoherence in the idea of necessary harmony between distinct persons. So PBT is unable to demonstrate that there must only be one omnibeing, and thus is unable to demonstrate that there can only be one God.

WWT is in the same predicament. Whatever properties are implied by the idea of being supremely worthy of the highest worship, those properties will not rule out multiple instantiation. As a result, WWT will be unable to demonstrate that there can be only one God.

For both positions, there is one small sliver of hope remaining. Since Creator Theology (CT) can explain why "the Lord our God is one," these alternative metatheologies could piggy-back on the success of CT in this regard if they could show how to derive the claim that God must be the asymmetrical source of all else from their alternative starting points. We will take up this question in Chapters 8 and 9 of Part III, which take up the possibility of deriving the starting points of alternative metatheologies. It is worth noting a justified pessimism about this possibility, however. Once we notice that the starting point for CT involves uniqueness from the outset, it would be surprising to be able to derive CT from either PBT or WWT without already having found resources within PBT or WWT for defending monotheism.

As noted before, however, this failure to sustain monotheism may be surmountable, if there is some way to keep the polytheistic society from overpopulation and the drama of the Greek pantheon. On the latter score, WWT has a useful response. For WWT, the highest and most exalted worship should not be given to beings with such embarrassing and regrettable interactions with other divine beings, so given such drama, a defender of WWT would rightly judge that such beings might be divine but clearly not deities. Thus, for WWT, if there are multiple deities, the society of deities will need to be harmonious, and necessarily so.

Something similar may be said usefully by defenders of PBT as well, though things are more complicated. PBT's calling card appeals to perfections, but what is needed is not an explanation of attributes to include in one's theology, but an explanation of what to exclude. The exclusionary principle for PBT appeals to a rank-ordering of possible beings, so that nothing that is superceded by anything else gets to count as a deity. So, to rule out the drama of the Greek pantheon, PBT needs to defend that there are possible beings that are greater than beings that participate in such drama. While it is not hard to see why it is either imaginable or conceivable that there are beings that share the perfections of the members of pantheon without also sharing their faults, it is harder to show that what is conceivable or imaginable is, at least in this case, also possible.

In any case, both PBT and WWT need not only to be able to exclude such drama, but also have some way of avoiding a polytheistic population explosion. As we saw in the last chapter, PBT has significant difficulty with this issue, deriving from a desire to find a collection of perfections to which can be appended one additional perfection: that of being necessary if possible. WWT holds no brief on this issue, and thus can avoid this way of generating a population explosion of deities.

A defender of PBT may avoid this problem by dropping the appendage that generates it. Doing so eliminates hope for the ontological argument, since what generates the problem is adding to a coherent mix of great-making properties the additional property of being necessary if possible. Dropping that appendage will undermine the ontological argument, but perhaps that hope was bound to disappoint anyway.

Dropping that property raises another problem for PBT, however, for one can't simply drop the appendage unless the property in question fails to count as a perfection and fails to be entailed by anything else on the list of perfections. Thus, for bottom-up PBT, simply cutting off the offending property can't be done. Moreover, for top-down PBT, it can only be done if the greatest metaphysically possible being lacks that property, just as one can only drop various omni-properties, for top-down PBT, if the greatest metaphysically possible being lacks that property. In all such cases, though, if the property is great-making or is entailed by great-making properties, an explanation is thereby required as to why that property is missing in the greatest metaphysically possible being.

So, PBT still needs a bit of theoretical fancy footwork here, and WWT is not in the same predicament. The threat of polytheistic population explosion that arises for PBT does not arise for WWT, precisely because it contains nothing in its starting point that implicates any re-envisioning of the line between the contingent and the necessary. WWT lacks the resources of CT for defending monotheism, but two points are in order before moving on. First, WWT comes in no worse than second on the issue of uniqueness. There still remains the issue of how many deities is too many, but that's not as problematic as having to explain why there are not infinitely many deities if there is one. Second, since the preference for monotheistic implications is defeasible, there remains the possibility that WWT ends up at no disadvantage to CT on this issue, all things considered. But our provisional conclusion is that on the issue of uniqueness, the advantage goes to CT, with WWT faring at least as well as, and perhaps somewhat better than, PBT even though both of them leave open the possibility of polytheism.

## 6.3 Personhood

WWT has the easiest time of all deriving a personal God. We saw in Chapter 1 Leftow's reason for endorsing this inference:

> I make only two claims about what worship is, both obvious given actual religious practice. One is that worship is a form of address: when we worship, we *say things to* what we worship.... The point of the practice is for these words to be heard and understood. The other is that worship always involves praising, at some point. Practice makes this clear, but it's even part of the word's etymology: it is from the Anglo-Saxon worth-ship, the proclaiming of worth. So if something is to deserve worship, it must deserve praise, at least in some respect.   Leftow (2016, p. 71)

We resisted this account of worship, however, in favor of one that puts submission and surrender, obeisance and deference at the heart of worship. This alternative agrees with Leftow in maintaining that worship involves communicative acts, though the path to this conclusion is a bit different. Worship is intimately connected with the bodily posture of bowing down, and such behavior is indicative of an attitude of surrender or subservience when done in a way that is truly worshipful. It is here, rather than in the notion of praise, that I think we find the central core of what worship is.

Part of the defense of this account of worship involves distinguishing it from closely related attitudes, for some of these attitudes can appropriately be taken toward inanimate objects, objects without intellect and will. For example, one can praise a work of art, one can be in awe in the presence of a grand landscape, one can acknowledge dependence on the order of things, and one can even show reverence for the vastness of the universe. One can also love and value to the highest degree inanimate things. None of these attitudes or responses need rise to the level of worship, for they bear no intrinsic connection to the obeisance and bowing down that is central to the nature of worship. Worship involves taking an attitude of surrender or submission toward another, where the attitude is displayed in some way or other, a way that constitutes a form of address. Worship is thus a communicative act, and such communicative acts make sense only when directed at things with intelligence and will—which is to say, to persons.

Some will object here that non-human animals turn out to be persons on this account, since they appear to have intelligence and will as well. What they lack, perhaps, is moral agency, but tracking that notion in the present context isn't on point, since we are not trying to distinguish human persons from lesser beings with minds and wills, but rather we are only identifying a necessary condition for appropriate worship. What matters is that the acts need to be directed towards things with minds and wills, and the rest of the story about appropriate worship is left open at this point, as is the quite interesting but ancillary issue of whether there are non-human animals that are persons. So even if there is a reason for distinguishing non-human animals from persons, that explanation won't undermine the requirement that worship must be person-directed.

The communicative acts involved in worship make sense only on the (Gricean) assumption that one's utterances are accompanied by an intention of some sort sensitive to whatever audience one's utterances are directed toward, where mind and will are constitutive of anything that can be an audience.[1] We can, of course, talk to anything, but when we knowingly talk to inanimate things, there is a detectable pretense involving personification that is present. Worship involves no such pretense. We can, of course, mistake inanimate things for persons and speak to them without pretense, but such possibilities don't show anything contrary to an account of communication that requires an intentional element concerning an audience of some sort or other.

So, the core feature of worship is the attitude of submission or surrender, often expressed in the bodily posture of prostration or bowing down. We can argue whether the mere presence of the attitude is sufficient for worship, or whether the attitude must be expressed in either thought or behavior in order for worship to occur. Note, though, that if an expression of the attitude will be a communicative act, the presence of the attitude is similarly person-directed. In language that is becoming more popular, the attitude of subservience or submission is not a *de dicto* attitude (one that is simply a relation to a propositional content), nor a *de re* attitude (one that has an object

---

[1] The details of the Gricean account are not as important as the general pattern of explanation they encode. The initial account from Grice (1968) begins by requiring that an utterance be aimed at belief formation in one's audience, but Grice later weakened that requirement to a recognition requirement only: that an utterance involve an aim for one's audience to recognize what one believes to be true. The general pattern, though, is what I'm relying on here, a pattern that explains semantic meaning at least partially in terms of speaker meaning, where speaker meaning requires an intention that presupposes intelligence and responsiveness in one's audience.

as content), but rather a *de te* attitude (one that has a special object as content, one that displays the consciousness involved in having a mind and will).[2] Such attitudes are central to the study of autistic spectrum disorders as well as the phenomenon of shared attention,[3] but the relevance of the attitude here is the way in which it yields the implication of personhood in the nature of the attitude in question, leading us to the same conclusion whether or not the attitude must be expressed in order to be an attitude of worship.

Since the requirements for personhood are here limited to mind and will, the expression of the attitude will count as interpersonal communication if directed toward a being with mind and will. When the attitude is expressed, an intention is present together with an intention that the expression be recognized for what it is, on the part of the being in question. Such recognition itself also requires the attribute of personhood, so the essential link between worship and personhood has multiple sources.

Of course, if the worship were somehow inappropriate, one might suggest that the expression of the attitude in question could be occurring without there being a person present to whom one was expressing surrender or submission. WWT needn't face such questioning, however, for the worship in question is something of which the deity is supremely worthy. So, no grounds can be found for the inappropriateness or incorrectness that would need to underlie some accusation of overreaching when deriving personhood for a being that is supremely worthy of the most exalted worship.

As already noted, CT is also able to sustain (defeasibly) that God is a person, so this argument on behalf of WWT generates no advantage for it over CT. Both of these positions share something of an advantage over PBT, however, since PBT can only derive the personhood of God by appeal to the idea that being a person is a great-making property or that persons are somehow higher on the scale of being than non-persons. As we saw in Chapter 2, however, such argumentation faces serious challenges, serious enough to lead us to the conclusion that PBT suffers a disadvantage on this score in comparison with both WWT and CT.

As a reminder of that argument the problems begin when we notice that some simply can't be persons. In such a case, it is not better for them to be persons, or at least, there is no reason to suppose that it would be better for them to be persons.

---

[2] Initial discussion of this attitude can be found in the work of Eleonore Stump. See, e.g., Stump (2010). Further discussion, and the language of *de te* awareness for this phenomenon, can be found in Kvanvig (2017a).

[3] For discussion, see Eilan et al. (2005).

What is left is for PBT to appeal to some ranking system for beings, arguing that persons are higher on this scale than non-persons. Even so, perplexity remains. The strategy for bottom-up PBT is to look for great-making properties with intrinsic *maxima*. And one would expect that, for top-down PBT, the ranking system is in some way a function of items on this list generated by the bottom-up strategy. So, one would expect, personhood should be on the list or play a role in PBT's story only if being a person is a great-making property with an intrinsic *maxima*. But the property of being a person is not such a property: it is, in the lingo, a digital property not an analog one. That is, it is a property that you either have or lack, not a property that comes in degrees. Without coming in degrees, however, a property isn't one with an intrinsic *maxima*.

Maybe one wishes to resist this last point, claiming that the maximum is simply to have the property rather than lack it. But if we start including non-degreed properties, counterexamples threaten. It is better to be a dog rather than a virus, but we don't want that property to be included in the features of deity. (If you are more a fan of viruses than I am, feel free to substitute any other comparative judgment having a first term that we don't want to attribute to God.)

I do not want to overstate how significant this puzzle is for PBT, but whatever its significance, it leaves CT and WWT with at least some advantage over PBT. The remaining item in the shared ground for our metatheologies is the issue of embodiment, so let us leave this discussion of personhood where it stands for now, returning to it in the next chapter that focuses in PBT, and turn to the question of what WWT has to say about the divine embodiment thesis.

## 6.4 Embodiment

Here we can be brief, in large part because of the extensive discussion of both PBT and WWT when considering the status of CT on this issue. As we have seen, there is no basis in any of the three major metatheologies for ascribing the having of a body to God. All three are compatible with that claim, but none of them require it. Defenses of the idea would have to come from some other source, and in such a case, any of our three major metatheologies can accommodate an argument for embodiment if such is required for being a person or being an object of any sort.

There could thus be a problem here for WWT only for those who think something stronger is required for metatheological adequacy. For example, those convinced that embodiment lands a being in the realm of decay and destructibility, one will want a metatheology to be able to derive the purely spiritual nature of deity. Either that, or a metatheology will have to provide some reason for distancing deity from the vagaries of contingency or concreteness that seemingly would plague any embodiment thesis. As we saw in Chapter 3, however, this issue presents a bit of a challenge to CT, but not to WWT or PBT. For PBT, the reason is straightforward: any being susceptible to these vagaries would be a lesser being than one who is not, yielding a PBT argument that no embodiment thesis can threaten the perfection of God.[4] For WWT, full details will have to await results from Part III, but a preview is in order here. In brief, WWT might piggy-back on this PBT argument if worthiness of worship is grounded in part in the perfections of God that are central to PBT. We will take up this line of thought in Part III.

How much of an advantage this result yields for PBT and WWT over CT is unclear, but we can say at this point that appears no worse for CT than the failure of PBT and WWT to derive the uniqueness of God. I'm inclined to think that the failure to sustain monotheism is a worse problem, but there is no reason to try to settle that issue at present. All we need, at this point, is an accounting of where the merits and demerits lie. A final accounting should be delayed until we complete our evaluation of the resources of each metatheology for all the issues already identified.

## 6.5 Conclusion

The results for WWT are thus encouraging. It has difficulty with the issue of monotheism but no difficulty with the issues of personhood or embodiment. Note, however, that each of the three major metatheologies has some difficulty or other with these items that constitute the shared ground. PBT has difficulty with personhood and with monotheism, CT has some issue with embodiment if there is a need to defend the pure spirituality of God, and WWT shares with PBT the issue with monotheism.

To summarize the results of Part II, we can say this. Regarding the shared ground, CT comes out slightly ahead, followed closely by WWT, with PBT coming up shortest. We turn in the next Part, Part III, to the question of the interderivability of alternative starting points for each metatheology.

---

[4] This argument is best suited to bottom-up PBT, since top-down PBT inevitably faces the issue of trade-offs among perfections. In such a case, we'd need an explanation why the lessening that accrues because of embodiment is worse than the lessening of whatever other lessenings are available.

# PART III
# TOWARD COMPETING STARTING POINTS

# 7
# Creator Theology's Disadvantages

## 7.1 Introduction

Creator Theology (CT) has advantages over both Worship-Worthiness Theology (WWT) and Perfect Being Theology (PBT). For one thing, it is able to be pristinely monotheistic, which neither WWT nor PBT is well suited to demonstrate, and it is able to sustain the viewpoint that God is a person in the sense of having both a mind and a will, an advantage it shares with WWT over PBT. It is time to see how far CT can go toward sustaining the starting points of PBT and WWT. I take up these issues in §7.2 and §7.3, respectively.

As we will see, the results are mixed, but better for CT than has typically been thought by those taking a more epistemological approach to metatheology. We will find limitations for CT in deriving the starting points of both WWT and PBT, a conclusion which should surprise no one. What matters, however, is the significance of this disability, and on this issue, I will argue that the limitations of CT are not sufficient to show that CT should be abandoned at this point in our inquiry. One reason for caution is that our approach is comparative, so even if CT can't derive the starting points of other metatheologies, that might be countered by a failure of those metatheologies to derive the starting point of CT as well. The conclusion I will defend, then, is that the gap that can't be closed between alternative metatheologies and one that begins with the claim that God is the asymmetrical source of all else may not be a decisive reason to conclude that God is not to be understood as fundamentally the creator of all.

## 7.2 From Creator Theology toward Worship-Worthiness

The first step in assessing whether alternative metatheologies can explain the worship-worthiness of the Almighty is to begin with an account of what worship involves and what it takes to be supremely worthy of the highest worship. Here we find little uniformity in the literature. Brian Leftow (2016) suggests that praise is central to worship, whereas Robert Merrihew Adams holds that "the soul of worship is *admiration*." Bayne and Nagasawa (2006, pp. 300–1) emphasize the role of awe (as a type of fear) and reverence as well as noumenal experiences of holiness and sacredness. While all of these elements are certainly important and perhaps even essential, I have argued that the central elements of worship are those of submission and surrender rather than praise, adoration, awe, or reverence. Moreover, to be worthy of such a response, the being in question must be impressive along a number of dimensions. One obvious dimension is power, but it is equally obvious that power alone doesn't make a being pre-eminently worthy of worship. Instead, it merely makes worship a wise and practically rational activity.

These points help us see that one cannot take a shortcut to worship-worthiness simply by citing the fact of creation itself. Richard Swinburne suggests such a shortcut:

> If there is a God and he has made and sustains the world and issued commands to men, men have moral obligations which they would not otherwise have. The grounds for this are as follows. Men ought to acknowledge other persons with whom they come into contact, not just ignore them—and this surely becomes a duty when those persons are our benefactors. We acknowledge people in various ways when we meet them, e.g. by shaking hands or smiling at them, and the way in which we acknowledge their presence reflects our recognition of the sort of individual they are and the kind of relation they have to us. Worship is the only response appropriate to God, the source of all being.     Swinburne (1981, p. 79)

The shortcut Swinburne suggests is that worship is "the only appropriate response" to the source of all being, though the first sentence of the quote adds a qualification to this shortcut. For it is not merely that God is the source of all being, but that he also "sustains the world and issues commands." Swinburne thus assumes, not only creation, but conservation in addition to the personhood of God in proposing the shortcut from CT to worship-worthiness. Here we should endorse Swinburne's additions; as we have already seen, personhood is derivable on CT grounds and the argument for that conclusion can also sustain the conclusion that divine creation requires divine conservation.[1] From these assumptions, Swinburne's shortcut suggestion is that worthiness of worship is a direct consequence.

---

[1] The argument linking creation with conservation in Kvanvig and McCann (1988). For further details and ramifications, see McCann and Kvanvig (1991).

Here we should balk. While it may be true that from these assumptions we can derive a *pro tanto* obligation to worship and a *pro tanto* worthiness claim as well, the claim that needs to be derived is the claim that, all-things-considered, God is worthy of worship in a way that makes such worship obligatory. Converting the *pro tanto* case into an all-things-considered case requires showing that no defeaters are present, and defending that claim requires showing something about God's goodness and the reasons for creation. For if the motives for creation are bad and the reasons diabolic, the *pro tanto* case that Swinburne cites will not convert to an all-things-considered case. As a result, the attempted shortcut to worship-worthiness from creation itself does not succeed: we must know something about the nature of God as asymmetrical source of all else if the derivation of worship-worthiness can be sustained.

So what else is needed besides power in order to make a being worthy of the supreme examples of submission and surrender (and what these might entail, including praise, adoration, reverence, and awe)? It is clear that the needed features are in the domain of the evaluative and the normative. Swinburne, in fact, hints in this direction when he discusses the duty of acknowledgement for our benefactors. It might be useful to worship an irascible and arbitrary potentate, but such a despot is not worthy of worship solely in virtue of having power to harm or benefit. What is missing is the good and the right: the powerful must also be good and do right if they are to be worthy of worship.

So, the attempt to derive worship-worthiness from CT will falter if CT can't show that God is not only powerful, but supreme in ways that include evaluative and normative dimensions as well. It is precisely at this point that CT struggles the most, though there are exaggerated concerns to avoid. In particular, we should avoid quick arguments against CT that are infected with Humean qualms about deriving an "ought" from an "is", with the implication that a perfunctory appraisal can be made with no further ado: there is no way to get from the descriptive CT to the axiological categories (comprised of the evaluative (PBT) and the normative (WWT)).

Humean concerns are often overwrought,[2] and here is a good example, for this Humean dictum needs careful articulation if it is defensible at all. For the supervenience of the normative on the descriptive is a standard assumption,

---

[2] Most especially these: there is no self to be found, no causation to be observed, no knowledge to be had. Pursuing these issues here would take us too far afield, but a hint might be in order. On the self, Hume introspects various intentional states and fails to find the self, but he looks at the wrong *relatum*: intentional states are a relation between a content and a person, so it should suprise no one that the self isn't found by examining the content of intentional states. On causation, I recommend Anscombe's discussion in Anscombe (1971). On Humean skepticism perhaps an common sense antidote would be helpful: Moore (1925, 1939) and Chisholm (1977).

where supervenience is thought of in terms of one-way entailment. For X to supervene on Y is for X to fail to entail Y, since multiple possible supervenience bases are possible, but for Y to entail X. So careless articulation of the Humean dictum founders on the rocks of the supervenience of the normative on the descriptive: no change in description, no change in the normative. A more careful articulation, however, might be this: in our best logic, there will be no proof available to get one from purely descriptive information to normative conclusions.

If we restrict the dictum in this way, however, it isn't a stumblingblock to CT's attempt to derive the worship-worthiness of God. For one thing, we might wonder exactly what we are supposed to be thinking about when we are thinking about our best logic. Is it standard, first-order extensional logic? As is obvious, intensional conclusions can't be derived in extensional systems! Second, we should note that the kind of necessity that is relevant to our project is metaphysical rather than logical necessity. Finally, we have scrupulously avoided requiring defenses, derivations, and explanations to use only truth-preserving tactics, but have instead granted that there are good non-monotonic inferences available for any proposed metatheology to use as well. Given these points, we need not be sidetracked any further by this Humean concern.

Since our issue concerns the derivation of evaluative and normative features from purely descriptive ones, I want to assume that God's power and ability to know are unlimited in order to focus on the central concern here. As we will see in the next section, there is an argument available to CT for showing this lack of limitation, but I'll postpone discussion of the argument here in order to keep our focus where it belongs. So for the present, we simply assume this lack of limitation, and we ask what might be available for generating the results about the good and the right that are needed for deriving worthiness of worship by CT.

Consider first the issue of whether such lack of limitation implies goodness. We can make some progress on this question by dividing the topic into two, where we distinguish between the metaphysical goodness of a being and the moral goodness of a being. On the metaphysical scorecard, goodness unequalled belongs to God simply in virtue of the aseity and independence God has as a result of being the asymmetrical source of all else. God's metaphysical pre-eminence is thus easily derived by CT.

One might wonder, though, whether such pre-eminence, combined with other metaphysical attributes of the sort involved in PBT, would leave open the possibility that God's metaphysical goodness, according to CT, is surpassable.

That concern will take center stage in the next section, when we consider the relationship between the starting points of CT and PBT, so I will postpone its consideration until then, to focus on the issue that is central to any attempt to derive WWT from CT.

The harder aspect is moral goodness, and here pessimism is the proper initial attitude. If God is the asymmetrical source of all else, there is no obvious connection to be found in that description for finding an ethical dimension to the fundamental nature of God. This point fits well with the history of monotheism in world culture. It is well-known that the distinctive ethical monotheism found in Judaism is not the first form of monotheism in human culture, and if CT is correct about the fundamental nature of God, one explanation of this development might be that it takes something beyond an understanding of the fundamental nature of God to generate an ethical component in one's monotheism. Of course, the possibility remains that this pessimism overreaches, for there are often hidden dimensions in a given thought that take serious intellectual effort to uncover, and the same could be true here. It could be that somehow there is a way to tie being the asymmetrical source of all else with moral goodness. But, if so, the link isn't obvious, so defenders of CT must shoulder the burden of trying to uncover such a hidden gem if there is one to be found.

In the remainder of this section, then, I will describe some possibilities that might be pursued in shouldering this burden. As we will see, all such possibilities face obstacles, but we will also see that there is no definitive argument that these obstacles cannot be overcome. Thus, our pessimism about the prospects for CT on this score needs to be a muted pessimism, one that remains open to the idea even though endorsing a tentative conclusion that CT comes up short on this issue.

Recall that we are assuming for present purposes the unlimited power and knowledge of God, postponing a defense of this lemma until the next section. Those familiar with the Platonic tradition will detect a ray of hope here deriving from the general Platonic stance that ethical failures receive correction by further education and learning. As Socrates claims in the *Protagoras*, "No one who either knows or believes that there is another possible course of action, better than the one he is following, will ever continue on his present course" (358b–c). So a ray of hope might be found if we could tie together the notions of rationality, knowledge, goodness, and rightness of action in something like the way Socrates suggests. If these ties could be sustained, as well as our assumption of the unlimited nature of God's knowledge, we'd be in a position to claim that God's moral goodness was similarly unlimited.

Here's an idea of how such argumentation might go. Suppose we think of knowledge as implying rationality, truth, and belief.[3] By assumption, God's knowledge is unlimited, so we can't explain any defect in what God wills in terms of ignorance, and thus we can endorse the idea that God is aware (knows) what is right and good in absolutely every circumstance, and thus rationally believes the same. Theoretical rationality of this sort is not the same as full rationality, for practical rationality is required as well. Is there a way to tie the purely theoretical rationality involved in knowledge to the practical rationality relevant to acts of will? Or is it possible for an asymmetrical source of all else to be perfectly rational from a theoretical point of view without that fact yielding any results about what is it rational to do, from a practical point of view?

There are theories of knowledge on which the answer is "No." Such theories of knowledge posit pragmatic encroachment into the nature of knowledge, tying reasons sufficient for knowledge with reasons sufficient for acting.[4] But even if we reject the identification here in favor of a purer form of intellectualism, as I argue in Kvanvig (2011a), we would end up with a conflicted self in the divine involving an incoherence in purely intellectual attitudes of just the sort that Socrates rejects. For in recognizing defects of the will, as happens when a person knows what is right and good but wills otherwise, a person also comes to recognize the importance and need to correct the defect and stop the madness of doing that which one recognizes to be wrong and which one knows one has the power to avoid. Whence then the defect? Such a being would be in a position of knowing on a given occasion that what is being done is not good, that avoiding doing it is easy (since the being in question has unlimited power), and that it is wrong to do what is being done. If that is possible, it is mysterious indeed.

Yes it is, but the issue is what CT can appeal to in order to rule out this possibility. One might place some hope in an appeal to a "guise of the good" thesis, according to which an action has to be motivated in a way that is seen as good. As Joseph Raz notes, a guise of the good thesis is a central plank in "bridging the theory of value, the theory of normativity, and rationality, and the understanding of intentional action" Raz (2010, p. 134). As helpful as such a bridge might be, it faces significant counterexamples concerning weakness

---

[3] For a defense of such an account of God's knowledge, with an explanation of why there is no Gettier problem to worry about for God's knowledge, see Kvanvig (1986).

[4] See, e.g., Fantl and McGrath (2009); Hawthorne (2004) and Stanley (2005).

of will and choosing the bad for its own sake.[5] Given the unlimited nature of God's power, counterexamples involving weakness of the will might be easy enough to dismiss, but examples such as Milton's Satan, as discussed in David Velleman (1992), are not so easily dismissed, whether considered in human or divine contexts.

Let me elaborate a bit on each point. First, when considering cases of weakness of will, we find a standardly noted oversight in the claim of Socrates that those who know the right will do it. Socrates failed to take into account the amount of effort needed to do what is right in certain circumstances, and the natural human predilection to shrink from the effort in such cases. Such weakness of will, however, is not relevant in our context, since we are assuming that the asymmetrical source of all else is a being of unlimited power. So if weakness of will could be involved in our context, it would have to involve some other explanation of failure to do what is right other than one that adverts to the needed effort involved. What could that explanation be?

It is probably best to view the phrase "weakness of will" as a misnomer, conjuring thoughts of limitations on power. For what is really at stake is acting against one's better judgment. In our case, the issue is whether it is possible to know that a given course of action is good and right and yet choose something contrary to it. If acting against one's better judgment is possible for the asymmetrical source of all else, what is needed is an account of how such a judgment can co-exist with a contrary, intentional action when done by a being of such unlimited power and knowledge. Ignorance can't explain it, and the needed effort to do what is right can't either. Whence then the action?

Perhaps we can find an answer by focusing on different motivational forces that underlie action other than the quality of the reasons one has for acting. In the case of ordinary human action, for example, proximate reward structures can swamp long-term ones, even for those who recognize the irrationality of such behavior, and emotional forces often tug on us in ways that we recognize are indefensible.

Here, though, CT has resources that are easy to overlook. Recall that central to CT is the claim that contingency is explained by the Divine will and necessity by the operations of the Divine mind, thereby securing the claim that God is the asymmetrical source of all else. On this account, however, the Divine will is explanatorily prior to the states of mind that, in our own case, function to

---

[5] For overview discussion, see Tenenbaum (2013) and Orsi (2015). For criticism, see, e.g., Velleman (1992); Setiya (2010), and Baker (2015). For attempts to formulate a version of the principle, or a related principle tying rational action to recognized motivating reasons, see Moss (2010); Raz (2010); Gregory (2013), and Singh (forthcoming).

generate our actions. We are familiar with explanations of action in terms of belief/desire complexes, or as in modern decision theory, confidence levels and preference orderings. In God's case, however, God's beliefs about the contingent realm result from awareness of God's own acts of will, making those acts prior to the knowledge of contingency that results. And something similar must also be said about any contingent preferences we find in God as well. Their existence is explained by God's acts of will, just as much as the beliefs about contingent matters are. The result is a picture on which all of God's preferences are the result of free, unconstrained acts of will, with input from states of mind taking priority only when it comes to that which is necessary.

Note as well the modal strength of these points. According to CT, the fundamental nature of God is that of the asymmetrical source of all else, and nothing could have this nature if it were possible for something else to exist sourced in a way independent of God. Thus, no matter what is or might be actual is dependent on God. Furthermore, given the dependencies just noted, there can be no possibilities that fall outside the divine purview in deciding what to create, so no divine decisions could be made on the basis of ignorance.

A couple of important things follow from these points. First, it is impossible for God's preferences or will to contravene what is necessary. This point follows because reality has to be consistent, and thus what God wills has to be consistent as well. For God to will that, for example, $2 + 2 = 5$ is impossible, since God's power is of the sort that cannot be resisted. So if God wills something, that thing becomes actual, but it isn't possible for it to be actually true that $2 + 2 = 5$. In addition, since the realm of contingent truth obeys the laws of logic, God's will has to be consistent as well. Since contingency results, according to CT, from God's acts of will, there is no possibility of incoherence between what God wills, what God believes, and God's preference orderings. For all of these are explanatorily consequent on God's acts of will.

Second, since God's willings are the source of all contingency, God's beliefs and preference orderings displayed in these willings must cohere as well. For divine beliefs and preferences have the same explanatory source. Our own affections and cognitions have different sources, and because of that fact, can be in conflict with each other. Our beliefs generally arise from sensory experience, but what we care most deeply about has a different source. So acting against our better judgment, as well as having vile and despicable fundamental motivations, is possible for us because of the different sourcing. But if we envision the entire created order as arising from one enormously complex act of the Divine will, that entire complex must be consistent and coherent on pain of the created order itself being incoherent.

It is in the completeness and consistency of the Divine will that CT finds resources for resisting the idea that God might not be morally good. Moreover, plumbing the depths of these resources is intellectually demanding enough that it is no surprise that ordinary, casual thinking about God would not reveal it, even for those who find it quite natural to think of God in personal terms. For ordinary persons, the ones we meet on our way, have affective and cognitive aspects that are sourced differently, leading to the possibility of conflict between our best judgment and what we care about most deeply, to say nothing of our capacity for ignoring what we find inconvenient and the power of self-deception. Suffice it to say, though, that the fact that ethical monotheism isn't one's first thought when thinking one's creator is no ground in itself to question whether CT might do better in sustaining ethical monotheism than what such first thoughts might include.

This explanatory machinery thus generates a system of preferences and a system of beliefs that is coherent and exhaustive, in a way that leaves no room for the kind of failure of fit between the affective and the cognitive that is essential both to the phenomenon of *akrasia* as well as to Milton's Satan. We can't find inconsistency or incoherence in either preferences or beliefs, since all necessities are grounded in the operations of the Divine mind, and such incoherence would render impossible the operations generating them. Consistency, coherence, and completeness are also to be imputed to the realm of contingency, this time on the basis of the Divine will, since incoherence or incompleteness would similarly render impossible the posited acts of will that generate it. Finally, no failure of fit between the affective and cognitive could arise, for precisely the reason that both are grounded in one and the same coherent, consistent, and complete system of willings.[6] In our own case, no such inconsistency is derivable, given our limitations and our capacity to ignore what we suspect might make us question courses of action that we are intent on. In the case of God, however, the divine preferences must be

---

[6] Astute readers will notice that I am here showing a preference for excluded middle and the law of bivalence. It is worth noting that there are important, but minority, positions in the philosophy of logic that jettison these principles, most notably, the intuitionist tradition deriving from L. E. J. Brouwer (1907), and developed most famously in the work of Michael Dummett. See especially Dummett (1977, 1978) and Dummett (1991). I relegate this point to a footnote, however, since to pursue these issues fully is beyond the scope of the current project. We will rest content here by noting that CT should not be rejected at this early stage by noting some minority possibility that would threaten these conclusions. Instead, we should view the matter as showing another of the ways in which our investigations always remain open to the possibility of being undermined by further learning, even when we can, as in this case, cite the weight of philosophical tradition in favor of the premises CT needs to derive the completeness and well-ordering of the (maximally specific) divine preferences. It is an independent and worthy project to see what each of these metatheologies would look like under intuitionistic scruples or any other assumptions that undermine the completeness of the world, one that I hope to pursue later.

complete with respect to the realm of contingency, supporting the idea that divine judgment about what is good and right, better and best, can't come apart from what God chooses as it can with us, on pain of God's preference orderings becoming incoherent. CT thereby finds some hope for generating as unlimited an account of divine goodness as it can sustain regarding God's knowledge and power.

This result is comforting for defenders of CT, but those familiar with the history of discussion of the freedom/foreknowledge problem will detect an issue. For, among the competing positions here is Molinism, which claims that there are counterfactuals of creaturely freedom (CCFs) that are contingently true, but not because of any act of will on the part of God.[7] The value of such a proposal, it is claimed, is that it allows one to embrace a libertarian account of freedom for humans while also retaining full and complete providential control in one's theology. The sticking point for CT, as described above, then is whether CT succeeds in the effort to derive a strong account of divine goodness only at the expense of abandoning human freedom.

Prospects for CT are not as dire here as one might think. First, there are accounts of human freedom that reject libertarianism, to which a defender of CT might appeal. I do not find such accounts attractive,[8] but it is one option open to a defender of CT. Even without abandoning libertarianism, however, the problem noted could only be pressed at this stage if Molinism were the only possible position that allows full providential control while also maintaining libertarianism. That claim, however, is provably false, as I have argued in Kvanvig (2011c). One such alternative is the view I defend in that work, which I call "Philosophical Arminianism," a position designed to allow both full providential control and libertarianism, while also resisting the idea that there are contingent truths, such as CCFs, that have to be explained in ways that are incompatible with CT's schema of explaining necessity in terms of the Divine mind and contingency in terms of the Divine will.[9]

None of these remarks show that CT won't have difficulties here, perhaps even irresolvable difficulties. This point, however, is true of all our claims about what is derivable from any given metatheology. We have claimed, for example, that we can derive monotheism and the personal nature of God from CT, but this claimed derivability involves defeasible support only, where what

---

[7] The best account of the view is in Flint (1998).

[8] For reasons roughly of the sort articulated in van Inwagen (1983).

[9] For criticism of this position, see Hasker (2016). This sustained opposition to my deserves a careful response, which I have not provided, and won't pursue here since it is ancillary to this current project. I thank Bill, though, for taking the time to understand and offer critical commentary on my thought.

looks to be a good derivation still might disappear under further learning. The same is true of the defense of divine goodness that CT can generate above: it presents evidence that a being of unlimited knowledge and power will also be of unlimited goodness, but the derivation is not itself incorrigible, incapable of being undermined by further investigation.

There remains one element of WWT that we have not yet addressed. For central to WWT is a normative dimension, that of the obligatoriness of worship. Merely defending God's goodness, power, and knowledge does not translate immediately into an argument for the obligatoriness of submission and surrender to our Maker, so we need to know whether it is possible to get from the results already achieved for CT to this further element.

Here we encounter a problem familiar in the metaethics of the last century, where various ethical naturalisms are claimed to be defective for failing to undergird the motivational component of judgments about right and wrong. The idea is that to see something as wrong is to be motivated, directly and immediately, to avoid doing it; and to judge that something is right to do is to be motivated, not indirectly through some desire to do the right thing, but directly by the judgment itself, to do the right thing. To the extent that ethical naturalism founders on this point, to the same extent so will CT. For the proposed grounds of the obligation to worship that are available to CT are descriptive claims about the nature of God, plus an evaluative claim about God's goodness. But just as with versions of ethical naturalism, none of these features provide the motivational element that some think is needed to account properly for the normative realm itself.

Things get worse if some expressivist/attitudinalist view is the correct one to talk about normativity, for on those views, the derivability of the obligation to worship will be threatened in ways similar to those that undermine attempts to derive, e.g., imperativals from declaratives. The generic point is that derivations seems to rely on items of the same ontological type, and if the substance of normativity is a different kind of thing than the substance of that from which we hope to derive it, the derivation will be problematic.

The issues involved here are enormously complex, and delving into them cannot be done in a sound and responsible way within the scope of this project. So, what I think we must do here is simply to note this issue for CT, making no pronouncements about how successful or unsuccessful CT might be in solving the problem. We thus cannot conclude at this point that CT can successfully derive the starting point of WWT, primarily on grounds for skepticism that the constitutive binding character of the normative is sufficiently different from the descriptive and evaluative to be explained solely on such bases. This puts CT in the same boat with various versions of Ethical Naturalism, so perhaps there is some comfort there.

If we find that no stronger position can be defended, the next question is how problematic this failure is. Here, we should draw a distinction. If we could show that, given CT's starting point, there is no basis for holding that God is worthy of worship, that result would be disappointing precisely because worthiness of worship is such a positive feature for a metatheology to be able to sustain. Perhaps, though, we can't have what we want, and this lesser result is all we can get. In that case, the limitation on CT here would not constitute a good enough argument for rejecting CT on its own. Instead, what would be needed is a comparative judgment that the disappointments we have to live with, given CT, are worse than the disappointments we have to live with given alternative starting points.

So the difficulty here for CT is serious enough to push us on to compare its lack to any that we might find for other positions. The next step is to see if we need to add to the list of CT's deficiencies in the context of the attempt to sustain the starting point for PBT.

## 7.3 From Creator Theology toward Perfection

We've already seen an argument for the conclusion that the best version of CT will endorse an agential conception of God as asymmetrical source of all else. We can begin our evaluation of the gap between CT and the starting point of PBT by noting how high a conception of God results from this starting point. Most significant is the strong metaphysical link present between source and outcome. Once we are conceiving of this link in agential terms, the strength of the link between divine intentional acts and outcome must involve necessity in what Aquinas refers to as the absolute, rather than relative, sense of the term: what we are used to referring to as "metaphysical necessity." Nothing short of that will satisfy the theoretical need for explanation. But if God's power is such that God's acting under the intention to produce a given outcome metaphysically necessitates that outcome, it is easy to see that such power is unlimited. For there is no power beyond that of a metaphysically necessary connnection between intention and realization of that intention. There is nothing that can interfere with it or prevent it from achieving its intended purpose, and that conclusion allows limitations on the power in question to arise only if there are limitations on what God can intend or will. But again, if there are such limitations, they will have to be limitations that are themselves metaphysically necessary (anything less would require some contingent source of the limitation, contravening the fully general sourcehood claim constitutive of CT), and any such limitations would also have to find their source in God. On the standard version of CT we are considering at this point, the one involving a divine conceptualist explanation of necessity, it would have to be something about the operations of the Divine mind that generated the posited limitations on what God can intend or will. There will be such limitations from the perspective of what is logically possible, since some things that are logically possible are not metaphysically possible.[10] These limitations aren't relevant here, since what we are looking for are metaphysical possibilities that nonetheless could not be willed by God.

Since nothing can frustrate God's intentions, and any limitations on what God can intend that arise from God's other attributes only generate logical possibilities that are nonetheless metaphysically impossible, it looks like we'd have to appeal to something like the paradox of the stone[11] to give us reason to say that there might be metaphysical possibilities that fall outside the scope of what God might intend. If so, CT is no worse off than is PBT, since PBT must answer to the paradox of the stone as well.

It is worth noting as well that CT may do better in sustaining a high conception of God's power than does PBT. PBT's hope is to show that God is an omni-being, with a fallback position getting close enough to an omni-being to be the best possible being. But this strategy presupposes being able to show that God is a person, for without cognitive states there is no omniscience, and without agency there is no moral goodness nor is there any of the power of agency. So the hopes and dreams for PBT are one thing, and the reality might fall considerably short. In such a case, the unlimited power CT can sustain might vastly surpass anything PBT can support.

Let us suppose, however, that PBT's hopes can be realized. If so, it would be premature to conclude that CT can defend the omnipotence of God as easily as PBT can. The considerations noted suggest this conclusion, but do not provide the kind of detailed analysis that would be needed to draw that conclusion. Instead, what we can note is that CT is in a position to endorse the conclusion that God's power is unlimited, since there cannot be any force or

---

[10] Examples of such are nearly always controversial, but here are a few: water not being $H_2O$, Superman not being Clark Kent, and Hesperus not being Phosphorous.

[11] That paradox that begins from the question whether God can make a stone too big for God to move. The paradox arises from the assumption that God can do anything, so presumably could be able to make such a stone, but in that case we can derive that there is something God cannot do. Hence, the paradox threatens to show that it is a mistake to think God can do anything. For discussion and possible responses, see Hoffman and Rosenkrantz (2017).

power to prevent something from coming to be that God wills to be. Whether such unlimited power amounts to omnipotence is a topic for further discussion and investigation, part of which involves the enormous complexity of trying to figure out what omnipotence actually involves.[12] The conclusion we can draw, however, gets CT's account of God's power quite close to PBT's notion of omnipotence.

So much, then, for the worry that CT can generate only a limited account of God's power. What of the other omni-properties? Can CT say anything about the extent of God's knowledge and goodness? We saw above the resources of CT for endorsing a doctrine of the unlimited scope of God's goodness, on the supposition of unlimited knowledge and power, so we need to see what to say about the issue of whether God's knowledge is limited in any way. On this issue, note first that among the powers of an agent is the power to know, and if God's power is unlimited in the way described above, God will have as extensive a power to know as any being can have. Such power would be unlimited as well, so that anything God wanted to know about, God would know about, unless such knowledge were metaphysically impossible. Note further that all truths, on the conceptualist story above, depend on God as their source, either in the will of God or in the operations of the Divine mind. And so merely by knowing his own will and how his mind works, God can know all truth. The only question remaining, then, is whether God actually knows everything that God can know. Here, a defender of CT can appeal to the lack of explanation for any such limitation. For a being of unlimited power, there is no cost of effort in doing what can be done, with limitations on this score arising only on the basis of things that can be done individually but not jointly. So long as there is no joint incoherence in knowing everything true, there is no reason for supposing that God doesn't know all truth, since that only requires a full understanding of God's own being. Moreover, since knowledge is itself a good thing,[13] there would be (defeasible) grounds for knowing what can be known for any morally good being. So, it appears, there is some basis available to CT show show that not only God's power, but also God's knowledge is unlimited.

There is more to discuss concerning the starting point of PBT, but the results to this point put us in a position to give a more detailed response on behalf of CT to the claim that CT can only sustain a limited conception of God. Showing how to avoid this complaint about CT will put us in a better position to see the central concern that needs to be addressed before drawing any conclusions

---

[12] For a taste of the complexities, see Flint and Freddoso (1983).
[13] For a defense of the universal value of knowledge, see Kvanvig (2008b).

about how close CT can get to the starting point of PBT, so let's examine the limited deity objection in a bit more detail.

As described earlier, there is the Millian worry that only a deity of limited knowledge and power can be sustained from the evidential basis for positing such a deity. As noted earlier as well, this picture of deity is derived by using the cosmological and teleological features ascertainable in nature to predict what kind of a being might be responsible for the existence of the cosmos. The central difference between that methodology and the present methodology is the difference between epistemology and metaphysics. Here, we are not attending to the question of whether there is evidence for a creator, but rather to the question of what is involved in the nature of a being who is the creator of all, or as we have refined that idea, who is the asymmetrical source of all else. What can be derived is obviously determined by whether one's project is epistemological or metaphysical, and if the latter, we have resources that no epistemological methodology can offer. In particular, the model of sourcehood developed makes God's actions akin to basic actions, where the success conditions for the action are built into its intentional component. The defense of this approach is that there are no limits on the power of a being who is the source of all else, since there is nothing which could interfere or limit the expression of such a will. We thus endorse the strongest possible reading of claims such as, "And God said, 'Let there be light,' and there was light." Not the slightest tinge of contingency is involved in the conditional relationship between God saying or intending a thing and its realization. Contrary to Millian concerns that only a God of limited power and ability can be derived from teleological and cosmological considerations, our more metaphysical version of Creator Theology reveals a personal being of unimaginable power, of such extensive power that exceeding it in effectiveness is impossible. Finally, the fullest version of this view traces contingency itself to operations of the Divine will, with necessity explained in terms of the operations of the Divine mind, even though it is worth noting that some qualifications will be needed, depending on the presence of freedom and indeterminacy in the created order. We need not delve into these issues at present,[14] however, for our goal is not

---

[14] The standard way of addressing this issue distinguishes betweeen God's antecedent will and his consequent will, with the latter activity operative in light of his knowledge of what indeterminacies are present. A first issue, though, is whether CT is itself compatible with the existence of indeterminacy, or more carefully, whether the full conceptualist version I've been discussing here is compatible with it. If this hurdle can be cleared, one way of explaining the idea of antecedent and consequent willing in the face of indeterminacy is Molinism, but not the only one. Moreover, Molinism, as standardly formulated, applies only to the indeterminacies that result if libertarianism about human freedom is correct. One alternative to Molinism is the view I defend in Kvanvig (2011b, especially ch. 8, "An Epistemic Theory

to find the best version of CT, but rather to see what limitations there are on CT for deriving the starting points of alternative metatheologies.

It is important also to note what I am not claiming at this point concerning CT. I am not claiming that this conception of divine power is metaphysically coherent. What I am doing, instead, is tracing how CT should be developed, as a metaphysical position in metatheology. The result may turn out to be incoherent, which of course would be so much the worse for CT. An analogy with PBT can help here. For bottom-up PBT, the characterization of deity goes through the method of finding great-making properties with intrinsic *maxima*. The result, supposing PBT can explain the personhood of God, involves the properties of omnipotence, omniscience, omnibenevolence, and necessary existence, among other things. This result, however, carries with it no guarantee of metaphysical coherence, not for the omni-properties themselves nor for their mutual exemplification, nor for their coherence with the property of being necessary if possible. The results, instead, are simply the tracing of the proper development of (bottom-up) PBT, with the next explanatory burden being that of defending the metaphysical coherence of the resulting theory. Just so here, with CT: we first develop and articulate what can be derived from the metatheology in question and then face the issue of whether the subsequent theory is metaphysically coherent (as well as whether it passes epistemic muster along whatever other dimensions are needed for a fully defensible theology).

So the first element of the theory that results from CT metatheology is the limitless power of God, where there are no external constraints of any sort of what God is capable of willing nor is there any metaphysical gap between trying and succeeding when it comes to acts of will on the part of God. Such power implicates superior intellectual ability as well. Having unlimited power would seem to include the power to discover what is true and what is not, and as we saw earlier, there is reason to see this ability as displayed as well.

From this point, there are two directions that might be pursued to link these ideas about power and knowledge to the axiological domain. The first way is through what I have called "integration principles," principles that link certain mental states, attitudes, and behavior with other mental states, attitudes, and behavior. Such principles are philosophically interesting in their own right, independently of our specific context, and include proposals such as: (i) in order to hope for something, you have to believe that it is attainable; (ii) in

---

of Creation"), and one of its advantages is that it applies to other types of indeterminacies in nature, besides those that arise from the powers of free agents.

order to perform an action, you have to see that action as good in some sense; (iii) to have an intention to do something requires believing that one will do that thing; and (iv) simply to desire or prefer something requires believing the object of desire or preference to be desirable or good.[15] We can think of these proposals in terms of attempts to ascertain what are the minimal requirements of coherence and unity in order for any organism to count as a person, a fascinating issue of deep significance for our understanding of our own natures.

We can also consider the possibilities involved in suffering failures of integration but not of sufficient force to undermine personhood. Regarding such failures, we look for what makes such failures possible, and in many cases, it looks like the answer required is always finitude or fallibility of some sort. Consider, for example, Φ-ing intentionally, but not knowing what one is doing; or intending to Φ-ing but not believing that one will Φ. For the former, one can engage in intentional behavior, under a certain description, but not realize that what one will be doing is also something under another description. For example, if I intentionally shift bike gears when going uphill, I may not know that I just shifted from the sixth ring to the fifth in my chainring set. Moreover, one might intend to exercise in the morning, but think that when morning comes, the intention will have disappeared as well as the willpower to carry through on the plan to exercise.

When we can trace such failures of integration to finitude and fallibility, it gives hope to the idea that integration principles for beings not bound by finitude might be strong enough to link power and knowledge to the axiological domain, allowing an explanation of how CT can derive positive evaluative and normative claims about the nature and behavior of God. Perhaps such considerations will allow a defender of CT to adopt the Socratic idea, at least for deities, that acting against one's better judgment is impossible, an argument pursued at some length in the prior section.

In this way, the metaphysical project of CT metatheology generates a complete answer to Mill's worries that considerations deriving from creation itself will sustain only a limited ascription of power, knowledge, and goodness to the creator. By replacing the epistemological project with a metaphysical one,

---

[15] For literature on these matters, see Bradley and List (2009); Bradley and Stefánsson (2016); Collins (1995); Cross (2008); Campbell (2018); Daskal (2010); Humberstone (1987); Hájek and Pettit (2004); Lewis (1988, 1996); Lauria and Deonna (2017b,a); Orsi (2015); Prince (1989), and Weintraub (2007). For related literature on the links between cognition, action, intending, and trying, see, e.g., Bratman (1984, 1999, 2001); Brand (1984, 1987); Garcia (1987), and Marušić and Schwenkler (forthcoming).

we end up with a much higher conception of deity, one where the properties in question are not limited in the way Mill claims.

Even so, responding to the Millian project in the way envisioned is not the same thing as showing that the starting point of PBT can be derived from CT. Note especially that I have been intentionally vague about the power, knowledge, and goodness of God, leaving open the possibility that the unlimited, unqualified features in question do not obviously amount to precisely the same thing that PBT offers in terms of the essentiality of the omni-properties of omnipotence, omniscience, and omnibenevolence. That vagueness leaves open the next stage of the dialect here, for we want not only to see what conception of God can be derived from CT, but we also want to consider whether the conception so derived is respectable enough to count as a complete and adequate theology. And here it is easy to imagine two Anselmian complaints. First, the vagueness regarding power, knowledge, and goodness shows that they are not really the same properties as the omni-properties; and second, even if they are the same properties, it is better to have those properties essentially rather than accidentally, and nothing in the derivations above generate that result.

Tom Morris gives voice to what such an Anselmian argument would look like. We assume that there is a being of the sort CT describes, and we call this being 'El'. We then consider whether El could be God, on the assumption that the greatness of El does not go as far as Anselmians would wish. We can then argue that El cannot be God, as follows:

> Now if in W there is a being who is omnipotent, omniscient, and all the rest, surely El is not God, but rather, at best, the vicegerent or deputy of God, a sort of demiurge. If El is less than omnipotent, and there is an omnipotent, omniscient individual, then clearly anything El accomplishes is done only at the good pleasure, or according to the wishes, of the Anselmian being. El would not be the ultimate reality. He would not be God. I think. this conclusion is fully in accord with the properly religious usage of 'God' in Judeo-Christian orthodoxy, and in fact that it is a conclusion forced on us by that usage. If the object of worship in the western tradition of theology is intended to be the ultimate reality, and if the Anselmian conception of God is coherent, the God of religious devotion is the God of the philosophers.
> 
> Morris (1984, p. 183)

Morris's argument is instructive, but needs modification. Note that Morris concludes that if El does not possess the Anselmian characteristics, "El would not be the ultimate reality." If this claim is correct, a defender of CT can evade this Anselmian objection, since being the asymmetrical source of all else entails immediately being the ultimate reality, and hence the attempted *reductio* would be a non-starter. But Morris need not have run the argument in this way. All his argument needs is the claim that if El is not the Anselmian being, then El is a vicegerent or deputy of the Anselmian being.

Even so, the argument, as presented, doesn't withstand scrutiny. In our context, El is first identified in terms of aseity and asymmetrical independence from all else. These characteristics lead straightforwardly to the conclusion that nothing can frustrate El's will. So how is it that there could be a being with more power than El? Answer: there couldn't be. So if El is not the Anselmian being, it is not because the Anselmian being would be more powerful than El.

In response, Morris could still claim the following. It is one thing to have maximal power and another to have it essentially. Perhaps El has maximal power and yet the Anselmian being has it essentially. Such a possibility requires that it be possible for there to be two maximally powerful beings, and some have doubted such a possibility. They have worried about what happens if the wills of the two conflict, but that argument requires assuming that their wills can conflict. Perhaps, instead, what we should conclude is the more limited claim that if there are two beings that are both maximally powerful, their wills cannot conflict.

If so, we can still ask if El would be, as envisioned, a mere deputy. This conclusion could be evaded if El were actual, but the Anselmian being was only possible. Let's assume, though, that Anselmians are correct, that an Anselmian being has to be actual if possible. So, we assume, both El and the Anselmian being exist, but whereas the Anselmian being has maximal power in every world (in which this being exists), El is not essentially so.

Notice, though, a competing claim. El is the asymmetrical source of all else, so is also the source of the Anselmian being. If the distinction between accidental and essential power inclines one toward the conclusion that El is merely a vicegerent of the Anselmian being, the dependence of the Anselmian being on El inclines one toward the opposite conclusion.

The thought experiment thus becomes a philosophical tug-of-war. We assume that the asymmetrical source of all else is not an omni-being, but that the Anselmian being is. But if both beings were actual, the Anselmian being would be a dependent being. Conundrums multiply: how could a limited God be responsible for the existence of something more impressive than God? The Anselmian being is, by nature, the greatest possible being; but equally by nature, El is the asymmetrical source of all else.

What remains, if one wishes to press the Morrisian objection, is to turn holistic, and claim that this advantage for El ends up disappearing once we pay attention to the entire panoply of great-making properties that the Anselmian being exemplifies. Such an approach endorses the top-down Anselmian strategy taken in Nagasawa (2017), in opposition to the usual bottom-up strategy common in the history of Anselmianism. On the bottom up strategy, no possible being can be God unless that being exemplifies all great-making properties with intrinsic *maxima*.[16] It will be hard to avoid the conclusion that being sourced by another being makes it impossible to exemplify all great-making properties, and so the bottom-up strategy would seem to require that neither being is, in fact, a deity.

What remains, then, is the top-down strategy, but a couple of points are in order about the limitations of this strategy. First, as we saw in Chapter 4, that strategy has no resources for explaining why the greatest possible being has to be necessary if possible. If the Anselmian being is merely possible, however, the description of that being no longer gives a reason for denying the status of deity to El. Second, if the existence assumption remains in place, the value judgments needed to draw the conclusion that the Anselmian being is the only deity in the story are not compelling. The Anselmian being won't have any actual advantage over El in terms of knowledge, power, or goodness, but only a modal advantage, if such it be. El, though, will have an actual advantage, in virtue of being the source of the Anselmian being. It is hard to come away from this contest without leaning toward the position that CT occupies.

So, as I see it, the Morris thought experiment is undermined in two different ways, one focusing on bottom-up construals of the Anselmian being and the other focusing on top-down construals. Even given this undermining, however, a bit of discomfort remains, for the undermining leaves open the epistemic possibility that El is God but is not the greatest possible being. For if the Anselmian being is more impressive along a number of dimensions, but this impressiveness is swamped by the fact that El is the source of this Anselmian being, we can still ask about the epistemic possibility of there being a different being that has all the virtues of the Anselmian being plus the sourcing features of El. That being, it would seem, would be the greatest possible being.

Here I have described this problem as one concerning epistemic possibility, but perhaps it is not merely an epistemic possibility but a metaphysical one as well. To consider this objection, then, we will let 'El' name the being who is, by

---

[16] As an example, and for a defense of this claim, see Plantinga (1974).

nature, the asymmetrical source of all else, and ask whether it is possible, either metaphysically or epistemically, that El is not the greatest possible being. If the answer to either question is "yes", we then need to consider if and how much of a mark against CT this fact reveals. I turn first to the metaphysical option.

Note first that El is characterized in a way that is purely extensional, at least on first inspection. There are no modal features involved in the claim that El is the asymmetrical source of all else. So, whereas PBT insists that God is the greatest possible being and (thus) a necessary being, perhaps El is only a contingent being. In such a case, it would follow that El is not the greatest possible being.

Let's consider first whether El is, as described, a merely contingent being. If we look merely at the definite description that indicates the fundamental starting point for CT, it might seem so. Yet, once the implications of this description are traced, the appearance changes. For if God is the asymmetrical source of all else, we find in God both the source of contingency and the source of necessity itself. Upon deriving that God is best understood as a person, we the find the source of contingency in the will of God and the source of necessity in the operations of the Divine mind. Since necessities obtain in every possible scenario, we must either suppose that God exists in every possible scenario in order to be the source of such necessities in each scenario in which they obtain; or we must suppose that God is contingently the source of necessities in actuality, but need not be so in other possible scenarios. Yet, if necessities are so in virtue of the operations of the Divine mind, such metaphysical dependence is not something that obtains in some metaphysically possible scenarios and not others. Rather, since the explanation involves such metaphysical dependence, it is the kind of dependence that has full modal significance: it is dependence that explains an essential feature of the thing in question and thus obtains in every possible scenario, since the thing in question is necessary. CT thus begins from a phrase that is intensionally pregnant, even though the language initially appears to be merely extensional.

Moreover, it is fairly easy to understand why it might seem plausible that CT, unlike PBT, can't imply that God is a necessary being. For the focus in ordinary thinking about God as creator of all is on the realm of contingency: the flowers, the streams, the animals, the planets, stars, and the very cosmos itself. If we focus on contingent things, and claim that God created them all, that alone gives us no reason to think that there couldn't be possibilities in which other explanations are appropriate. A more philosophically sophisticated understanding of God's asymmetrical sourcehood of all else, however, doesn't merely have the existence of contingent things depending on the will of God, but rather the realm of contingency itself explained in terms of the will of God. In this way, the relation between contingency and the will of God mirrors the relation between necessity and the mind of God: in both cases, the explanatory relationship is metaphysical in nature, telling us about an essential feature of each region of metaphysical space, leaving no room for explaining the existence of contingent things in other possible scenarios in terms that don't appeal to the will of God.

We can conclude then that the answer is "no" to the question of whether it is metaphysically possible that El does not exist. This result blocks the first version of the worry that El might not be the greatest possible being, since on one version, the issue was whether we could find a possible scenario in which a different being existed that had all the virtues of El plus those of the Anselmian being. Since El is necessary, however, the answer is straightforward: there is no such possible scenario, since it would require two beings each of which is individually the sole source of all else.

We need, then, to consider the second version of the concern, the version that appeals to epistemic rather than metaphysical possibility. Before doing so, however, it is worth noting how close we are to being able to show that one can derive the starting point of PBT can be derived from CT. We, of course, have seen no basis in CT for claiming that God is an omni-being. Recall, however, that there are two versions of PBT, a top-down version and a bottom-up version. Only the bottom-up version is able to derive the conclusion that God must be an omni-being, and it derives this conclusion in a way that invites opponents to challenge the coherence of the theology that results. Top-down PBT does not wish to depend on the omni-being claim, precisely because of the possibility of coherence failure.[17] To the extent that it is an open question whether PBT can coherently maintain that God is an omni-being, it is no objection yet to a claim that CT might be able to show that God is the greatest possible being. So, even though it is hyperbolic to claim that the starting point of PBT follows from CT, there is a more careful point to be made that reveals the strength of CT as a metatheology. CT subsumes versions of PBT that are most easily shown to be coherent.

There remains, however, the other version of the objection to CT, the one that appeals to an epistemic rather that metaphysical notion of necessity. We need to see whether CT can respond adequately to this version of the objection.

The language of epistemic possibility is plausibly taken to be found in natural language in the form of claims about what might be true, and this

---

[17] See Nagasawa (2017) for an extended argument of precisely this sort.

feature of natural language is among the most controversial issues in recent philosophy of logic and language. The beginnings of the controversy are found in the epistemic logic of Jaakko Hintikka from the early 1960s.[18] Hintikka, like others to follow, takes the language of 'might' typically to be an expression of epistemic possibility, which he defines as:

EP: $\Diamond_K \Phi =_{df.} \neg K \neg \Phi$

Where ⌜$K$⌝ is the knowledge operator (read as "it is known that") and ⌜$\Diamond_K$⌝ expresses epistemic possibility.

Since this beginning, a number of attempts have been made to improve on this account of epistemic possibility.[19] In our context, however, most of this discussion is beside the point, for if we have already determined that it isn't metaphysically possible that there is a being greater than El, any account of epistemic possibility that makes knowledge rule out such possibilities will not be able to explain any sense in which El might not be the greatest possible being. For such a possibility is ruled out without appeal to any knowledge at all.

What this shows, I think, is that if we want to endorse something in the spirit of Hintikka's original proposal, we will also have to allow that there are other uses of 'might' in natural language that cannot be characterized in this way. For example, we can appropriately use the language of 'might' to express the idea that even our most impressive knowledge is fallible. As we might put it, our knowledge is fallible precisely because we might be wrong. To understand such uses, the knowledge in question has to be bracketed, since it obviously entails that we are not wrong (on the supposition that knowledge is factive).

Just so, if we want to interpret the possibility that El may not be the greatest possible being, we can do so by bracketing the information available that shows that such a possibility is not metaphysically possible. In doing so, however, we undercut the significance of the worry, it would seem. Consider an analogy. Skeptics want us to admit that we can always be wrong, and fallibilism is characterized in terms of this possibility. Any skeptical celebration, though, is premature, since the fallibilist admission includes a precise denial of what the skeptic was hoping to get from the possibility in question (when the admission is that even what we know best is fallible). Just so, a defender of CT can admit

---

[18] See Hintikka (1962).
[19] See, e.g., Fetzer (1974); Hacking (1967); Teller (1972); DeRose (1991); Huemer (2007), and MacFarlane (2011).

the possibility, in some sense, that El is not the greatest possible being, but any celebration by defenders of PBT would be as premature as that of the skeptic, since the admission by defenders of CT includes the resources to show the asymmetrical source of all else cannot be surpassed in greatness. In this way, defenders of CT can endorse the caution implicit in Morris's concern about whether El is the greatest possible being while deflating the concern at the same time. They can do so in a way that mirrors the way in which fallibilists can endorse skeptical caution without endorsing skeptical conclusions.

## 7.4 Conclusion

We can close this chapter with two points. The first is a somewhat provisional conclusion that the defender of PBT will find it hard to show that CT is inadequate. The resources of CT on this issue are vastly better than those impressed with Millian concerns have imagined, leaving it hard to see any suitable grounds for concern that the asymmetrical source of all else fails to be adequate enough to satisfy Anselmian intuitions. The second, point, however, is that the derivation of worship-worthiness is a more contentious issue for CT. So at this point we cannot claim that CT is impressive enough to be declared the victor in the competition among metatheologies.

Even granting this limitation, it is worth reminding ourselves that the elements of sourcehood central to CT are not mere accouterments to a theology that make these elements somehow optional. Instead, the central elements of the metatheology of CT are elements to which PBT and WWT must answer. It is thus encumbent on these alternative approaches to show that the the aseity of God as well as the dependence of all else on God can be sustained on their approach. The point to note, then, is that CT has considerable advantages as a metatheological position, both in terms of the conditions of adequacy it imposes on other metatheologies and also in its capacity to sustain an understanding of God that goes considerable distance in deriving the starting points of PBT and WWT.

# 8
# Perfect Being Theology's Difficulties

## 8.1 Introduction

The purpose of this chapter is to consider the degree to which Perfect Being Theology (PBT) has resources for generating the starting points for Creator Theology (CT) and Worship-Worthy Being Theology (WWT). We already have a partial answer, for we have seen that PBT is not well suited to deriving the starting point of CT. We turn to this task in §8.2, followed by more extensive discussion of the starting point of WWT in §8.3.

Though our goal is more in terms of finding data at this point than drawing conclusions from it, we can at least compare the results achieved in the last chapter for CT with those obtained here for PBT. As we will see, PBT is considerably less adept at generating the starting points of competing metatheologies than is CT. We will wait until the next chapter to comment on the comparison between PBT and WWT.

## 8.2 From Perfection in Being to Sourcehood

Perfect Being Theology is designed to show that God must be an omni-being, perfect in power, knowledge, and goodness. As we have seen, there is a bit of a hiccup to be faced here, one concerning the personal nature of God, which is a task that defenders of PBT have not addressed sufficiently. And the case of the hiccups might worsen, for there is no guarantee that the notions of omnipotence, omniscience, and omnibenevolence are coherent, nor that they are mutually consistent. As with other metatheologies, however, these concerns about coherence are issues to be addressed later in the process of theory development. Our initial concerns about metatheologies is what they have to say about the shared ground and what they have to say about the starting points of competitors. So the first hiccup is relevant to our current assessment concerns, with the other issues left to the side for now.

The difficulty concerning the derivability of the personhood of God from PBT occurs again when it comes to the claim that God is the creator of all. Here is Anselm's discussion of it:

> God is whatever it is better to be than not to be; and he, as the only self-existent being, creates all things from nothing.
>
> WHAT are you, then, Lord God, than whom nothing greater can be conceived? But what are you, except that which, as the highest of all beings, alone exists through itself, and creates all other things from nothing? For, whatever is not this is less than a thing which can be conceived of. But this cannot be conceived of you. What good, therefore, does the supreme Good lack, through which every good is? Therefore, you are just, truthful, blessed, and whatever it is better to be than not to be. For it is better to be just than not just; better to be blessed than not blessed.
>
> Anselm (1998 [1077–8], ch. V)

Anselm claims to establish that nothing else exists through itself except God, and that all other things are created by God from nothing. The argument for this conclusion has as its premise that God is whatever it is better to be than not to be. So Anselm is committed to the claim that it is better to be the independent, asymmetrical source of all else than not to be.

This argument looks worst when we take the Anselmian slogan to apply to each individual item in our ontology, claiming that it is better for each individual thing to be the independent asymmetrical source of all else than not to be such an asymmetrical source. If we try this route, we end up saying that the best version of you is one that is self-existent. I resist. I'm all for the advice of aiming to be the best you can be, so would respond by claiming that the best version of you can't be one that is self-existent, since that version of you is impossible! This point generalizes: if we want to rank-order various versions of any given thing, from worst to best, what we find is an ordering among possibilities, from which it follows that being self-existent isn't really a great-making property for individuals.

We need not intepret the Anselmian as arguing in this way, however. Instead, we can understand such talk in terms of the properties themselves, as does bottom-up PBT, looking for great-making properties with intrinsic *maxima*. Typical examples of such properties include things like power, knowledge, and goodness. Such properties come in degrees, and the highest degree in each case generates an omni-property, if all goes well. This approach is useful, because it provides a basis for responding to parodies of the ontological argument, such as the perfect lost island example in Gaunilo (1998 [1078]). One can undermine such parodies if one can show that the properties are gradable but have no maximum (as Plantinga (1974) claims) regarding the properties that make some islands better than others.

As noted in Chapter 4, reliance on gradable properties such as power, knowledge, and goodness creates a difficulty for PBT, since some of these properties presuppose personhood, which is not a gradable property. Furthermore, the fact that some of these properties presuppose a non-gradable property raises the possibility that the supposedly gradable properties are only gradable relative to a context. In the evaluative context of persons, more power, knowledge, and goodness is better; in the evaluative context of buildings, they are not. For this reason, the Anselmian needs a way to derive the personhood of God independently of an attempted derivation of the claim that God is an omni-being.

The implications for the Anselmian derivation of the property of being the asymmetrical source of all else are clear. This property is not a gradable one since the aseity involved in it is an all-or-nothing kind of thing. Gradability does enter into the property in one way, for sourcehood can range from being the source of just one particular thing all the way to being the source of all things. But a complex property doesn't itself become gradable simply by having component parts that are gradable. So if great-making properties need to be gradable, Anselm's argument that God is the asymmetrical source of all else fails.

This problem derives from the dialectical strategy of avoiding a certain problem for Anselmianism, and in a way that yields some hope for defending the ontological argument. It is worth noting, though, that even though PBT originates in a desire to demonstrate the existence of God, there is no more reason to require PBT to defend the ontological argument than there is to require CT to defend version of cosmological and teleological arguments. Each of these metatheologies is fundamentally metaphysical in character, leaving open the possibility that approaches to the nature of God are combined with a skeptical stance about the epistemic quality of any of the arguments for the existence of God. So, if the above dissatisfaction for Anselmian methodology arises simply because of the demands of the ontological argument, a defender of PBT can simply endorse PBT without wedding that endorsement to any affirmation about the ontological argument itself.[1]

---

[1] A recent example of such a version of PBT can be found in Murphy (2017).

Even so, divorcing PBT from the ontological argument won't help with the needed derivations of personhood and sourcehood. Deriving any particular property from the claim that God is the greatest possible being requires a principle about which properties go into making something be the greatest possible. A first requirement is to distinguish between good, better, and best, since we don't want to impute less than the best to the greatest possible being. Resisting a temptation is good, but perhaps it is best not to be subject to temptation at all. In addition, we need to distinguish between context-relative evaluation and context-independent evaluation: it is good for humans to have two arms, but it is not good for tigers or giraffes or redwood trees. Once these two elements are combined, however, there is no longer any clear path from PBT to personhood or sourcehood, since the evaluations being made are no longer obviously context-independent. Nor should this difficulty be surprising. We initially moved away from an evaluation of properties instanced in individuals, since it is implausible to think that great-making properties have to answer to the requirement that, for any individual whatsoever, having that property would make that individual better. For precisely the same reason, we have no grounds for thinking that the crucial properties under discussion meet the requirement of context-independent evaluation.

What is left for PBT, then, is to abandon a bottom-up strategy for defending personhood and sourcehood, pursuing instead a top-down strategy. Such a strategy involves some construction of a great chain of possible beings,[2] and then we simply look at the nature of the being that is at the top of the chain to see what the greatest possible being is like.

For such a top-down strategy to succeed, there needs to be some compositional function on properties that contribute to the greatness of a being. This function must at least allow pairwise comparisons to be made between any candidate greatest possible being and everything else. When we find that no comparison is possible, we are able to discard that candidate as a candidate for greatest possible being. In the best case, comparisons are always present between any two individuals, allowing a linear ordering of all possible beings. But there are concerns about such a linearity assumption,[3] on grounds of value incommensurability (which is greater, an avacado or an aardvark, an envelope or an elevator?), so PBT would be better off not tying its wagon to this beast. Abandoning the linearity assumption still leaves another hurdle to overcome,

---

[2] "Chain" may not be the best term to use here, for there is no need for there to be a well-ordering among all possible beings. All that is required is that the greatest be comparable with everything else. For discussion, see Nagasawa (2017).

[3] As argued initially in Broad (1939) and more recently in Morris (1987a).

for the top-down methodology still requires that no being is the greatest who is not value commensurable with every other being. For whenever $x$ and $y$ are value incommensurable, it is false that either is better or greater than the other. I have no idea how to argue for the claim that there must be at least one such being, but without it, top-down PBT has no hope of success.

This point may be overstated, but not in a way that can eliminate the problem. Suppose that for every being except one, there could be found another being whose value exceeded the value of the first being. Then there is one being regarding whom there is no greater, and only one such being. If so, perhaps that being should be regarded as the greatest possible. That being, after all, is the only unsurpassable being, with every other being falling into the category of surpassable beings. (And if there is more than one such being, they are all greatest possible beings, a polytheistic possibility left open by PBT already, as noted in Chapter 5.) This result could obtain even if this greatest possible being is not value-commensurable with every other possible being.

Still, the problem doesn't disappear either way. First, it is no easier to argue for the claim that there is an unsurpassable being than it is to argue for the claim that there is a being value commensurable with all other beings. As a Christian theist, I of course endorse both of these claims, but I derive them from a substantive theology quite a ways down the road of theory development from any initial metatheological starting point that hopes for a derivation from that starting point alone. Even worse, however, is this point. Suppose then that we grant that there is an unsurpassable being, but with no guarantee of uniqueness. That is, we suppose that we find two beings that are unsurpassable. If so, however, PBT faces a dilemma. The methodology identifies two beings as equally impressive, and then we ask whether being the asymmetrical source of all else contributes to the greatness of these beings. Here's what we know: whatever goes into greatness of being, being the source of all else can't go into any such function that leaves open the possibility of ties for greatest possible being. For we have already seen that this description secures monotheism. So, the function could, at most, allow the property to contribute to greatness for only one of the two beings. That is not a promising result.

To see why, consider the prime examples of great-making properties cited by defenders of PBT, those involved in being an omni-being. Let's even grant that personhood is included in the mix. Assume as well, though, that no uniqueness proof will be forthcoming from the collection: if there is an omni-being that is a person, there might be more than one; if no such personal omni-being is possible, there are different, equally good combinations of power, knowledge, and goodness that are possible. Call each such combination a "collage of great-making properties", and then take each collage and add to it the property of being the asymmetrical source of all else. The coherence of this version of PBT requires that adding this property to a collage generates an enhanced collage* that is possible in at most one case. What is far from obvious is why this would be possible in at most only one case. Instead, what would seem to be true is that turning a possible collage into an impossible collage* would be possible and perhaps frequent, but not almost completely ubiquitous. So, there is no reason whatsoever for concluding that the needed value function can be found, and without such a reason, there is no reason for thinking that this version of PBT is in a position to derive this characterization of God.

Notice, too, that this difficulty has been developed and articulated in the context of considering top-down PBT, but it isn't clear how bottom-up PBT would be immune to the problem, either. In our context, though, there is no need to delve further into the matter. What is important is that all versions of PBT suffer the same fate. They have no basis for claiming that God is the asymmetrical source of all else, and the fundamental reason for the failure is that such descriptive features of God are difficult to derive on the basis of evaluative considerations alone. For those impressed with the idea that the evaluative strongly supervenes on the descriptive, this result should not surprise at all, for such supervenience tells us only that there will be no change in the evaluative dimension without some change in the descriptive dimension (but not the other way around).

We turn, then, to the remaining starting point, that of WWT. In this case, prospects seem more promising from the outset, and our task is to see if appearances are misleading.

## 8.3 From Perfection in Being to Worship-Worthiness

The prospects for deriving worship-worthiness from PBT might seem more promising, for it is standard fare among defenders of PBT to make such a claim. We find such a claim by Tom Morris, a good representative of the view. He writes,

> Worship-worthiness, for example, can be held to supervene upon, or to consist in, some of the properties ingredient in perfection. The idea of worship-worthiness can thus be subsumed within the idea of perfection, which can in turn act as a guide to our understanding of the conditions of proper worship, the characteristics required for a being to merit this ultimate attitude and treatment.    Morris (1987b, p. 24)

It is clear that Morris intends to explain worship-worthiness on the basis of PBT. His derivation is remarkably pithy, but also indefinite: either supervenience or constitution is the needed basis for the derivation, not to mention the vagaries of the phrase "can be held". Such language invites suspicion about whether the inference is too quick.

Tim Bayne and Yujin Nagasawa think so.[4] They maintain that perfection is not sufficient for being worthy of worship. They write,

> It seems possible for a world to contain two beings, each of whom instantiates those properties included within M [the properties defining maximal excellence]. Call one of the two beings 'God' and the other 'God*'. If worshipfulness supervenes on the possession of M-properties then we would have obligations to worship both God and God*.
>
> (Bayne and Nagasawa 2006, p. 308)

This objection begins with the idea that there is nothing in the collection of properties that defines maximal excellence that guarantees that there is only one maximally excellent being. Suppose we grant this premise.[5] The problem they see is that we need not have obligations to worship both beings, and so perfection in being does not imply worthiness of worship.

Fortunately for defenders of PBT who agree with Morris, this argument is not persuasive. There is no necessity to the idea that one can only have obligations to worship one being, nor is there any impossibility to the idea that if there is more than one perfect being, one must worship all of them. There is, perhaps, a hint of a reason for denying the latter claim in some contemporary Christian practices that prohibit praying to any member of the Trinity except the Father, on the basis of the teaching by Jesus about prayer that points to the beginning of the Lord's prayer: "Our Father who art in heaven...". The restriction on prayer is a bit of an inferential stretch, however, since it would make little sense for Jesus to answer the disciples' request ("Teach us to pray") by talking to himself! Moreover, even if prayer must be addressed only to the Father (and if we assume that all members of the Trinity are equally perfect beings in the sense defined by PBT), there is no reason to think that one can't worship without praying. So the central

---

[4] See Bayne and Nagasawa (2006). See also Bayne and Nagasawa (2007).

[5] Bayne and Nagasawa go on to argue that even if this premise is denied by a defender of PBT, the same problem remains in virtue of plausible *per impossibile* reasoning. Distinguishing between acceptable and unacceptable reasoning of this sort, however, is something no one has a good theory about, and it is painfully obvious that not all such reasoning should be accepted (nor should it all be rejected). We can bypass this issue here, however, for I think we should grant the premise in question, as I argued in Kvanvig (2021a) and in Chapters 4 and 5.

assumption of the counterexample to the sufficiency of perfection for worship-worthiness need not trouble Morrisians until and unless a further argument is produced showing that at most only one being can be worthy of worship or that worthiness of worship can be selective with respect to a mutiple group of deities.

Regarding the latter possibility, the discussion of selectivity among beings displaying maximal excellence is confounded a bit by the introduction of the thesis that only God is worthy of worship. The authors note that most monotheists would endorse such a thesis, and this is especially true if we are thinking about the supreme worthiness of the most exalted worship that defines WWT. But the selectivity point doesn't follow from any commitment by monotheists to the restrictive thesis, since the selectivity point clearly involves what to say about a situation in which monotheism has to be abandoned (if PBT is still being assumed). So, some other explanation, other than monotheism's predilection for the singular desert of God for the kind of worship under discussion is needed to undergird the selectivity claim.

It is worth making this point as carefully as we can. The claim that only one being is supremely worthy of the ultimate worship follows from two claims: (i) to be God is to be worthy of worship, and (ii) there is but one God. Once the conjunction of these two is abandoned, it is not clear why or whether one should retain the claim that only one being is supremely worthy of the ultimate worship. For perhaps claim (i) is the central one with claim (ii) being ancillary, so that if the conjunction is to be given up, it is claim (ii) that goes first. To retain the stricture Baynes and Nagasawa need—that only one being can be supremely worthy of the highest worship—would require giving up (i) when the conjunction is abandoned, and that strikes me as forced and not the most appealing strategy for revising a theology in the face of theoretical tension.

I note, though, that this discussion presumes that both 'God' and 'God*' denote deities in the Bayne/Nagasawa thought experiment. If that assumption is false, the above discussion won't address their perspective adequately, but we need not pursue that possibility here, for if both beings aren't deities, it is clear that PBT has been abandoned. For both beings are assumed in the thought experiment to be maximally excellent, and thus tied for the title of greatest possible being.

There is another way in the literature that appears to resist Morris's plan to derive worship-worthiness from perfection of being. One might here borrow from Mark Murphy's train of thought in Murphy (2017, ch. 7). Murphy holds that perfections alone can't ground the obligation of allegiance, since such allegiance involves an assumption of shared goals that doesn't follow from the perfections alone. What is needed in addition is for a perfect being to adopt a contingent ethics that puts in place the sharing of goals needed to generate an obligation of allegiance. Murphy writes,

> Now suppose that the Anselmian being has a contingent ethics such that (a) the An-selmian being does not will that we act in ways that the norms of practical reasonableness forbid of us and (b) whatever further the Anselmian being wills with respect to created rational beings is such that for each creature, subordinating the creaturely will to the Anselmian being's will enables that creature to act in a rationally preferable way with respect to the ends set by those norms of practical reasonableness. In these circumstances, it seems to me that there is an overwhelmingly strong case for the worthiness of the Anselmian being for us to be obedient to that being's will.
>
> Murphy (2017, p. 168)

Murphy cites two conditions concerning practical reasonableness that he claims are sufficient for generating obligations of obedience to God, among which, according to WWT, we find the obligation of worship. What is important here for our context is that the form of argument used gives a buttressing reason for the selectivity claim central to the argument by Bayne and Nagasawa that perfections are not sufficient for worship-worthiness. Moreover, Murphy's argument is fully general, not relying on the uniqueness claim used by Bayne and Nagasawa, but only on the idea that the perfections of God do not include the elements of willing described in conditions (a) and (b) in the passage above.

Here, a defender of PBT might balk, claiming that it is a perfection to have one's will conform to the conditions in question. Murphy's answer is that perfect being thinking should "press outward" (p. 21), characterizing the perfections in as expansive a way as one reasonably can.[6] Though such a description is vague, we can get an idea of what is intended by noting that Murphy thinks this characterization is satisfied by noting that God would be greater in a case where counterfactuals of freedom exist and are known by God than in a case where such knowledge is absent because metaphysically impossible. Generalizing on this example, the idea seems to be that when there is more than one way of characterizing deity, the Anselmian has a reason to prefer the one that makes the reach of metaphysical possibility greater. In the present context, that idea is honored by letting the possibilities of what God might will range wider than what would be required for it to be a perfection

---

[6] Murphy (2017, p. 21).

for God's will to be constrained in a way that makes conditions (a) and (b) be honored automatically.

This explanation should be resisted, I think. To see why, consider the argument about knowledge of counterfactuals of freedom. We consider two beings in two different cases. In case 1, there are true counterfactuals of freedom and they are known by being 1. In case 2, counterfactuals of freedom are metaphysically impossible and are thus not known by being 2. (It is compatible with this description that being 1 is identical to being 2, but such identity doesn't seem to be needed for the argument.) All else being equal, the idea is that being 1 in case 1 is greater than being 2 in case 2. But that is the claim to be resisted. Not knowing what isn't true isn't even remotely lamentable. If it is true that you can't know what isn't true, we don't generate a reason for thinking that it is greater to know falsehoods by reasoning of this sort. What's metaphysically possible is to be sorted out first, and then greatness assessed within the modal space in question; thinking about what would be fantastic if true is not a way of finding a reason for thinking the space in question is wider than what we might otherwise have thought. It wouldn't make a being greater if that being could square a circle, and reasoning by cases in the way just described doesn't give us a reason of any sort—*pro tanto, prima facie*, defeated, or defeasible—for thinking that squaring a circle is possible.

Perhaps, though, the impossibility of knowing counterfactuals of freedom arises because the claims are true but still unknowable. Some claim that omniscience requires only knowing what is knowable, and so perhaps the thought experiment is supposed to be that both beings would then be omniscient, but the first would be greater nonetheless. I grant that the first would be greater, but the reason is that restricted accounts of omniscience aren't defensible.[7] Two cryptic reasons: first, if radical skepticism is true, this account confirms that my truck is omniscient; second, whereas power is a modal concept, knowledge isn't, so when we refine the ideas of being able to do anything and knowing everything, we should honor the difference, limiting the omnipotence claim modally (being able to do all that can be done, not the stuff that can't be done) and omniscience non-modally (knowing all that is true, not the stuff that is false). If we take the example in this way, however, there is no pressing outward that needs to be resorted to. All that is needed is to note that perfection of being involves omniscience rather than something falling short of it.

So I think there are grounds for rejecting Murphy's methodological principle. What is true of being 1 and being 2 is that being 1 would be greater if there

---

[7] For a full accounting of reasons against, see Kvanvig (1989a,c).

are known counterfactuals of freedom, but if there are no such counterfactuals, both beings are equally impressive.

Moreover, it isn't quite clear that Murphy's account threatens the derivation of WWT from PBT. Even if granted, what his account shows is only that there are special obligations of allegiance that need not be present, dependent as they are on God's free willings. In order to threaten the derivation of WWT from PBT, one would need to argue that among these obligations of allegiance is the obligation to worship. It is true that the obligation to worship is one kind of allegiance obligation, since what is central to worship is the surrender and submission displayed in acts of obeisance. But just because some obligations of allegiance might be contingent, it doesn't follow that they all are. So even granting Murphy's claims isn't enough unless and until we have grounds for claiming that the special kind of allegiance obligation involved in worship is also contingent.

To address that issue, we need further information about what properties of deity such an obligation supervenes on, something we haven't determined to this point. What we can note, however, is that the usual ideas advert to elements of both PBT and CT: submission and surrender are appropriate because God is the source of all and the most perfect being. Since these characteristics are not contingent, neither is the obligation to worship. What such submission and surrender involves may turn out to depend contingently on what God wills, so that Murphy's point about conditions (a) and (b) can be accommodated. In such a case, the obligation to worship would not be contingent, but the particular forms such worship must take or the particular ways in which these obligations are grounded might vary between different possibilities concerning what God has willed.

So, to the benefit of PBT so far, I don't think that Murphy's account gives adequate grounds for denying that the starting point of WWT can be generated by PBT, and the selectivity point on which Bayne and Nagasawa rely remains unsupported as well. We can thus view these disagreements with Morris's argument as failures to undermine that argument. We can thus return to Morris's pithy derivation to consider its merits directly. We will see that there are other reasons available for thinking that argument does not succeed.

The suggestion is that worship-worthiness can be derived from PBT using either the conceptual resources of supervenience or constitution. A couple of examples will aid us in seeing the pitfalls of each possibility.

Take supervenience first. The most straightforward account of supervenience understands it in terms of one-way entailment: regarding our topic, the instance of the slogan is that there can be no difference in worthiness of worship without a difference in great-making properties. But one-way entailment, absent an explanatory connection, is much too easy to find. It holds between *I am of Scandinavian descent* and *2 + 2 = 4*.

In other cases, supervenience coincides with explanatory priority. For example, David Lewis (2001) maintains that truth supervenes on being. Hence, he claims, there can be no change in what's true in a world without a change in what exists in that world. This relationship between truth and being mirrors an explanatory relationship as well: whatever truth is, it answers to being in some sense.

Since the goal of PBT is to make the perfections derived from perfect being methodology function to explain the key elements needed in an adequate account of the nature of God, it is committed to thinking of worship-worthiness as depending on and being explained by these perfections. This result supervenience alone cannot provide. At best, supervenience is compatible with this commitment of PBT, but does not entail or confirm it.

What of constitution? Examples of constitution are often examples of material constitution: the statue is constituted by the clay from which it was formed, the highway is constituted by the asphalt out of which it is made. In these examples, the clay and the asphalt are explanatorily prior to what they constitute, and Morris's idea is that we might say the same about the relationships between the divine perfections generated by PBT and the property of being worthy of worship.

The problem is that, though the language of explanatory priority is quite natural when discussing objects and their nature, the language of constitution, applied to properties, is not. What does it mean to say that the property of being worthy of worship consists in, or is constituted by, the omni-properties, for example? I understand what it would mean to say that the latter explain the former, but I do not see how it could be true that the former consists in, or is constituted by, the latter.

The concern here is that constitution is explained most naturally as a relation between an object and its parts or components. So, for example, water is constituted by hydrogen and oxygen parts in a certain ratio and relation. The engine in my truck is constituted by its component parts. The statue is constituted by the clay, shaped in the right way. A set is constituted by its members, a team by those persons who play on it, and a mereological sum by its parts.

Perhaps, though, it is easier to traverse between the land of objects and the land of properties than I am assuming. Perhaps we can also say that the property of being water is constituted by the properties of having hydrogen and oxygen parts in a certain ratio and relation. We can treat attributions of constitution as interchangeable between objects and properties, but one would have thought that the constitution of objects takes priority here, with property constitution being derivable on the basis of the kinds of objects in question. If so, one won't be able to argue that the perfections of God function so as to constitute the worship-worthiness of God without first identifying some object constitution claim from which this claim follows. One can, of course, meet this standard by gerrymandering. Just say, "Oh, I was thinking that the being worthy of worship is constituted by the most perfect being," but such language is forced, awkward, and sounds mistaken.

The alternative would be to insist that object constitution piggybacks on property constitution whenever such object constitution occurs. One can detect a hint of Platonism here, and Platonism had better not be needed to sustain a derivation of worship-worthiness from perfection of being. Let us bypass that issue, however, in order to focus on the nature of this constitution relation. To get the needed result, we need some notion of structure in properties that allows the identification of certain properties as elements of another property. Here, I think, we find mystery instead.

Consider some cases where no such mystery is present. If we have propositions in our ontology, we can say that the proposition *2 + 2 = 4* has the numbers 2 and 4 as constituents, as well as the summing and identity relations.[8] And, if we have properties in our ontology, we might have the property of being a circle constituted in part by the property of being a closed-plane figure. But these examples don't give us anything helpful when it comes to the property of being worthy of worship. They provide examples to support claiming that this property is constituted in part by the property of being worthy and the property of worshiping. They provide no support for identifying perfections as the constituents in question.

So my inclination here is to go back to the priority of the constitution of objects, where we can easily understand the claim that the statue is made of clay and the highway of asphalt, just as we can understand the claim that a set is composed of its members and a team by its players. The idea here is that there is some material that gets formed in a certain way so as to yield something else. To the extent that we can apply such an idea to the realm of properties, we get nothing that could support the contention that worship-worthiness is constituted by the perfections of God.

---

[8] That's not all there is to the proposition, of course. There is also the uniting of all these things into one thing, and such unity is not itself any of these constituents or the totality of them.

Defenders of PBT need not despair at this point, for there is available alternative metaphysical language to the language of constitution that could be used instead. We might talk of grounding relations, or dependence relations, or of what is fundamental, in just the way that we described in Chapter 1. The idea there was that, for example, the property of being a bachelor is not fundamental but is grounded in the properties of being an unmarried male eligible for marriage (among other things).

In application to our context, the idea would then be this: the property of being worthy of worship is grounded in the more fundamental properties that are great-making properties of the greatest possible being. Presumably, this grounding relation can't obtain without involving metaphysical entailment, so we should expect that the property of being supremely worthy of the most exalted form of worship is entailed by the perfections in question. This point may be plausible, though it is perhaps equally plausible to claim that the entailment runs in the other direction. But neither direction of entailment is obvious enough to be endorsed without further explanation, since the grounding claim alone doesn't yield either entailment.

An example from metaphysics and the philosophy of science will help. Those who share the Aristotelian conception of metaphysics as an investigation of what grounds what[9] split into two quite different groups when considering the claims of the British Emergentists, culminating in the work of C. D. Broad in the first few decades of the twentieth century, especially Broad (1925).[10] According to Emergentism, there are properties or aspects of reality that are irreducible to the more fundamental properties out of which they arise, properties that introduce an element of novelty over and above the properties that ground them.

It is controversial exactly what this idea of emergence involves, and it is controversial whether there are such properties.[11] Defenders of PBT might take comfort in the controversies, thinking that the literature might give grounds for rejecting the possibility of emergent properties, but such optimism needs more than controversy to sustain it. For the general issue remains, and that issue is that things that are fundamental might still be grounded, so that an appeal to grounding doesn't settle the question of fundamentality. We saw just

---

[9] An excellent introduction to this way of thinking can be found in Schaffer (2009).

[10] For an excellent introduction to the history of British Emergentism, see O'Connor and Wong (2015).

[11] See, e.g., Humphreys (1997a,b); Wong (2005); Kim (2006); Clayton and Davies (2008); Wilson (2013), and Humphreys (2017). It is also worth nothing that, though the natural home for the language of emergence concerns emergent *properties*, the idea can and has been extended to talk of substances as well, as in Hasker (2001) and Merricks (2001).

such an example in Chapter 1, the example of Williamson's epistemology. On his account, knowledge is fundamental but its fundamentality is compatible with it being grounded in belief and truth (and perhaps some other, distinctively epistemic, properties). It retains its fundamental status in virtue of not being reducible to some conjunction of such properties.

The same possibility arises here. We have noted WWT's normative starting point and PBT's evaluative stance, and are considering whether this normative starting point can be derived from the evaluative one. The possibility of emergent properties in metaphysics and the philosophy of science mirrors conversations in the history of ethics about how to ground the normative in the evaluative. Cognitivists maintain that moral obligation is grounded in, and reducible to, some descriptive or natural property or other (perhaps a calculus on pain and pleasure as utilitarians maintain, perhaps by a consistency in willing as Kant would have it), but non-cognitivists insist that there is something central to morality that no cognitive account can explain. The idea here is that judgments about right and wrong are thought to be intrinsically motivating, and thus not capable of being purely cognitive, since motivation comes only from our non-cognitive features. Call this latter view the "Humean" view, to honor its source.

Since the notion of being worthy of worship is clearly a normative one, one might expect this issue to play a role in philosophical theology as well. For example, a Humean will want us to consider what to make of a situation in which a person comes to recognize an experience as an experience of God. Think, for example, of Moses and the burning bush. A Humean approach to the story will understand it in terms of Moses's coming see the burning bush as that of being in the presence of one-to-be-worshiped. Non-Humeans might grant that the experience will be motivating in this way, but only indirectly, but being routed through some desire, say, to honor God or to acknowledge his greatness.

Suppose, then, that Humeanism is true concerning the nature of normativity. If so, defenders of WWT will insist that any attempt to derive worthiness of worship from a list of properties generated by the methods of PBT cannot succeed unless the properties so generated are already normative properties. The only plausible suggestion for such a property here would be that of omnibenevolence, but that property won't be suitable for addressing Humean inclinations.

To see why, note that moral theory involves two subparts (at least): the theory of obligation and the theory of value. Part of the goal of a full moral theory is to say how these subparts are related, but whatever the answer is to that issue, it is clear that evaluative judgments fall under the theory of value whereas normative judgments falls under the theory of obligation. So, Humean inclinations arise when something within the theory of obligation looks to be intrinsically motivating, not something within the theory of value. I suppose one could be a Humean about attributions of value or goodness to an object, but such a view would be much less attractive than the Humean view we actually find in metaethics, which is a thesis about the motivational force of normative judgments.

Thus, any inclination toward Humeanism should incline one to treat experiences like those of Moses and the burning bush as intrinsically motivating, motivating simply on the basis of the fact that one is in the presence of *God*, rather than in some indirect fashion, such as would happen if one first recognized the perfections of God and was so attracted to such perfections that a motive for worship arose. On a Humean approach, mere recognition of deity is, by itself, intrinsically motivating, and the motivation is one toward worship. Hence, according to this brand of WWT, part of the WWT story is that the mere recognition that one is in the presence of God is motivation enough for worship.

The key question for such a version of WWT is analogous to one that faces Humeans in ethics when they attempt to move from Humeanism to attitudinalist/expressivist positions.[12] The question concerns the relationship between the two positions, and the point to note is that attitudinalism/expressivism (A/E) is constructed precisely to explain the Humean position about the intrinsically motivating character of normative judgments. Part of the argument for A/E is that cognitivist views, at least extant ones, fail to provide good explanations of the Humean point.

These two features are independent of each other: the complaints about cognitivism might be correct and yet A/E inadequate; and the complaints might be mistaken and yet A/E adequate. Most relevant in our context is the way in which Humeanism provides an argument against cognitivism, for on this point metaethical concerns are equally metatheological. Non-normative understandings of God, at least when combined with a Humean account of motivation, are ill-equipped to explain how experiences of and judgments about the divine are intrinsically motivating of worship. Moreover, the Humean view here is attractive: to see, judge, or experience something as

---

[12] Such views descend from the earlier emotivist rejections of cognitivist positions in ethics, such as we find in Ayer (1936) and Stevenson (1944). Two leading expressivist figures are Simon Blackburn (1984, 1993, 1998) and Allan Gibbard (1990, 2003).

God inclines one toward the surrender and submission that are the heart of worship. Such inclinations can, of course, be resisted, and the drama here fits well with a further theological understanding of the fundamental temptation being that of rebellion against such inclinations. To the extent that one is drawn to such a portrayal of God, to that extent one will be inclined to think that the starting point of WWT is not going to be derivable from PBT, even if the worship-worthiness of God is grounded in the perfections that are central to PBT.

In addition, as we saw earlier in our discussion of Murphy's concerns, the natural point to look in trying to derive worship-worthiness is not simply in the perfections of God. If the obligations of allegiance and obedience are grounded anywhere, they seem to be grounded in the source of all, in creation and conservation, not perfection alone. If that is correct, then perfection of being is not sufficient to undergird worthiness of worship, and Murphy's point is sustained. So, perhaps there is more than one basis for skepticism about deriving the starting point of WWT from PBT.

If we endorse this agnosticism about the derivability of the starting point of WWT from PBT, then neither CT nor PBT seem well-suited to explaining the nature of the divine. For they could only generate an account of worthiness of worship on which an experience of the divine would be extrinsically or indirectly motivating, routed through some desire or preference in favor of divinity.

So here again, just as with the idea of emergent properties, we can see the possibility that worship-worthiness has an aspect to it that is not and cannot be encoded in non-normative features of God, even if it is grounded in these features. As a result, the perfections of God that are the stock-and-trade of PBT cannot be used to derive the worship-worthiness of God. For some, pushing hard on the ethical analogy might incline toward non-cognitivist accounts of religious language, but the path to such a conclusion is long and treacherous, and outside the scope of this inquiry. For our interest is limited to the issue of whether the starting point of WWT can be derived by PBT, and the examples of ethical judgments and emergent properties spawn a story as to why such derivations cannot be counted on.

## 8.4 Conclusion

The combined results of the two parts of this chapter present disappointing conclusions for perfect being theologians, since neither starting point of alternative metatheologies can be derived on the basis of PBT. All hope for PBT is not yet lost, however, for we also had to be skeptical about the capacity for CT to derive the starting points of its competitors. In addition, we need to consider whether a similar pessimism plagues WWT. We turn, then, in the next chapter to see what level of success WWT can muster.

# 9
# Worship-Worthiness and Its Drawbacks

## 9.1 Introduction

So far, we have seen disappointing results from both Perfect Being Theology (PBT) and Creator Theology (CT) in their efforts to derive the starting points of competitor metatheologies. CT is able to derive God's unlimited power, knowledge, and perhaps even goodness, but the vagueness of this language about limits will be troubling to those who were hoping to derive the omni-being of PBT. Moreover, the same difficulties plague the effort by CT to derive the starting point of Worship-Worthiness Theology (WWT) as plague the effort by PBT: in both cases, the normative dimension might be grounded in either the evaluative or descriptive dimension, while leaving the normative dimension fundamental. In addition, PBT lacks the resources necessary to preserve monotheism and the personhood of God, and is unable to sustain the idea of God as creator of all.

These points can serve to make WWT quite attractive, and the idea that judgments, thoughts, and experiences of God immediately and intrinsically motivate worship of God is a pleasing one. This idea links directly to the notion that God is supremely worthy of ultimate worship. Moreover, the notion of supremacy here is to be understood in such a way that the impetus toward worship is not merely under the guise of the evaluative, but of the normative: it is not merely a good idea to worship God, but it is our required response. There is thus considerable attractiveness for WWT, for here we find an understanding of deity on which the recognition and experience of the divine are appropriately intrinsically motivating of worship. Such a route to WWT is not the only one, but it is enough for present purposes to find one way of approaching the question of the nature of God that makes the view attractive.

Such a version of WWT will draw a distinction between grounding and fundamentality, thereby resisting the efforts of PBT to derive the starting point of PBT, but also for the purpose of showing that the starting points of PBT and CT can be derived from WWT. For, to the extent that the grounding claims are correct, WWT has a place to start in deriving the starting points of alternative metatheologies. It has a place to start since grounding relations are necessary relations. In the scientific domain, the grounding relation may only be nomologically or scientifically necessary; but once in the metaphysical domain, grounding relations appear not to change from world to world. If so, and if worthiness of worship is grounded in the perfections of God, there would seem to be a straightforward argument for concluding that the starting point of PBT can be derived from WWT.

The central question, then, for WWT is how far these points can be taken in the attempt to derive the starting points of both PBT and CT. We take up these issues in §9.2 and §9.3. A side benefit of this order of inquiry will be to see the extent to which WWT has been presupposed even by those whose focus is on the perfections of God, raising the possibility that once the distinction between WWT and PBT is made clear, there are more defenders of WWT than we might initially suppose.

## 9.2 From a Worship-Worthy Being to a Perfect Being

I begin here with a source of discontent about the idea of deriving the perfections of God from WWT. A central part of the history of theology over the past century or so is a recognition of the differences between Greek and Hebrew ways of thinking, together with an acknowledgment that Christian theologians throughout history have interpreted Scripture in ways that depend too much on Greek rather than Hebrew ways of thinking. Once the cautionary note has been sounded, we find a chorus of complaints about confusing Jerusalem with Athens and the God of the Bible with the God of the philosophers.[1] Since PBT is the poster child for the God of the philosophers, we need to keep in mind the possibility that it would be a *hindrance* rather than a *benefit* to be able to derive too much of the starting point of PBT from either CT or WWT.

As one might expect, philosophers and philosophical theologians who discuss this concern tend to see the tension as overwrought. The point to note, however, is that we have two issues to consider here, not just one. One issue is the derivation itself, and the second issue is the significance of the first issue. The complaints noted signal a possibility that we have not highlighted to this point, the possibility that attempted derivations of the starting point of PBT might be better off if their success is muted.

---

[1] A representative sample of this literature includes Kenny (1979); Goodman (1996); Meconi (1999); Rehm (1999); Ward (1999); Polka (2015), and Stump (2016).

The dominant strain in the literature concerning a perceived tension between biblical theology and philosophical theology defends the compatibility of the God of the philosophers and the God of the Bible, so let us take up the first issue about derivability before delving into the significance issue. A nice summary statement of the compatibility claim is given by Edward Wierenga, together with a defense of the derivability of notions of perfection from worship-worthiness:

> A suggestion Wainwright considers is that the demands of worship support this identification, and it is worth considering in this context because Augustine himself held that God is uniquely deserving of worship.... According to the proposal to be considered, the God of Abraham, Isaac, and Jacob deserves to be worshiped, but only a fully perfect being is worthy of worship; so the God of Abraham, Isaac, and Jacob is a perfect being.
>
> Wierenga (2011, pp. 147–8)

This remark is instructive in two respects. First, it is intended to relieve concerns about any perceived tension between biblical and philosophical theology. But it is equally informative about the resources of WWT for deriving the starting point of PBT. Wierenga and Wainwright commit to the view that if a being is worthy of worship then that being must be perfect, so God is a perfect being.

Before considering the merits of the view, it is worth pausing a moment to notice the order of derivation here. It begins from the standpoint of WWT, argues from worship-worthiness to perfection of being, and concludes that the God of the Bible is a perfect being. Once we are clear on the distinction between PBT and WWT, this defense of the compatibility of the God of the Bible with the God of the philosophers is not a version of PBT at all, but more congenial to WWT. So even though WWT gets very little attention in philosophical theology in comparison with PBT, perhaps the lack of attention is a result of lack of clarity about the positions rather than some opposition to it.

Once we take note of the order of derivation, we find it elsewhere as well. For example, we find it in Wierenga's discussion of Calvin's view of the innate awareness of the divine [*divinitatis sensum*]:

> It may not be beyond controversy that all people are instinctively aware of divinity, as Calvin suggests, but it is certainly true that many people find themselves with the conviction that there is a higher being, a being who is worthy of worship. Reflection on what is involved in being worthy of worship

can lead to views about God's nature, for no being is worthy of worship unless that being is supremely excellent.   Wierenga (1989, p. 3)

As in the earlier quote, the order of explanation here begins with the idea that God is worship-worthy, from which we obtain certain conclusions about the nature of God, to wit, that God is supremely excellent. As before, this form of inference is what we expect to find from defenders of WWT rather than as a defense of PBT.

Not just Wierenga's summary of Calvin represents him as an example of WWT, but Calvin himself endorses the inferences central to the attempt by WWT to derive the starting point of PBT. He writes,

> ... it will not suffice simply to hold that there is One whom all ought to honor and adore, unless we are also persuaded that he is the fountain of every good and that we must seek nothing elsewhere than in him. This I take to mean that not only does he sustain this universe (as he once founded it) by his boundless might, regulate it by his wisdom, preserve it by his goodness, and especially rule mankind by his righteousness and judgment, watch over it by his protection; but also that no drop will be found either of wisdom and light, or of righteousness or power or rectitude, or of genuine truth, which does not flow from him, and of which he is not the cause.
> 
> Calvin (1960 [1536], I, 2, 1)

Calvin claims here to be able to derive a host of features that perfect being theologians claim are needed in an adequate account of the nature of God. He claims to be able to derive these features from the claim that "there is One whom all ought to honor and adore." It is perhaps a remote possibility that Calvin does not take this phrase to express the idea of worship, but such an interpretation of this language would be strained. If we grant that the premise in question is the distinctive worship-worthiness that defenders of WWT claim is fundamental to a proper understanding of God, we find in this passage precisely the kind of inferential structure needed for a derivation of the starting point of PBT from WWT.

To some, claims of this sort are taken to support PBT, because the God of the philosophers is thought to be the perfect being of Anselmian thought. Such reasoning is confused, however, since the reconciliation proposed is better thought of as beginning from an appeal to worship-worthiness, taken to be a central or the central aspect to honor when thinking about the God of the

Bible, and deriving the perfections of God from such worship-worthiness. As I see it, the misperception here is the result of failing to distinguish fundamentality from grounding, but since we discussed that point at some length in the last chapter, we need not dwell on it further. What is worth noting, though, is the range of central figures that appear to argue in this way, suggesting that the attractions of WWT are much more widespread than one would think when noting how generally the God of the philosophers is identified with Anselmian perfect being thinking.

Even so, the above passages don't quite get us to the starting point of PBT, for they at most get us only to the conclusion that God must be a perfect being in order to be worthy of worship. PBT, however, has as its starting point that God is the most perfect possible being, not merely that God is perfect. On this issue, there is agreement even among those, such as J. N. Findlay, who reject theism, that the modal claim is what is needed:

> Not only is it contrary to the demands and claims inherent in religious attitudes that their object should exist "accidentally": it is also contrary to those demands that it should possess its *various excellences* in some merely adventitious manner. It would be quite unsatisfactory from the religious standpoint, if an object merely *happened* to be wise, good, powerful, and so forth, even to a superlative degree, and if other beings had, *as a mere matter of fact*, derived their excellences from this single source. An object of this sort would doubtless deserve respect and admiration, and other quasi-religious attitudes, but it would not deserve the utter self-abandonment peculiar to the religious frame of mind.     Findlay (1948, p. 180)

There are two things of note here, once we include worship and its worthiness among "the demands and claims inherent in religious attitudes." The first is the move from contingent possession of characteristics important for being an object of religious devotion and the worship involved in such devotion to the essentiality of such characteristics. The second is the pointing to a list of personal characteristics that might be cited as necessary for a being to be worthy of worship. According to Findlay, these characteristics include wisdom, goodness, and power of "a superlative degree."

I will return to the second point in a moment, but I want to highlight first the connection between Findlay's first point and the Calvin quote above. From Calvin we get the claim that God is "the fountain of every good" and that "we must seek nothing elsewhere than in him." It is the second of these descriptions ("we must seek nothing elsewhere than in him") that is especially inviting, since it signals the devotion that is at the heart of the kind of worship involved in WWT, the same kind of attitude Findlay described in terms of "utter self-abandonment." For it claims that everything worthy of being sought is somehow in God rather than elsewhere. Calvin proposes that such a claim might be used to derive divine conservation and providence, boundless power, great wisdom, and divine goodness; even stronger, that there is nothing of wisdom or insight, goodness, righteousness, or truth that "does not flow from him, and of which he is not the cause." And Findlay's point is that we need more than just the properties in question, we need to find those properties to be essential in order for the basis to be adequate to the religious frame of mind.

There is a way to deflect the concern about essential properties, however, and put the focus instead on the derivation itself. For if worship-worthiness is essential to the nature of God, as WWT would have it, then what follows from worship-worthiness, or what is required for it, will be similarly essential to the nature of God. So the point about essentiality is well taken, but handled directly by a focus on the derivation of the starting point of PBT from WWT. Thus, instead of being sidetracked by the essentiality concern, let's focus on the issue of the derivation itself and whether the claims made so far can withstand scrutiny.

One skeptical voice about the prospects for WWT here is that of Yujin Nagasawa (2008), arguing that a being worthy of worship need not be maximally perfect in every respect. Nagasawa imagines a being that is omnipotent, omnibenevolent, but not omniscient because of failing to know some truth. Nonetheless, Nagasawa claims, this being could still be worthy of worship.

There are two issues that confound this attempt to block the WWT strategy of deriving perfection of being from worship-worthiness. The first is that it is hard to make sense out of the idea of knowing everything except one truth, as Wierenga (2011, p. 149) notes: if $p$ is the unknown claim, then *anyone believing $p$ is alethically correct in that belief* is a claim that is distinct from $p$ and thus is known by the being in question, who also knows perfectly well that the latter claim entails $p$. Such a being would also then know that what this being knows also entails the first-person claim "if I don't believe $p$, I am making a mistake." A claim that such a situation is possible is far from obvious.

More important, however, is a second point. Nagasawa's version of PBT, as articulated in Nagasawa (2017), reveals that the example in question does not in fact threaten the derivation of perfection of being from worship-worthiness, but rather threatens bottom-up versions of PBT which claim that nothing can be a perfect being unless that being is an omni-being. On Nagasawa's top-down approach, we have no grounds for concluding that the being described, the one just short of omniscience, is not the most perfect possible being. So the existence and worship-worthiness of such a being is not a counterexample to the claim that only the most perfect possible being can be worthy of worship. Thus, even if the possibility of the case imagined is granted, it needn't undermine the derivation of the starting point of (coherent) PBT from the starting point of WWT.

Still, there are other skeptical voices as well that have to be acknowledged and considered. Tom Morris, for example, writes:

> Many people think of God as the singular, ultimate source of all contingent reality. This is the dominant idea behind what might be called "explanatory theism". Others characterize divinity primarily as that which is worthy of worship. Each of these controlling ideas, developed by means of a naturally associated method of explication, can begin to issue in a more or less well articulated conception of various divine attributes, but I think neither is capable of alone providing for a fully adequate conception of deity. There are important properties theists want to ascribe to God which bear no clear connections, logical, conceptual, or otherwise to either ontological ultimacy or worship-worthiness. The precise property of omnipotence might provide a good example of this.   Morris (1987b, p. 24)

Morris suggests that WWT will not be able to provide a "fully adequate conception of deity," since there are "important properties" to ascribe to God that cannot be derived from WWT.

A first point to note, by way of response, is Morris's earlier optimism about generating worthiness of worship from PBT. The best hope for such a view was to view worthiness of worship as fully grounded in the perfections of God, rather than as Morris suggested, that worship-worthiness supervenes on or is constituted by these perfections. Here, however, Morris's claims threaten the grounding claim, since Morris claims that these perfections "bear no clear connections, logical, conceptual, or otherwise to . . . worship-worthiness." Without some such connections, grounding isn't present, since grounding itself is one such connection. And if the only hope for deriving worship-worthiness from perfection of being lies in an appeal to grounding (rather than supervenience or constitution), then Morris's skepticism here will threaten the hoped-for derivation of worship-worthiness from perfection of being on the same basis as it threatens the derivation of perfection of being from worship-worthiness.

This *ad hominem* argument against Morris doesn't eliminate the concern expressed, so let's consider his claims independently of their effect on other positions he wishes to hold. When we look at the claims themselves, what we find is that Morris is not very specific about what perfections will be left out, noting only that the property of omnipotence "might provide" an example of such a property.

It is worth noting in passing, though, that it is far from clear that PBT itself can undergird the property of omnipotence. It is a controversial matter whether the property of being all-powerful is itself coherent, and it is also controversial whether the property of omnipotence is compatible with that of omnibenevolence as well as with certain known facts about the universe, such as the presence of evil. I myself am convinced that none of these problems undermines the doctrine of omnipotence, but it is worth noting that some defenders of PBT refuse to endorse the requirement that the most perfect being must be an omni-being. Given these points, Morris's concern may generalize, putting pressure not only on WWT but on PBT as well.

Here, though, amelioration is in order. If no metatheology can get us to the conclusion that God is omnipotent, one wonders about the plausibility of the idea that only a conception of God on which God is omnipotent can be a "fully adequate conception". In fact, if the derivations of any proposed elements of such a fully adequate conception can't withstand scrutiny, we should jettison the thought that a fully adequate conception requires them. So, to undertake this issue seriously and carefully, we need some candidates on the list of required features of deity that have to be sustained by any fully adequate conception of God.

Morris is not alone in failing to be specific on this score. Wierenga focuses on God's "supreme excellences," but doesn't identify them. Finlay lists some qualities, but focuses not on their derivation, but on the mode of essentiality for whatever qualities one selects. And the Calvin quote, once dissected carefully, offers little assistance. His claims offer quite a bit of content, however, and thus provide a nice context for seeing what properties might be thought important enough to need derivation, and to see what problems exist for the derivations themselves.

Calvin first wants a link between:

Worship-Worthiness: "there is One whom all ought to honor and adore" and

> Pre-eminence: "he is the fountain of every good"
> \+
> Exclusivity: "we must seek nothing elsewhere than in him."

The link relevant to our context is this: Worship-Worthiness cannot be supreme, according to Calvin, without Pre-eminence and Exclusivity. Calvin doesn't say why an understanding of the former would be insufficient without the latter, nor does he tell us what kind of insufficiency is at stake here. In the context of this project, however, we can supply a reason. If God is worthy of worship in a way that doesn't allow for derivations concerning the kind of being God is, WWT will be obviously inadequate as a metatheology. So at least one kind of insufficiency here might be metatheological.

It goes without saying that noting the need of the inference for the adequacy of WWT is no reason for thinking that the inference is sound nor for thinking that the properties that are claimed to follow are the ones needed by a full and adequate account of the nature of God. While it may be true, to use Wierenga's language, that "no being is worthy of worship unless that being is supremely excellent," we can't use that point to defend WWT's attempted derivation of the starting point of PBT without more specificity about what these excellences are. On this issue, Calvin proposes Pre-eminence and Exclusivity, but doesn't leave the matter there. Right after the first sentence asserting the link noted above, he writes, "This I take to mean...". The referent of 'this' is not clear, but let us assume that he is talking about the conjunction of Pre-eminence and Exclusivity. Let's also not get sidetracked by the imprecision of the phrase "take to mean," since it can red-herring us in pointless directions about speaker-meaning and semantic-meaning and the relevance of either to our metatheological project. Instead, let's understand Calvin to be drawing inferences here, which has the advantage of understanding the passage in a way that makes it relevant to metatheology.

I note as well that the inferred list is divided into two parts, and there is an affinity between the first part and Pre-eminence and between the second part and Exclusivity. So, I think the right way to understand Calvin here is that he holds that Pre-eminence implies creation, conservation, providence, and goodness; and Exclusivity implies that God is the source of all wisdom, light, righteousness, power, rectitude, and truth itself.

The first implication claim is relevant to the attempt to derive sourcehood from WWT as well as more standard perfections associated with PBT, and since we are already enmeshed in the passage, let's take note of the difficulties faced by both of these issues. Why exactly do the supreme excellences needed for worship-worthiness include creation, conservation, providence, and goodness? The passage merely makes the claim that they are needed, but what we seek is an explanation of why that is true.

Let's divide the cases, grouping creation and conservation apart from goodness and providence. For the former, the best WWT can offer will be to argue, first, that neither doctrine can be sustained without the other,[2] and, second, that God couldn't be supremely worthy of the most exalted worship if there were some other being responsible for the existence and continuation of the universe. The latter point thus requires some argument that worship-worthiness attaches only to the source of all. We will explore this idea further in the next section below, when we consider whether WWT can derive the starting point for CT, but we should be skeptical here. The argument just presented is, I think, the best we'll find, and it is silent about what to say if there is a perfect being but everything is unsourced. As noted already, though, there will be more to say on this issue in the next section.

Moreover, Calvin's claim about the doctrine of divine providence following from Pre-eminence seems to overreach. To be supremely worthy of the highest worship requires divine goodness, since a lack of such would support qualifications in the attitude of worship. But providence goes well beyond goodness, just as grace and mercy go beyond desert, and it is central to theistic traditions that much, perhaps even all, of the care and concern shown to us by God counts as undeserved favor. So full providence, involving grace and mercy, doesn't seem to be required of a being who is supremely worthy of the highest worship.

It is easy to become skeptical of this point when one conflates the related elements involved in typical worship. God is not only to be worshiped, but also praised and thanked, and a gracious God is an object of praise and thanksgiving in a way different from what we would find apart from grace. There is, of course, the grace of God displayed in creation itself, so perhaps it makes no sense to talk of the possibility of God showing no grace whatsoever. Even so, there are differences in kinds of grace shown. For example, it is an act of grace to select a chosen people; it is a different act of grace to select a different group as the chosen ones. In each case, what God is to be thanked for differs.

Once we are careful to distinguish the central worshipful attitudes of surrender and submission from the attitudes and activities involved in praise and

---

[2] For arguments to this effect, see Kvanvig and McCann (1988); McCann and Kvanvig (1991).

worship, we can see why the doctrine of providence need not follow from worship-worthiness itself. For that doctrine includes the elements of grace that affect patterns of praise and thanksgiving, but do not enhance the worthiness of worship for the one who displays such grace. Being supremely worthy of total surrender and submission should in no way be thought to require that God perform every supererogatory act possible nor the greatest possible combination of supererogatory acts. Hence, there is no good reason for thinking that any particular engagement with the domain of grace is required for worship-worthiness. What is true is that greater praiseworthiness and deservingness for thanks increase as supererogation increases, but worthiness of worship remains constant throughout.

So I think Calvin can't succeed in showing that the doctrine of providence follows from worship-worthiness, but there is something to be said in Calvin's defense nonetheless. For there is some attitude of gratefulness or adoration that is responsive to the grace of God, even if that attitude does not affect worship-worthiness itself. Moreover, Calvin's formulation of Pre-eminence doesn't use our language of worship-worthiness, but instead speaks of honoring and adoring. This way of escape for Calvin from the above problem, however, doesn't help in our context, since what was needed was an argument from worship-worthiness to the doctrines in question, and no such argument is available.

These woes for Calvin threaten to generalize to other properties. Consider, for example, omniscience and omnipotence. How much knowledge and power is required for pre-eminence in worship-worthiness? As with the issue of supererogation, if God is omniscient and omnipotent in some other world, but not the actual one, it is not clear that God's worship-worthiness would be diminished. Perhaps if God's knowledge and power were superceded in another world by some being other than God in that world, there would be a problem. For such a possibility raises the question of whether it is possible for this other being to also have whatever other properties ground worship-worthiness, and if such a combination is possible, then the supreme worship-worthiness needed for WWT can't be defended, since the supremacy isn't essential to the nature of God.

Such concerns need full and careful elaboration before being endorsed, but the former point is all that is needed in our context. If knowledge and power function in the way grace does when it comes to ascribing worship-worthiness, we will have reached a conclusion in accord with Morris's concern above, since omnipotence was the feature Morris noted as one that WWT would not be able to derive.

Recall, however, that Morris gives no argument that an adequate theology must include either omniscience or omnipotence nor that PBT has the resources for deriving these doctrines. His claim was only that properties like these are "important properties theists want to ascribe to God." We obviously need more than desire here, and the final issue we need to address concerns this issue of what significance to attach to failures by WWT to derive the doctrines that PBT seems better suited for deriving.

A first point to note is that the significance of failure depends quite a bit on what these properties are. For example, Augustine (Augustine, 1998 [426], X, x) claims that God is called "omnipotent" "on account of His doing what He wills". If that is the property in question, then WWT can derive the omnipotence of God merely from the fact that there can't be any power or force that impedes the will of a being having pre-eminent worship-worthiness. But I suspect that's not the property Morris has in mind. Instead, I suspect he has the omni-properties associated with PBT metatheology in mind. Deriving those understandings is something much more difficult than the Augustinian claim.

Here, I think defenders of WWT have two responses. The first is to note that PBT may not be able to show that God is an omni-being. As we have seen from Nagasawa (2017), such bottom-up versions of PBT face special difficulties, and as we saw in Chapter 4, placing hope in PBT as an adequate metatheology disappoints. If no such derivation is available for PBT, there is a second response on behalf of WWT that becomes more plausible. That response is to question whether omnipotence so understood is one that is needed, one that is really necessary for a theology to be adequate. If PBT faces the same difficulty here, as well as CT as discussed in Chapter 6, it becomes a bit of a surprise to be told that no metatheology can be adequate apart from endorsing these doctrines.

We are not at that point yet, and it is important to remind ourselves of our dialectical location. We are looking for promising derivational paths from a given metatheology to various other kinds of claims, with no assumption here that what is promising at this initial stage will hold up under further and more complete scrutiny. So even though there is the prospect that no metatheology will be able to derive that God is an omni-being, that prospect should not lead us to think that PBT has no advantage on this issue in comparison with the other two metatheologies we have considered. There is thus an advantage for PBT here, though it remains unclear how significant the advantage is. What is clear is that we want to be able to endorse the idea that God's power, knowledge, and goodness are supreme, and leave for further argument whether such supremacy is best thought of in terms of the omni-properties of the Anselmian tradition.³

For an idea of why it should be controversial whether supremacy requires omni-properties, return again to what we learned regarding grace and supererogation. In these cases, there is a baseline of divine goodness essential for theological adequacy, and beyond the required baseline optionality is present regarding what dimensions of grace are actual. For divine power and knowledge, we may have a similar necessary baseline, in terms of the supremacy of God's knowledge and power. Such supremacy may or may not amount to omnipotence and omnscience as understood in the bottom-up PBT tradition, depending in part on whether those understandings are paradox-free. But even apart from the coherence of such Anselmian understandings, there is also the possibility to consider that God engages in acts of will that are self-limiting in a way that leaves supremacy in place but makes omniscience or omnipotence mere possibiities for God, in worlds where these acts are not undertaken.⁴

There are sticking points that will need to be considered if a defender of WWT takes this route. The case just described is one in which we compare God's knowledge and power in one world with God's knowledge and power in another. But there are also cases to consider where the beings in the two worlds are not the same. One such example is a case where a non-God has more knowledge or power in another world than God has in this world. In such a case, there is pressure to conclude that a greater level of worship-worthiness would be present if there were no such possibility.

There are several options to consider in determining what to make of such a possibility. The obvious one, I think, is one in which one being is supreme in this world but less than supreme in another world, coming in behind some other being. In that case, the fundamental nature of the first being would not be that of supreme worthiness of ultimate worship, so WWT would founder if such a possibility were a metaphysical possibility. A second case is more intricate, a case where one being is supreme in all worlds, but has a lesser degree of the supremacy qualities in the actual world than some distinct being in another world. Even so, the first being remains unsurpassable in these qualities: there is no world where such a being comes in second to any other being.

---

³ Something along these lines is central to the understanding of God's power in Peter Geach (1977, 2002), where he claims that God is almighty as distinct from omnipotent.

⁴ Open Theism is a position endorsing this line of thinking. See, e.g., Swinburne (1977); Hasker (1989), and van Inwagen (2008) for positions that get close to endorsing the language in the text.

What to make of such a scenario isn't quite clear to me. Perhaps, for example, being actual carries overriding weight in assessing supremacy so that the case, as imagined, fails to threaten the starting point of WWT and fails to threaten the derivation of (top-down) PBT from this starting point. Instead it might merely involve another scenario under which the worship-worthiness of God fails to require that God is an omni-being. If PBT also doesn't guarantee that God is an omni-being, the case doesn't conclusively show that the starting point of PBT cannot be derived from WWT.

We thus reach a conclusion affirming some measure of hope for WWT to explain how and why a being maximally worthy of ultimate worship would suitably approximate the perfect being of PBT. The limitations on the explanation are these. First, there is no guarantee that a being worthy of worship will be an omni-being, but rather only essentially supreme in knowledge, power, and goodness. As we saw above, there is no definitive basis in PBT for finding this result problematic, though bottom-up PBT offers a promise of derivation that WWT simply cannot achieve. Second, the supremacy in question guarantees that God is the most perfect being there is, but the stronger Anselmian position about the most perfect possible being cannot be derived. Defenders of WWT can take refuge in the fact that what can be derived from WWT may be able to withstand scrutiny when addressing the question of whether this gap reveals any theological inadequacy. The qualification that remains requires a closer look at the prospects for WWT to generate the starting point of CT, so we turn to that issue in the next section.

## 9.3 From Worship-Worthiness to Sourcehood

Regardless of the links between WWT and the idea of perfection at the heart of Anselmianism, there is still the need to generate whatever aspects of sourcehood are essential to an adequate theology as well. For example, if we are seeking to satisfy the aspirations of typical theologians in religions of the Abrahamic tradition, we will want to be able to show any deity worthy of worship is also the creator. Can this conditional be sustained?

One might think that the derivation cannot succeed, since one might hold that God would be worthy of worship even in that possibility in which nothing at all exists other than God. Recall, however, that the sourcehood at the heart of CT isn't sourcehood about contingency only, but rather about everything. And there is no possibility of there being nothing at all except God. So this quick attempt to reveal a problem here for WWT fails.

There is, however, another issue, and it concerns an imagined situation in which there are contingent beings not dependent on the will of God for their existence. If God is nonetheless worthy of worship in such a scenario, then we have a case where sourcehood is not necessary for the starting point of WWT to obtain, and thus no derivation of sourcehood will be possible by WWT. This possibility is one raised Bayne and Nagasawa (2006) in the context of challenging the claim that worship-worthiness can be grounded in the dependence on the Divine will that creation involves. They write,

> A first objection to grounding worshipfulness in creation concerns the status of beings uncreated by God. The creation-based account would suggest that such beings have no obligations to worship God, at least if we take the account to specify the sole ground of worship. We think that this result will strike most theists as the wrong result. Presumably theists hold that any possible entity (apart from God) would have an obligation to worship God were it to be actual (and capable of worshipping God).
>
> Bayne and Nagasawa (2006, p. 304)

The authors here speak of grounding worship-worthiness (they call this property "worshipfulness") in creation, which requires that creation itself is necessary for worship-worthiness. But such a result leaves unexplained the idea that God would be worthy of worship even for uncreated beings.

I suspect that the authors are correct in noting the centrality of worship-worthiness for monotheists, but that point alone gives no reason for their conclusion if monotheists hold that conclusion in part because they think it impossible for there to be uncreated beings. It is this assumption that provides some hope to WWT for defending the claim that worship-worthiness is partially grounded in sourcehood. The quote above expresses a concern about the relationship between sourcehood and worship-worthiness, and puts this concern in terms of the language of grounding. In our context, the partial grounding claim commits a defender of WWT to the idea that being supremely worthy of the most exalted worship involves being the source of all else.

A defender of WWT who is hoping to derive the starting point of CT from WWT will thus want to resist the argument in the passage above. Such resistance will have to go beyond the context of the quote above, for in that context the issue is whether God would be worthy of worship by uncreated contingent beings. Even if the answer to this question were "Yes", that claim would fall short of the hope of deriving the starting point of CT from WWT. For such a derivation would show that any possible scenario in which there is a deity supremely worthy of ultimate worship is a scenario in which that being is also the asymmetrical source of all else. Of course, if the answer to the question is "No", then hope for the derivation evaporates.

We can thus view the claims above as stronger than are required for undermining the derivation of CT from WWT. That point is worth noting, since the problem will still remain even after developing some skepticism about the claims in the quote.

Suppose, then, that a defender of WWT wishes to maintain that if there are unsourced beings, no being however divine would be supremely worthy of ultimate worship. The plausibility of this suggestion depends, I will argue, on whether the beings in question are assumed to be unsourced or alternatively sourced. For consider the second possibility. Under this assumption, the imagined scenario is one where the beings in question have a source in something other than the focal candidate for deity. So, assume first that $X$ is claimed to be supremely worthy of maximal worship but not the source of all else, while there is another being $Y$ that is the source of all else. Central to worship is the surrender/submission attitude, of a supreme sort. If so, however, $Y$'s sourcehood status undermines the assumption is $X$ is supremely worthy of the maximal value of the surrender/submission attitude, since the relation to $Y$ places a competing demand on the objects of creation. Each such creature would need to place a mitigated attitude of some sort in order to rightfully acknowledge some element of the same attitude as appropriate for the source of one's being.

This point is not undercut if we minimize $Y$'s sourcehood so that $Y$ is the source only of some creatures but not all, with $X$ the source of other creatures, where $X$ is the candidate for deity. In such a case, at least some creatures would be subject to competing demands of allegiance, submission, and surrender, underming the assumption that $X$ is God, given WWT.

What happens, though, when we consider the possibility of unsourced beings? In such a case, there can be no reliance on the competing demands used to undermine the argument under the assumption of alternative sourcing. So perhaps here we find a case where worthiness of worship remains undiminished even in the face of lack of sourcehood.

Here the objector might appeal to the fact that such beings, even though unsourced, remain destructible. One might then maintain that the surrender/submission attitude involved in worship can be supreme even if arising from this sense of dependence on God, rather than from being sourced in God.

Here, though, such a claim is not compelling. Why wouldn't the appropriate attitude be greater, more heightened, if both one's existence and continued well-being depended on God, rather than just one's continued well-being? If so, the attitude that is central to the worship-worthiness of God is diminished in the case of such unsourced inexplicables. Such diminution then provides a basis for a defender of WWT to claim that the example doesn't give a reason for thinking that the starting point of CT cannot be derived from WWT.

The complexity of the argument here has gotten great enough that a summary is in order. We are looking at an objection to the claim that the starting point of CT can be derived from WWT. That objection involves inexplicables, things not sourced in God, and the objection claims that God's worthiness of worship would be undiminished for such beings. The strategy for defenders of WWT in responding to this objection is to try to find grounds for claiming that worthiness of worship would be diminished in such cases. This diminution is easiest to find if the unsourced find their source elsewhere, so the most forceful version of the objection requires that the unsourced be inexplicable. In order for the objection to be sustained, we have to show that God's worthiness of worship is still supreme, even for such inexplicables. Here, the argument on behalf of the objection appeals to dependence relations that still generate such supremacy. One intent on defending WWT against this objection, however, seems to have a reply: supremacy is not achieved in this way, because a greater would obtain if the dependency involved sourcehood as well as dependence for continued well-being.

So, there is no clear path for concluding that the consideration raised by Bayne and Nagasawa shows that WWT lacks the resources for deriving the starting point of CT. Moreover, closer inspection of the passage reveals why. That passage reveals no sensitivity to the ways in which worship comes in degrees of ultimacy and the ways in which worthiness also comes in degrees. Even if the authors are correct that worthiness of worship would not be eliminated for unsourced beings, a defender of WWT can point out that if the degrees just noted are diminished in any way, that is sufficient for showing that alternative sourcing is incompatible with WWT.

One might rightly note, however, that blocking objections to an inference is not the same thing as defending the derivation in question, and thereby grant the responses above but still doubt the central claim that sourcehood can be derived from the starting point of WWT. The responses above, though, give us an idea about how a defense of the derivation might proceed. We start with the assumption that God is worthy of worship, in the exalted sense that characterizes WWT. We then assume for *reductio* that the sourcehood claim central to CT is false. For it to be false, we need to find entities that are either unsourced or find their source in something other than God. As argued above, however, neither option presents a credible possibility in which no diminution of worship-worthiness occurs. Hence we have an argument that WWT can derive the starting point for CT.

Although promising, there is a caveat to mention here. For nothing in this argument says anything about whether the unsourced or other-sourced entities are necessary or contingent, nor whether they are agents or non-agents, nor whether the lack of sourcing is an essential properties of the things that are unsourced. If we are talking about agents, contingent or not, the above argument can stand as is, but suppose we are talking about unsourced or other-sourced non-agents, either contingent or necessary. To illustrate the issue, let's assume we are talking about some abstract entity such as a proposition or a set (where the set is contingent in virtue of having some contingent thing as a member). In order to derive the starting point of CT from WWT, the degree of worship-worthiness will need to be diminished by the lack of sourcing in God for such a proposition or set.

An initial response to this argument is that it would seem that the supremacy of worship-worthiness can only be under threat from things capable of worship that are not sourced in God. But, one might maintain, there is simply no call of any sort for worship by entities not capable of worship, for precisely the same reason that non-agents cannot have obligations to worship.

This response, however, is confused. The issue isn't, at bottom, an issue about whether unsourced beings have an obligation to worship, but whether supreme worship-worthiness is partially grounded in God's being the source of all else. If God is not the source of all else, then the partial grounding claim is false without an explanation of how supremacy of worship gets compromised by the lack of sourcing, even if merely for abstract entities such as propositions or sets.

The kind of response that would be relevant might go like this. One might hope to argue that God's greatness is diminished under the hypothesis in question, and then maintain that such diminution also weakens the degree of worship-worthiness in question. Alternatively, one might pin one's hopes on defending the claim that even abstract entities have to be sourced in God, as our initial characterization of CT has it.[5] These kinds of responses are at least

---

[5] For discussion of this issue, see Morris and Menzel (1986); Davison (1991); Davidson (1999); Craig (2012); Davidson (2015); Menzel (2016); Craig (2017a,b).

relevant to the issue at hand, even though we are in no position to endorse either approach at this point.

Here, however, a comparison with the degree to which WWT can yield an explanation of the starting point of PBT is helpful. As we saw at the end of §9.3, we don't know exactly what is involved in the idea of perfection of being, but when we consider the issue of supremacy of worship-worthiness, we find two points to consider. Suppose that the unlimited power, knowledge, and goodness involved in worship-worthiness doesn't quite reach the heights of the perfections of the greatest possible being. We need to ask, then, whether the worship-worthiness is actually supreme, or whether it is diminished somewhat by this fact. If in fact the degree of worship-worthiness is diminished, to that extent we have grounds for maintaining that the gap disappears between the perfections of the most perfect being and the perfections arising from the absence of limit on them. For the supremacy of worship-worthiness would require it.

This possibility is most obvious when we are imagining a case where the possible perfect being is also actual, for if there is a being purported to be supremely worthy of ultimate worship while there is also another being more exalted in perfection, it is clear that we have an inconsistency. But what if the possible perfect being is non-actual? Here one might consider defending the idea that supreme worship-worthiness doesn't answer so much to what is true about the entire space of modality, but rather to the nature of perfections that we actually find. The idea would then be that the supreme degree of worship-worthiness can be possessed even if there is a non-actual possibility in which a more perfect being would be found. That being, were that possibility realized, would also be supremely worthy of the most exalted worship, but actual desert regarding worship is not diminished simply on the basis of a possibility of something greater.

Note what is required of this thought experiment. We are assuming that the starting point of any adequate metatheology identifies an essential property of deity that is fundamental. If it is supreme worship-worthiness, then there is no possible circumstance in which that being exists and lacks this property. Yet, if there was a possible circumstance in which such a being exists and there is a more perfect being as well, then the first being would lack the requisite property, and WWT would be undermined by that possibility. But suppose, however, that there is no possibility of both beings co-existing, but rather that each is possible in non-overlapping scenarios. Such a possibility does not obviously threaten WWT, though it would show that the starting point of PBT cannot be derived from supreme worship-worthiness.

Similar options re-appear when considering WWT and the starting point of CT. Suppose abstract entities might not be sourced in God. This would happen if the sourcing were only contingent if present. It would also happen if being unsourced were essential to *abstracta*.

The second option is less troublesome to WWT. For if such objects are essentially unsourced, then the starting point of CT should perhaps be amended, to restrict the quantifier to the realm of what can be sourced. The argument for this claim is basically the same kind of an argument for the claim that omnipotence should not be thought of as requiring that an omnipotent being be able to do what can't be done. Just so, CT would then be the metatheology that begins from the idea that God is the source of all else, but gets precisified once we take into account the existence of essentially unsourced things. This option is present since each metatheology should be thought of in terms of a family of alternative precisifications, and even though the most beautiful version of CT makes the quantifier unrestricted, it is not an abandonment of this metatheological perspective to retrench in the face of impossibilities, just as it is not an abandonment of PBT to retrench if the notion of omnipotence is itself incoherent. We might have been hoping that such eventualities did not need to be accommodated, but they must be, they can, without detriment to the metatheological perspectives in question.

Moreover, if CT is amended in this way, the existence of essentially unsourced things would not present an obstacle to deriving the starting point of CT from WWT. For that new, revised starting would involve no commitments regarding God's relationship to essentially unsourced things, except of course for the commitment that God is not their source.

What about the other possibility, the possibility in which there is the possibility of contingently unsourced things? A defender of WWT will want to divide the cases again, distinguishing cases of actually unsourced things from potentially unsourced things. In the former case, it is not difficult to see how to argue for some diminution in worship-worthiness, on grounds that more supremacy is achieved in the possible case where the things in question are sourced. A resister of WWT might claim otherwise, though, claiming that supremacy answers to actuality more than to the totality of modal space, so that the mere potentiality in question doesn't generate any such diminution.

At this point, however, I don't think we are in a position to settle this issue. I don't think we know enough about the notion of supremacy in worship-worthiness to say how much that notion answers to modal space in its entirety. Until we know that, we can't conclude that supremacy in worship-worthiness demands that the object of worship is the greatest possible being, and we can't conclude that supremacy in worship-worthiness demands that the object of worship is the asymmetrical source of everything that can be sourced.

Where this leaves us, then, remains murky. We cannot close off the possibility that the starting point of CT can be derived from WWT, but we have found no unproblematic way to complete the derivation, either. So, the proper conclusion to draw is that WWT may not be able to show that the starting point of CT can be sustained.

## 9.4 Conclusion

We thus can endorse the conclusion that WWT is a formidable metatheological stance to take. In comparison with both CT and PBT, it does no worse than the alternatives, and in some ways shows more promise of preserving the starting point of alternative metatheologies. There are ways to argue that it is unsuccessful in deriving the starting points of alternative metatheologies, but these arguments aren't conclusive. Moreover, there are at least somewhat plausible arguments for the contrary conclusion as well. We are thus not in a position to endorse WWT, but we are closer to that conclusion than we are to the claim that WWT provides an inadequate metatheology.

We turn in the final substantive chapter to wrapping up what we have learned from the first two sections of this book and then to an investigation of the relationship between our best metatheologies and the complete theologies that we find in the literature. The central question is the extent to which a kind of theoretical integrity can be retained when attempting to move from the former to the latter.

# PART IV
# CONCLUDING PARAMETERS

# 10
# Theological Systems and Their Derivations

## 10.1 Introduction

We have collected data from the most important areas of philosophical theology to use in assessing the plausibility of our competing metatheologies. Our first task is to assess what we have learned to this point, and then to note the attributes of deity that carry weight in assessing a metatheology that don't fall under the starting points of the metatheologies we are considering and weren't covered in our discussion of the initial shared ground. These attributes taken together with the attributes involved in the shared ground and alternative starting point comprise the basic ingredients in a complete theology. Our task will be to see the degree to which complete theologies are derived from our best metatheologies, and what to make of the matter if we find significant independence of the former from the latter.

For this task we can begin by listing some of the common attributes of God that we have not discussed to this point. Among the metaphysical attributes that we have not focused on are immutability, infinity, eternality, simplicity, transcendence, and immanence. Among the moral attributes that we have mentioned only in passing or not at all are wisdom, truthfulness, justice, mercy, love, grace, faithfulness, freedom, holiness, and righteousness. After summarizing what we have learned in the first two parts of this work in §10.2, we will turn to a discussion of various types of theism in §10.3, followed by discussions of the metaphysical and moral aspects of each in §10.4 and §10.5, respectively.

## 10.2 Summary

In Parts II and III, we considered what each of our three primary metatheologies (Creator Theology (CT), Perfect Being Theology (PBT), Worship-Worthiness Theology (WWT)) could sustain concerning the common ground of monotheism and personhood and concerning the starting points of competing metatheologies. Using ✓s and ✓s to mark different degrees of positivity, from close to full confidence for the former to cautious optimism for the latter, and using Xs and Xs to stand for negative results from mild to extreme, the conclusions drawn are summarized in Table 10.1:

**Table 10.1** Scorekeeping

| Category | Specific Feature | CT | PBT | WWT |
|---|---|---|---|---|
| Common Ground | monotheism | ✓ | X | X |
|  | personhood | ✓ | X | ✓ |
| Competing Starting Points | creator | NA | X | X |
|  | perfect being | X | NA | ✓ |
|  | worship-worthy | X | ✓ | NA |

The table is, of course, a coarse-grained instrument for summarizing discussion in Parts II and III of this work, and as a result elides the important qualifications that are central to our investigation. For example, the chart expresses optimism about the relationship between WWT and PBT, claiming that each shows some promise in deriving the starting point of the alternative. Our discussion, however, showed difficulties standing in the way of such a conclusion. What the chart represents, then, is that we found some grounds for derivation, but also some concerns that need to be resolved before endorsing the derivation. Such a stance is stronger than simply not having any information either way on the matter, so it gets represented as a slight positive for each. The same point bears emphasizing for slight negatives as well. For example, we saw that CT comes much closer to showing that God is the most perfect possible being, by sustaining the necessity of God's existence plus the unlimited character of central divine attributes. Here, though, we'd need an additional reason for thinking lack of limits is sufficient for being the most perfect, and we have found no such assurance. So our conclusion has to be mildly negative on this issue, even though the resources of CT in this area are much stronger than typically supposed.

Inspection of this table shows that, contrary to common assumptions in philosophical theology over the past half-century, PBT fares the worst by these measures. WWT is better, in virtue of being able to show that God is a person and that worship-worthiness is partially grounded in the perfections that are at the heart of PBT, and CT is surprisingly at least tied for the best, and is perhaps best of all if we let strength of positivity break any tie. I suspect our surprise here has two sources. The first is that philosophical theology spends too little time on issues involving monotheism and personhood, and it is here that CT has an unblemished record in contrast with both WWT and PBT. The second results from the usual practice of considering straight away the question of whether the creator of all has to be a perfect being, and usual epistemological approaches deriving from what can be gleaned from cosmological and teleological considerations fall far short in being able to find perfection from such sources. Yet, even once we recognize the need to replace the usual epistemological approach with a properly metaphysical one, we cannot get the full starting point of PBT any more than we could get the full starting point of WWT from CT.

We must acknowledge, however, that some of these derivations are on shakier ground than others, and the shakiness of some of these derivations might incline one toward some version of MAF. Here, the best version of MAF would seem to be a combination of CT and WWT starting points. Such a version of MAF would have as its shakiest component the demonstration of perfection being a partial ground of worship-worthiness. It is worth noting that defenders of PBT often cite as one of its charms that worship-worthiness follows from, or is grounded in, perfection in being, and this hope underlies the promise available to WWT for deriving the starting point of PBT. The one remaining cause for concern was whether modal space could be split in such a way that there is a more perfect possible being who inhabits a region of modal space that does not intersect with that part of modal space occupied by the being supremely worthy of worship. (If overlap is present, then supremacy would be compromised.) Such a case presupposes little to no credit on the greatness of being calculation for being actual rather than being merely possible, and though we should find such a valuation function highly suspicious, there is no obvious route to showing that it is impossible for modal space to be divided as envisioned. For that reason, we have to include some caution in our optimism about deriving perfection from WWT, and by implication, from CT as well. In the face of such uncertainties, one can see the attraction for endorsing the WWT/CT version of MAF, since such a combination rules out the bifurcation of modal space just described, since CT requires that God sources everything else in every possible scenario.

Whether we endorse CT or the WWT/CT version of MAF, the right attitude here is to see these results as a strong vindication for thinking of God primarily in terms of the creator of all rather than in Anselmian terms involving "that than which a greater cannot be thought." The Anselmian formula is philosophically intriguing and generates a philosophically engaging attempt to prove the existence of such a being. As we have seen, however, hope sometimes disappoints, and such is the case here.

Our task, then, is to see if our assessment changes in light of the need to move from a metatheology to a complete theology. To prepare for that discussion, we consider in the next section the most common complete theologies in recent times within western Christianity, since they provide a nice test environment for determining the prospects and limitations that arise in the attempt to derive a complete theology from a metatheology.

## 10.3 Theological systems

Among the competing outlooks on the nature of God are those of classical theism and neo-classical alternatives to it, open theism, pantheism and the related panentheism, and process theology. This list is historically rather than logically oriented, generated by looking at what has been defended in the literature rather than describing the space of possibilities that are available, but that fact isn't a defect at this point. For our interest is in seeing the relation between metatheological options and various types of completed theologies.

We can begin with characterizations of each of these approaches, though some of what I will say here will be partially stipulative, since labels have a way of coming to have honorific status so that labeling can become an exercise in futility. Some bristle at not being included in various camps, and the capacity for bristling is widespread enough that no characterizations are likely to be forthcoming that puts everyone where they want to be found. So I will resort to partial stipulation if needed, in order to have some basis for discussion.

I begin with classical theism, with central characteristics not discussed in previous chapters of impassibility, immutability, eternality, and simplicity.[1] In combination with God's aseity, these qualities imply that God is pure actuality, cannot suffer, and is the omni-being of strong versions of Perfect Being Theology.

These four characteristics are noteworthy since it is difficult if not impossible to deny some but not all of them, and such denials are the defining feature (in combination with the rest of the exalted conception of God found in classical

---

[1] This view is defended variously by Augustine, Boethius, Anselm, Peter Lombard, Aquinas, and others. Contemporary defenses include Rogers (2000); Mawson (2005); Helm (2010), and McCann (2012).

theism), as I use the term, of neo-classical theism.[2] Not all neo-classical theists explicitly deny all four of these central features, though (as argued in Mullins (2016c)) there are plausible lines of reasoning from denials of any to denials of the others.

For example, denying impassibility obviously implies denying immutability, and once changes of any sort are occurring in God, simplicity will be hard to defend. That leaves only the doctrine of eternity, and though there are ways to forestall its denial,[3] the best reason for the doctrine in classical theism is the doctrine of simplicity itself. So once that doctrine goes, it is hard to see why one would want or need to retain timelessness.

Moreover, once simplicity is given up, we lose the basis for insisting that there is no potentiality in God, and if there is potentiality, there is a capacity for some sort for change, undermining classical versions of immutability and impassibility. Once again, eternality is still open to defense, but it will be a view left without defense even if coherent.

If timelessness is abandoned, however, we also end up with an account that makes God part of the dimension that involves change, and if God is merely everlasting rather than timeless, then if God acts in any way at all, including the act of creation, God cannot be immutable or simple. And once these are abandoned, one loses any basis for thinking that impassibility should be retained.

Finally, if we abandon immutability, we lose a reason to retain impassibility, and we introduce potentiality into the nature of God, resulting in the loss of simplicity as well. Moreover, as above, the grounds for eternity go as well.

Such are the plausible, though perhaps not compelling, connections between the four characteristics in question. And it is these four that form the core dispute between classical and neo-classical theisms.

Open theism shares with neo-classical theism this predilection both to preserve elements of classical theism and also to abandon the four central metaphysical doctrines of classical theism, but goes further in denying that God is the omni-being of classical theism. The usual form for the latter is to deny that God has exhaustive knowledge of the future, but other possibilities

---

[2] Neo-classical theisms are defended in Plantinga (1974, 1980); Woltersdorff (1975); Morris (1991); Wolterstorff (1991); Craig (2001); Zagzebski (2006), and O'Connor (2012). Relevant literature on the distinction between classical and neo-classical theism includes Mullins (2016a,b,c); Göcke (2013); Mullins (2018), and Timpe (2013).

[3] See, e.g., Stump and Kretzmann (1981) and Kvanvig (1986).

have been endorsed as well, including that God's goodness is contingent rather than necessary.[4]

Pantheism and process theology share no such attraction for classical theism. On the latter view, God is in the process of becoming just as much as the world is,[5] and the resulting view is one version of panentheism. Pantheism, as I will use the term, identifies God with the world,[6] whereas panentheism refuses to endorse the identity claim in favor of the view that the universe is, in some sense, in God or part of God.[7]

## 10.4  Issues of Derivability

The above sketches of the central types of theological systems we find in the literature are enough to raise the central question of this work, a question about the relationship between the metatheologies we are investigating and extant theological systems concerning the nature of God. We have already noted the paucity of attention to the class of competitors when it comes to metatheology as well as a penchant for substituting an epistemological project for what is most properly understood to be a metaphysical one. It is worth noting here also the lack of attention to the kind of theoretical rigor and discipline we might have hoped for in generating a theological system from a given metatheological standpoint.

Consider, as an example, the systematic development of the Thomistic version of classical theism which identifies God in terms of the notion of pure act. As I understand this system, it begins from a CT metatheology, and if it is to be faulted, it is for its failure to generate the complete theology from this metatheological starting point. Instead, it adverts to the metaphysics and philosophy of science of Aristotle, relying on the distinction between form and matter and on the notion of a complete explanation that prevents explanations from coming to an end when encountering any further instance of formed matter. We thus find in God a stopping place for explanation only if there is no compositionality, no admixture, of form and matter in the nature of God,

---

[4] Relevant literature includes Swinburne (1977); Hasker (1989); Pinnock et al. (1994); Sanders (1997), and Hasker (2013).
[5] See, e.g., Hartshorne (1984).
[6] The obvious historical source is Spinoza, but see also Levine (1994); Oppy (1997); Mander (2000), and the articles in the first section of Buckareff and Nagasawa (2016).
[7] For relevant literature, see Peacocke (2004); Peters (2007); Clayton (2010, 2013); Biernacki and Clayton (2014), and Atmanspacher and Sass (2017). For the conceptual problem of defining panentheism, I have found the Göcke-Lataster debate most helpful. See Göcke (2013); Lataster (2014, 2015); Göcke (2015), Mullins (2016c), and Culp (2020).

and thus we get both that God must be simple and must be pure act, with no potentiality at all.

We could take quite a while plumbing the intricacies of this system, and would reap great benefit from doing so, but here we only need this sketch to see the signs of alloy in the system. What would be more elegant, simple, and pure would be to carry out the derivation from the metatheological starting point alone. Moreover, it isn't really fair to describe the approach in terms of MAF, since a rejection of fundamentality of that sort is still at the metatheoretical level, and the Thomistic version of classical theism isn't a result of adding elements of PBT, WWT, or any other metatheology to CT. Instead, the system results from alloying alien elements to a pristine metatheology in order to derive an admittedly powerful and impressive theological system.

The tinge of alloy can always be removed by doing the basic work in philosophy to defend the philosophical elements used to generate the complete theology. Here, however, the Aristotelian metaphysics of form and matter has not withstood scrutiny, and without it, the explanatory principles about what needs explanation and what doesn't have no foundation. So, the point above remains, though it is a relatively banal endorsement of a point long acknowledged in assessments of Thomism.

I note in passing that it is difficult to find a Protestant theology with such power and scope, in large part because the focus in Protestant thought is on systematic theology, conceived in terms of what Sacred Writ teaches us about the nature of God. Ignoring a distinction doesn't make it go away, however, so the domain of philosophical theology doesn't disappear nor does the distinction within philosophical theology between a metatheology and a complete theology of the nature of God. So what we should expect to find, and do find, in Protestant thought is that the primary issue concerns the degree of skepticism one should take toward the significance of metatheology for deriving a complete theology concerning the nature of God. On one end we find Karl Barth and Cornelius van Til representing a strongly skeptical Reformed strand against the possibility of knowledge of God from philosophical theology,[8] to the more strident apologetic efforts by many within other branches of Evangelicalism.[9] One will be hard-pressed to find anything remotely approaching the kind of disciplined effort needed to characterize the metatheology and show what elements of the complete theology endorsed

---

[8] See, e.g., van Til (1976, 1977) and Barth (1968).
[9] I'm thinking of people such as Josh McDowell, Ravi Zacharias, Lee Strobel, William Lane Craig, Gary Habermas, etc.

are derived from the metatheology. What we find instead is an interest in the epistemology of religious belief, with an interest in determining whether any of it is defensible from a purely theoretical point of view.

We can speculate, though, about what such perspectives would generate if engaged in the project of metatheology. One would expect a complete theology that is an amalgam of bits of metatheology with a strong element derived from sacred texts. Though Thomism is no more an unalloyed derivation of an account of the nature of God than we find on this approach, the difference is in the alloy. Skepticism about the need and importance of metatheology undermines itself, since the arguments needed for the skepticism partake of the same philosophical dimension that is being argued against, and limitations on what is derivable from a given metatheology cannot be properly assessed without engaging in the project itself, instead of substituting some other project in its place. Here, Thomism shines for its honesty and effort.

Could we ask for something better, something unalloyed? The aspiration is understandable, but articulating what is desired turns out to be quite difficult. The ideal would be where the metatheology is all that is needed to generate a complete theology, but that ideal is hopelessly naïve. Imagine making the same kind of demand on a complete scientific account of the world. Even if one thinks that physics is fundamental for such an understanding, it would be wildly implausible to think that a complete account could be derived from physics alone. Dependence relations are one thing, reducibility another.

To make progress, we can note that it is one thing to grant unavoidability of alloy and quite another to refuse or minimize engagement with the needed task of defending the philosophical theses included in one's metatheology and of articulating and arguing for the implications of such for a completed theology that depends on that metatheology. Our issue is one squarely within philosophical theology, so if additional resources are needed to move from a preferred metatheology to a complete theology, we will want to see what kind of general philosophical fit we find between the metatheology and the other sources. So, for example, if appeals to sacred texts are going to be used, such a source doesn't come free of a philosophical need for defense.

There is a legitimate concern here that no such enterprise can succeed, and that all we can ever hope for is to holistically incorporate information from any source whatsoever in moving from a metatheological starting point to a complete theology. Before drawing this pessimistic conclusion, however, we want to see if something better is available, beginning by seeing whether any of the metatheologies being considered have resources relevant to what divides the major theologies above. In this process, we will consider each metatheology individually, but also the version of MAF that previous chapters have shown to be superior to any of the individual non-MAF metatheologies we have considered. That version is a combination of WWT and CT, claiming that God's nature is fundamentally that of the worship-worthy source of all else. The power of this version of MAF is that it can generate a preference for monotheism and for the personhood of God, and since worship-worthiness can plausibly be claimed to be partially grounded in the perfections of God that are central to PBT, WWT/CT gets the best of PBT derivatively. WWT/CT thereby yields a preference for an account of God on which God is the most perfect being and essentially an omni-being as well. The WWT/CT version of MAF thus generates the full power of a version of MAF that takes all three starting points as equally fundamental, but with greater parsimony. It therefore holds a privileged position in metatheology, once we have seen the results of prior chapters concerning the derivational capacities of each of the major metatheologies. Our task, then, is to see how each non-MAF metatheology compares with this WWT/CT version of MAF in moving from metatheology to a complete theology.

## 10.5 Metatheological Resources

Once we begin to compare the major three metatheologies with major theologies from two sections ago, one should begin with a pessimistic inclination about the capacity to derive the latter from the former, except in special cases. Noting the special cases is a good place to begin.

We have seen, for example, a defense of the personhood of God for both WWT and CT, and pantheism suffers in the face of such defenses. Moreover, for versions of PBT strong enough to show that God is an omni-being, open theism is put on the defensive. The issues are complex, but open theists are forced to insist on a weaker account of omniscience, along the lines articulated in Swinburne (1977), or argue against bivalence or excluded middle regarding future contingents, as in Geach (1977). Though there is an undercurrent of support within the philosophy of logic for these latter views, the overwhelming stance is in favor of the standard first-order requirements in favor of bivalence and excluded middle. The reasons here are simple: we bet on the future, we predict the future, we worry about the future, and sometimes we win our bets, our predictions are true, and our worries are misplaced. All such phenomena point to truth-values for future contingents, and motivations for overriding this evidence focus not on semantics for ordinary language[10] but on arguments for logical and theological fatalism under the assumption in question. Those grounds, however, are less than compelling, arising from scope ambiguities in key premises in the argument for logical fatalism,[11] and also in some versions of arguments for theological fatalism. Moreover, when the arguments for theological fatalism are properly constructed, they don't reveal any need or preference for denying truth-values for future contingents but instead merely make this one option among several for avoiding the unwanted conclusion. In the face of ordinary semantic data concerning future contingents, a better route is to pay attention to the best arguments against bivalence and excluded middle, which come not from considerations about future contingents, but from considerations involving vagueness and semantic indeterminacies that might result from it.[12] Those grounds, however, do not align with the considerations involving future contingents, so are of little use to open theists needing to maintain that God is omniscient. In addition, there are difficulties of other sorts for any view aiming to sustain a limited account of omniscience, as I've argued in Kvanvig (1985, 1986, 1989a,c) and most recently in "Open Theism and the Future," in Kvanvig (2011b), where I argue that the asymmetry between past and future that open theism relies on vanishes on closer inspection, leaving nearly all of the past and future unknowable on precisely the same grounds as those involving future contingents. Hence, there are good explanations for an aversion to open theism by defenders of PBT, explanations that generate a preference for some other complete theology.

As we have seen, however, the major metatheologies are silent on the issue of whether God has a body and whether the universe is that body. The only hope for such a demonstration is if there were an essential connection between bodies and corruptibility, and that claim is difficult to defend. It is noteworthy in this regard to consider versions of theism that include a doctrine of the resurrection of the body, for on such versions, there is theoretical pressure to deny the needed link. It is possible, of course, to supplement such views with a claim of miraculous continuous regeneration of such bodies to counteract entropy, but such an addition looks more like special pleading than something for which we have sound independent evidence.

---

[10] Geach (1977) is an exception here, but his account is logically untenable, as I argue in Kvanvig (1986).
[11] For details, see Plantinga (1974); Kvanvig (1986); Flint (1998).
[12] For extended discussion, see Williamson (1994).

This point leaves open the sound conclusion that this dispute is matter for resolution within basic metaphysics rather than a special issue to be resolved within philosophical theology. On certain metaphysical views, combinations of form and matter are always contingent and in need of sustenance in one form or another, leading to a conclusion that the sustainer of such had better not be a combination of form and matter and had better be something in which essence and existence are the same. But such Aristotelian systems must be defended in their own right in terms of basic metaphysics, rather than being derived from some metatheology within philosophical theology. So none of the major metatheologies is going to have much to say about the divide between panentheists and defenders of more classical theisms that affirm that God is a purely spiritual being.

The final issue is what separates classical theists from neo-classical theists, on the issues of immutability, impassability, eternity, and simplicity. It is here that the topic of alloy in a complete theology is most pressing, for none of the metatheologies show great promise in settling which side of the fence to be on regarding these attributes. The best hope here is for a PBT-generated affirmation of classical theism, but the Thomistic example cited earlier points in a different direction. To get a PBT resolution here, we would need to be able to show the intrinsic superiority of each of these properties, so that being timeless, changeless, incapable of suffering, and non-composite in the extreme were all better features to have than lack. So, one might argue, stability of character and Stoic endurance in the face of pain are good qualities to have, and the scale on which such stability and endurance falls has a maximum value which is immutability and impassability. As soon as we give this argument, however, it is clear that things are not that simple. For we have not only metaphysical attributes to consider, but also moral ones, which include, as noted earlier, wisdom, truthfulness, justice, mercy, love, grace, faithfulness, freedom, holiness, and righteousness. Some of these generate an obvious counterargument to this attempted demonstration of divine immutability and impassability.

To see how and why, let's divide these moral attributes into those that are essential to deity and those that are optional. Those that are essential to deity—arguably including justice, holiness, righteousness, wisdom, and truthfulness—are compatible with the above argument. But not so with optional qualities, such as those signaling divine responsiveness to our circumstances and plight, generating grounds for gratitude and thankfulness. Among these qualities are grace, mercy, and love. These features give pause regarding the above argument, for such responsiveness is evidence of God's being moved by our plight and engaging in various accommodations aimed at solving the problems of sin and misery, as the Westminster Catechism characterizes it.

I am not claiming that these considerations settle the matter, for they do not. What I have described is merely the opening salvo in the conflict between classical and neo-classical theists. What is important in our context, however, is not who will win, but the rules of engagement for the conflict. To minimize the alloy in the complete theology being endorsed, the rules of engagement counsel uncompromising commitment to settling disputes within the scope of the metatheologies involved. Thus, for WWT, PBT, and the WWT/CT version of MAF, settling disputes by appeal to the notion of what a perfect being would be like is perfectly appropriately and capable of minimizing alloy in the final product.

Intrusion from outside the system is, however, unavoidable. Central to CT's metatheology is the aseity and independence of God, an aspect of deity that all metatheologies have reason to sustain. But there will be strong pressure outside of philosophical theology, from general metaphysics to the theories of explanation and confirmation in philosophy of science and epistemology, for thinking that a full and complete explanation of all of reality cannot succeed without requiring divine transcendence from the cosmos itself, on pain of making God be just another being as much in need of further explanation as we find in all other cases.

Once we have such a basis for aseity, independence, and transcendence, one question to ask is whether the combination of metaphysical traits favored by classical theists fits better with these qualities than do their complements. On that score, the answer would seem to be "yes," since the complements in question are so broad in scope that they hardly delimit logical space at all. That is, merely telling me that God is capable of change, suffering, undergoing the experience of time, and like everything else in being subject to distinctions of various sorts doesn't communicate anything distinctively God-like, except for the aspect of suffering which implies sentience. In this respect, neo-classical theists, of which I am one, can be objects of ridicule of the same sort rightly aimed at apophaticists. In both cases, nothing short of a positive account of the nature of God gives us anything intellectually robust enough to ground a life of devotion, loyalty, and faithfulness that is at the heart of true religion.

As this last remark signals, unavoidable alloy will arise from other sources as well, including the lived experience of religious communities and the spiritually sensitive. Complete theologies have no escape from the holistic web of experience and belief that provides the input for our general sense-making attempts, and there are no general principles governing such sense-making to limit where relevant information can come from. So, complete theologies will also answer to sacred texts as well as metatheology, and in the process, the "better fit" argument for classical theism over neo-classical theism may be overridden. If we think of the phenomenon of fallibilistic support for a position being negatively affected by further information in terms of defeaters and diminishers,[13] the face-value of descriptions of God in both the Christian and Hebrew Bibles is clearly a diminisher of the power of the "better fit" argument above for classical theism, for the portrayal of God in these scriptures is clearly one who is passionally moved by our plight and actively involved in response.

Those familiar with the conversations in philosophical theology will know that these remarks are not even close to the end of the story, for "of making many books there is no end."[14] Here is not the place to engage that literature nor to attempt to resolve the disputes. Instead, the central point to note here is that of structural and methodological awareness and transparency, together with some ordering of sources of information used in the process of moving from a metatheology to a complete theology.

Here is what to expect. Philosophical theology begins with a clear endorsement of a metatheology, followed by a documenting of what aspects of a complete theology can be generated from that metatheology. The next step is to identify what more is needed in an adequate complete theology, noting the sources of such information together with an assessment of the ways in which information from different sources interacts so as to provide details for the question of whether and when defeat or diminution of evidential support results from conflicting information.

We can go further and demand a complete philosophical underpinning for the above, which would involve a complete epistemology and metaepistemology as well as an ethics and metaethics, but the general point is clear enough as it stands. That point is one of perspicacity in theory construction.

## 10.6 Conclusion

The primary result of this chapter is to sustain a kind of independence for metatheology from the questions of adequacy for a complete theology. We have seen the argument for the superiority of the WWT/CT version of MAF,

---

[13] As I argue in Kvanvig (2014).
[14] The need to footnote has no apparent end either: Ecclesiastes 12:12, NIV.

and noted that it, together with all other metatheologies, lacks the resources to settle all disputes between various competing complete theologies. Rather than being a defect in our metatheology, this result is to be expected. It accords perfectly with the holistic character of explanation and confirmation that we see throughout intellectual life (and all other rational domains, for that matter). This conclusion is less pristine than we might have wished, and the proper response to it is greater perspicacity in philosophical theology than we find in its history.

# 11
# Conclusion

In the religious and intellectual climate in which I was raised, the history of philosophical theology goes back to St. Paul, especially the book of *Romans*, develops greater refinement with the rise of polemics and the need to articulate carefully the central doctrines of the Christian faith, and reaches full maturity by the time of Augustine. Though there never was a time during this period in which it was controversial or questionable whether God was the most perfect being,[1] none of this early philosophical theology generated any clear endorsement of Perfect Being Theology (PBT). Equally true is that this history assumes that God is the creator of all and worthy of worship, but none of it counts as a clear endorsement of either Creator Theology (CT) or Worship-Worthiness Theology (WWT).

My own sense of the history of metatheology is that its significance doesn't become obvious until we get to Anselm and his attempted ontological argument for the existence of God, in the latter part of the eleventh century. Moreover, the position Anselm endorses becomes controversial over the next two centuries, in large part because of the rejection by Aquinas of the ontological argument, which has seemed to many to be intimately wedded to Perfect Being Theology. Hence, to reject the ontological argument is tantamount to being suspicious of Perfect Being Theology.

Yet, the Thomistic opposition generated no clear focus on metatheological assumptions, though as I understand the history here, Thomism arises as a version of Creator Theology and matures to a complete theology in combination with various aspects of Aristotelian metaphysics together with sacred texts. Though Aquinas never puts things in the way I am putting them, there is no attempt to obscure the role played by these various input sources. If any methodological inelegancies are to be noted, it is that it isn't always clear what sources have trumping power or how that issue is being navigated. That is not surprising, since the epistemology concerning defeasible reasoning won't be a matter of concern until the rise of fallibilism in the latter part of the nineteenth century.

---

[1] For an excellent summary and discussion of the history of perfect being thinking, see Nagasawa (2017).

With the rise of Protestantism and its focus on *sola Scriptura*, things become even more muddled. It is fair to say, I think, that mantras of this sort betray a false consciousness, since there is no intellectual enterprise of any sort lacking in philosophical commitments and assumptions. It would be better to acknowledge and bring them to the light of day to be examined than to pretend there is a way to avoid them. If one wishes to heed the Scriptural admonition to "beware of philosophy and vain deceit," the right way to do that is first to be *aware* of philosophy and vain deceit.[2]

The result, in my own tradition, is that philosophical theology outside of Catholicism makes no progress on metatheological issues nor on the relation between metatheologies and complete theologies. And Catholic philosophical theology faces the daunting issue of fundamental changes in underlying metaphysical assumptions when the rise of modern science and philosophy threatened the Thomistic synthesis. Descartes's metaphysics rejected the distinction between form and matter and took powers out of objects and put them back in the divine being by making interactions a matter of laws of nature enacted and sustained by God. So, no longer is there a metaphysical underpinning for the doctrine of simplicity arising from the theory of explanation where, for Aristotle, explanation can only stop where we find no admixture of form and matter. Moreover, the rise of Empiricism, though sympathetic with Aristotle's epistemology, provides no comfort to Aristotelian metaphysics, either. Finally, since I'm painting with such broad strokes, once we get into the post-Kantian era, obfuscation becomes an end-in-itself and we can all be forgiven for being perplexed by nineteenth- and twentieth-century post-Kantian philosophy and philosophical theology. More seriously, though, the Kantian and post-Kantian tradition leans heavily enough toward anti-realist metaphysics that direct inquiry into the nature of God, from standard realist assumptions, was not high on theology's agenda, whether via philosophical theology or some other route.

Then we enter the golden age for philosophical theology and metaphysics more generally, in our own post-Kripke era.[3] Even here, however, close attention to the types of metatheology and the issues of fundamentality did not happen. It is fair to say that the dominant streams of thought in this revival understand the nature of God in Anselmian terms, fascinated as we have been over the past half-century or more with the prospects for a successful

---

[2] A neat turn of phrase I owe to Norman L. Geisler, from Geisler (1999). His admonition remains even once we notice the hendiadys for what it is: Paul's warning is one about falling prey to vain and deceitful philosophy, and no one needs to object to that!

[3] Though I grant it is easy to see one's own era as much more special than it really is. So the reader can deflate the claim as appropriate—it's still a much better time for philosophical theology and metaphysics than during the heyday of Logical Empiricism.

ontological argument and for a better understanding and clarification of what it is to be an omni-being.

As I have argued here, however, Anselmianism is not only a latecomer on the scene of philosophical theology, but also certainly not the sole option. There are passing observations that show up occasionally in the literature about other possibilities, but even then the views mentioned get corrupted by an unwarranted substitution of an epistemological approach for some alternatives to Perfect Being Theology, instead of holding fixed the metaphysical character of metatheology. In addition, the attention to alternatives is piecemeal: there is no sustained effort to survey the landscape or to see exactly the fecundity of each approach.

Once we turn our attention to the landscape in question, we should expect to find illustrative examples of metatheologies within the domains of the descriptive, the evaluative, and the normative. That is exactly what we find when we note the descriptive character of Creator Theology, the evaluative character of Perfect Being Theology, and the normative character of Worship-Worthiness Theology. There may be other possibilities to consider in each of these categories, but if there are, they are quite hidden from view in our history of thinking about God.

With these options to consider, first steps in evaluating each option require finding conditions of (defeasible) adequacy on a metatheology, and the two categories for such conditions argued for here are ones concerning divine ontology—in particular, the issue of monotheism and the question of the personhood of God—and the starting points of alternative metatheologies. With these conditions of adequacy in place, we discover a mixed bag of results, with no decisive victory for any of the three metatheologies mentioned. Of particular note, however, is that Perfect Being Theology fares the worst in the face of these conditions of adequacy. Given its presumptive status in recent philosophical theology, this result is surprising.

The failure of any of these to show clear superiority raises the possibility of a mixture of them as a version that denies that there is to be found a fundamental feature of God that is singularly descriptive, evaluative, or normative. As we have seen, the best version here is one that combines descriptive and normative features: that version of anti-fundamentalism that holds that God is, fundamentally, the worship-worthy creator of all.

In a way, this result is a comforting one for those who wondered whether the God of the philosophers is not the God of the Bible, since the concepts of creator and worship-worthiness clearly take center stage in our thinking when considering the nature of the God of the Bible. The Bible begins with

God as creator, as does the fourth gospel. And the most common response to the experience of God in the Hebrew Bible is the kind of bowing down and prostrating of oneself that is the bodily expression of the surrender and submission that is at the heart of worship.

But worries about the contrast between the God of the Bible and the God of the philosophers can be overblown as well. If the worry is one about what is fundamental to the nature of God, the worry is well-taken, and our results side with those who reject the idea that God is fundamentally to be thought of as "that than which a greater cannot be thought." As we have seen, however, there is some plausibility to the idea that worship-worthiness is partially grounded in precisely the perfections that form the core of Perfect Being Theology, so if there is a concern that the God of the Bible simply is not the kind of perfect being that Anselmians focus on, there are grounds for rejecting that concern. What is true of God and what is fundamentally true of God are different things. On the latter, Anselm was wrong; on the former, both Anselm and the Bible are in substantial agreement.[4]

The implications of this conclusion about metatheology are yet to be plumbed, but one important result can be noted here. That result is a warranted suspicion of every version of the ontological argument. One need not be a fan of that argument in order to be a defender of Perfect Being Theology, but historically the two have been wedded. The reason for suspicion concerns the inability of Perfect Being Theology to take into account the distinction between contingent and necessary existence prior to any attempt to construct an ontological argument. The reason for this issue of priority is that the central premise of any ontological argument is a claim to the effect that some given nature is necessary if possible, and this property of being necessary if possible comes into play in Perfect Being Theology in the same way that omni-properties come into play: there is a great-making property and there is a maximal value that can be specified for that property.

Suspicion of this argument arises for any view that takes God as creator to be more fundamental than God as perfect being, for part of being the source of all is to be the source of the distinction between contingency and necessity, and once that distinction is in place, the property of being necessary if possible cannot coherently be appended to any nature unless that nature is already that of a necessary being. If that is so, however, the ontological argument can add nothing that isn't already in place before coming to that argument. Such a result doesn't show the argument to be unsound, of course, but merely useless. If God

---

[4] For details on the biblical record concerning the perfections of God, see Nagasawa (2017).

exists and is a necessary being, then this argument is sound, though in the same sense as this argument is sound: whether or not the rain falls mainly on the plane, God exists; so God exists. The soundness of the argument cohabitates with its uselessness.

The final step to address in any full philosophical theology concerns the path from preferred metatheology to complete theology. As we have seen here, there are no general methodological rules to be endorsed for traversing this path, precisely because of the holistic nature of explanation and confirmation. That holistic feature can rationally lead us to prefer some sources over others and then change the ranking as further exploration occurs, but what is central to the entire process is the story of fallibilist epistemology, involving defeaters and diminishers of rational standing as well as enablers, buttressers, and conferrers of rationality. The formal account of this structure can be gleaned,[5] but once beyond the structure and into the realities it defines, the language of holistic coherentism rings true: we are a ship at sea, trying for ways to stay afloat.

It is perhaps worth noting that nowhere is it less likely that we can stay afloat than when we aim for some understanding of divinity. Equally true, however, is that nowhere is it more important to try.

---

[5] See Kvanvig (2014).

# Bibliography

Adams, Marilyn McCord. 1987. *William Ockham*. Notre Dame: University of Notre Dame Press.
Alanen, Lilli. 2008. "Omnipotence, Conceivability, and Modality." In *A Companion to Descartes*, edited by Janet Broughton and John Carriero. 353–71. Malden, MA: Wiley-Blackwell.
Anscombe, G. E. M. 1971. *Causality and Determinism*. Cambridge: Cambridge University Press.
Anselm. 1965 [1078]. *Proslogion*. Oxford: Oxford University Press.
Anselm. 1998 [1077–8]. "Proslogion." In *Anselm of Canterbury: The Major Works*, edited by Brian Davies and G. R. Evans. 82–105. New York: Oxford University Press.
Aquinas, Thomas. 1948 [1265–74]. "Summa Theologica." In *Complete English Edition in Five Volumes*, edited by Fathers of the English Dominican Province. Vol. 1. Westminster, MD: Christian Classics.
Armstrong, D. M. 1983. *What is a Law of Nature?* Cambridge University Press.
Atmanspacher, Harald and Hartmut Sass. 2017. "The Many Faces of Panentheism: An Editorial Introduction." *Zygon* 52 (4): 1029–43.
Augustine. 1982 [396]. *Eighty-Three Different Questions*. Washington, D. C.: Catholic University of America Press.
Augustine. 1998 [426]. *The City of God against the Pagans* (ed. R. W. Dyson). New York: Cambridge University Press.
Ayer, A. J. 1936. *Language, Truth and Logic*. London: Victor Gollancz.
Baillie, James and Jason Hagen. 2008. "There Cannot Be Two Omnipotent Beings." *International Journal for Philosophy of Religion* 64 (1): 21–33.
Baker, Derek Clayton. 2015. "Akrasia and the Problem of the Unity of Reason." *Ratio* 28 (1): 65–80.
Barth, Karl. 1968. *The Epistle to the Romans*. Oxford: Oxford University Press.
Bauer, William A. 2019. "Powers and the Pantheistic Problem of Unity." *Sophia* 58(4), 563–80.
Baumberger, Christoph. 2014. "Types of Understanding: Their Nature and Their Relation to Knowledge." *Conceptus: Zeitschrift Für Philosophie* 40 (98): 67–88.
Baumberger, Christoph, Claus Beisbart, and Georg Brun. 2017. "What Is Understanding? An Overview of Recent Debates in Epistemology and Philosophy of Science." In *Explaining Understanding: New Perspectives from Epistemolgy and Philosophy of Science*, edited by Stephen Grimm Christoph Baumberger and Sabine Ammon. 1–34. Routledge.
Bayne, Tim and Yujin Nagasawa. 2006. "The Grounds of Worship." *Religious Studies* 42 (3): 299–313.
Bayne, Tim and Yujin Nagasawa. 2007. "The Grounds of Worship Again: A Reply to Crowe." *Religious Studies* 43 (4): 475–80.
Bennett, Jonathan. 1994. "Descartes's Theory of Modality." *Philosophical Review* 103 (4): 639–67.

Bennett, Karen. 2011. "Construction Area (No Hard Hat Required)." *Philosophical Studies* 154 (1): 79–104.
Bernstein, Sara. 2016. "Grounding Is Not Causation." *Philosophical Perspectives* 30 (1): 21–38.
Biernacki, Loriliai and Philip Clayton. 2014. *Panentheism across the World's Traditions*. New York: Oxford University Press.
Bigelow, John. 1988. *The Reality of Numbers: A Physicalist's Philosophy of Mathematics*. Oxford: Oxford University Press.
Bird, Alexander. 2007a. "Justified Judging." *Philosophy and Phenomenological Research* 74 (1): 81–110.
Bird, Alexander. 2007b. *Nature's Metaphysics: Laws and Properties*. Oxford: Oxford University Press.
Blackburn, Simon. 1984. *Spreading the Word*. Oxford: Oxford University Press.
Blackburn, Simon. 1993. "Errors and the Phenomenology of Value." In *Essays in Quasi-Realism*. Oxford: Oxford University Press.
Blackburn, Simon. 1998. *Ruling Passions: A Theory of Practical Reasoning*. Oxford: Oxford University Press.
Bohn, Einar Duenger. forthcoming. "Divine Foundationalism." *Philosophy Compass*.
Bradley, Richard and Christian List. 2009. "Desire-as-Belief Revisited." *Analysis* 69 (1): 31–7.
Bradley, Richard and H. Orri Stefánsson. 2016. "Desire, Expectation and Invariance." *Mind* 125 (499): 691–725.
Brand, Myles. 1984. "Intending and Acting: Toward a Naturalized Action Theory." *Journal of Philosophy* 84 (1): 49–54.
Brand, Myles. 1987. "Intending and Acting." *Mind* 96 (381): 121–4.
Bratman, Michael. 1984. "Two Faces of Intention." *Philosophical Review* 93 (3): 375–405.
Bratman, Michael. 2001. "Faces of Intention." *Philosophical Quarterly* 51 (202): 119–21.
Bratman, Michael E. 1999. *Faces of Intention: Selected Essays on Intention and Agency*. Cambridge: Cambridge University Press.
Broad, Charlie Dunbar. 1925. *Mind and Its Place in Nature*. London: Routledge and Kegan Paul.
Broad, Charlie Dunbar. 1939. "Arguments for the Existence of God." *Journal of Theological Studies* 40: 16–30, 156–67.
Brouwer, L. E. J. 1907. *Over de Grondslagen der Wiskunde*. Amsterdam: Maas & van Suchtelen.
Buckareff, Andrei and Yujin Nagasawa. 2016. *Alternative Concepts of God: Essays on the Metaphysics of the Divine*. Oxford: Oxford University Press.
Buckareff, Andrei A. 2016. "Theological Realism, Divine Action, and Divine Location." In *Alternative Concepts of God*, edited by Andrei A. Buckareff and Yujin Nagasawa. 213–34. Oxford: Oxford University Press.
Calvin, John. 1960 [1536]. *Institutes of the Christian Religion*. Philadelphia: Westminster Press.
Camp, Wesley Van. 2014. "Explaining Understanding (or Understanding Explanation)." *European Journal for Philosophy of Science* 4 (1): 95–114.
Campbell, Douglas I. 2018. "Doxastic Desire and Attitudinal Monism." *Synthese* 195 (3): 1139–61.
Carnap, Rudolf. 1962. *Logical Foundations of Probability*. Chicago: University of Chicago Press.

Chisholm, Roderick M. 1948. "The Problem of Empiricism." *Journal of Philosophy* 45 (19): 512–17.
Chisholm, Roderick. 1957. *Perceiving*. Ithaca: Cornell University Press.
Chisholm, Roderick. 1977. *Theory of Knowledge*. Englewood Cliffs: Prentice-Hall. 2nd edn.
Clayton, Philip. 2010. "Panentheisms East and West." *Sophia* 49 (2): 183–91.
Clayton, Philip. 2013. "Introduction to Panentheism." In *Models of God and Alternative Ultimate Realities*, edited by Jeanine Diller and Asa Kasher. 371–9. New York: Springer.
Clayton, Philip and Paul Davies. 2008. *The Re-Emergence of Emergence: The Emergentist Hypothesis*. Oxford: Oxford University Press.
Coleman, Sam. 2019. "Personhood, Consciousness, and God: How to Be a Proper Pantheist." *International Journal for Philosophy of Religion* 85 (1): 77–98. http://dx.doi.org/10.1007/s11153-018-9689-7.
Collins, John. 1995. "Desire-as-Belief Implies Opinionation or Indifference." *Analysis* 55 (1): 2–5.
Conee, Earl and Theodore Sider. 2005. *Riddles of Existence: A Guided Tour of Metaphysics*. Oxford: Oxford University Press.
Craig, William Lane. 2001. *God, Time, and Eternity*. London: Kluwer Academic Publishers.
Craig, William Lane. 2012. "Nominalism and Divine Aseity." *Oxford Studies in Philosophy of Religion*: 43–64.
Craig, William Lane. 2017a. "Absolute Creation and Divine Conceptualism: A Call for Conceptual Clarity." *Philosophia Christi* 19 (2): 431–8.
Craig, William Lane. 2017b. *God and Abstract Objects: The Coherence of Theism: Aseity*. New York: Springer.
Cray, Wesley D. 2011. "Omniscience and Worthiness of Worship." *International Journal for Philosophy of Religion* 70 (2): 147–53.
Cross, Charles B. 2008. "Nonbelief and the Desire-as-Belief Thesis." *Acta Analytica* 23 (2): 115–24.
Culp, John. 2020. "Panentheism." In *The Stanford Encyclopedia of Philosophy*, edited by Edward N. Zalta. Metaphysics Research Lab, Stanford University, fall 2020 edn.
Curley, E. M. 1984. "Descartes on the Creation of the Eternal Truths." *Philosophical Review* 93 (4): 569–97.
Dasgupta, Surendranath. 1940. *A History of Indian Philosophy: Volume 3*. Cambridge: Cambridge University Press.
Daskal, Steven. 2010. "Absolute Value as Belief." *Philosophical Studies* 148 (2): 221–9.
Davidson, Matthew. 1999. "A Demonstration against Theistic Activism." *Religious Studies* 35 (3): 277–90.
Davidson, Matthew. 2015. "God and Other Necessary Beings." In *The Stanford Encyclopedia of Philosophy*, edited by Edward N. Zalta. Metaphysics Research Lab, Stanford University, spring 2015 edn.
Davies, Brian. 2016. "Aquinas on What God Is Not." *Royal Institute of Philosophy Supplement* 78: 55–71. http://dx.doi.org/10.1017/s1358246116000230.
Davison, Scott A. 1991. "Could Abstract Objects Depend upon God?" *Religious Studies* 27 (4): 485–97.
DeRose, Keith. 1991. "Epistemic Possibilities." *Philosophical Review* 100 (4): 581–605.
deRosset, Louis. 2016. "Modal Logic and Contingentism: A Comment on Timothy Williamsons Modal Logic as Metaphysics." *Analysis* 76 (2): 155–72.
Donnellan, Keith S. 1966. "Reference and Definite Descriptions." *Philosophical Review* 75 (3): 281–304.

Drewery, Alice. 2005. "Essentialism and the Necessity of the Laws of Nature." *Synthese* 144 (3): 381–96.
Dummett, Michael. 1977. *Elements of Intuitionism*. Oxford: Oxford University Press.
Dummett, Michael. 1978. "The Philosophical Basis of Intuitionistic Logic." In *Truth and Other Enigmas*. 215–47. Cambridge, MA: Harvard University Press.
Dummett, Michael. 1991. *The Logical Basis of Metaphysics*. Cambridge, MA: Harvard University Press.
Dummett, Michael. 1995. "Origins of Analytical Philosophy." *Philosophical Quarterly* 45 (179): 268–71.
Dummett, Michael A. E. 1993. *Origins of Analytical Philosophy*. Cambridge, MA: Harvard University Press.
Edel, Abraham. 1942. "The Logical Structure of G. E. Moore's Ethical Theory." In *The Philosophy of G. E. Moore*, edited by P. A. Schilpp. Vol. IV, 135–76. Evanston: Northwestern University Press.
Eilan, Naomi, Christoph Hoerl, Teresa McCormack, and Johannes Roessler, eds. 2005. *Joint Attention: Communication and Other Minds*. Oxford: Oxford University Press.
Fantl, Jeremy and Matthew McGrath. 2009. *Knowledge in an Uncertain World*. Oxford: Oxford University Press.
Fetzer, James H. 1974. "On 'Epistemic Possibility'." *Philosophia* 4 (2–3): 327–35.
Findlay, J. N. 1948. "Can God's Existence Be Disproved?" *Mind* 57 (226): 176–83.
Fine, Kit. 2001. "The Question of Realism." *Philosophers' Imprint* 1: 1–30.
Fine, Kit. 2002. "Varieties of Necessity." In *Conceivability and Possibility*, edited by Tamar Szabo Gendler and John Hawthorne. 253–81. Oxford: Oxford University Press.
Flint, Thomas P. 1998. *Divine Providence: The Molinist Account*. Ithaca: Cornell University Press.
Flint, Thomas P. and Alfred J. Freddoso. 1983. "Maximal Power." In *The Existence and Nature of God*. 81–114. Notre Dame: University of Notre Dame Press.
Frankfurt, Harry. 1977. "Descartes on the Creation of the Eternal Truths." *Philosophical Review* 86 (1): 36–57.
Frege, Gottlob. 1879. *Begriffsschrift, eine der arithmetische nachgebildete Formelsprache des reinen Denkens*. Halle: L. Nebert.
Frege, Gottlob. 1893–1903. *Grundgesetze der Arithmetik*. 2 vols. Jena: Hermann Pohle.
Frigerio, Aldo and Ciro Florio. 2015. "Two Omnipotent Beings?" *Philosophia* 43 (2): 309–24.
Garcia, Jorge L. A. 1987. "Intending and Acting." *Review of Metaphysics* 41 (2): 375–7.
Gardiner, Georgi. 2012. "Understanding, Integration, and Epistemic Value." *Acta Analytica* 27 (2): 163–81.
Garrett, Susan R. 2008. *No Ordinary Angel: Celestial Spirits and Christian Claims about Jesus*. New Haven: Yale University Press.
Gaunilo. 1998 [1078]. "On Behalf of the Fool." In *Anselm of Canterbury: The Major Works*, edited by Brian Davies and G. R. Evans. 105–11. New York: Oxford University Press.
Geach, Peter. 1977. *Providence and Evil*. Cambridge: Cambridge University Press.
Geach, Peter. 2002. "Is God Omnipotent?" In *Questions about God*, edited by Steven M. Cahn and David Shatz. Oxford: Oxford University Press.
Geisler, Norman L. 1999. "Beware of Philosophy: A Warning to Biblical Scholars." *Journal of the Evangelical Theological Society* 42: 3–19.
Gentzen, Gerhard. 1969. *The Collected Papers of Gerhard Gentzen*. Amsterdam: North-Holland Pub. Co.

Gibbard, Allan. 1990. *Wise Choices, Apt Feelings*. Cambridge, MA: Harvard University Press.
Gibbard, Allan. 2003. *Thinking How to Live*. Cambridge, MA: Harvard University Press.
Gibbs, Jr., Raymond W., ed. 2008. *The Cambridge Handbook of Metaphor and Thought*. Cambridge: Cambridge University Press.
Glazier, Martin. 2016. "Laws and the Completeness of the Fundamental." In *Reality Making*, edited by Mark Jago. 11–37. Oxford: Oxford University Press.
Göcke, Benedikt Paul. 2013. "Panentheism and Classical Theism." *Sophia* 52 (1): 61–75.
Göcke, Benedikt Paul. 2015. "Another Reply to Raphael Lataster." *Sophia* 54 (1): 99–102.
Goodman, Lenn Evan. 1996. *God of Abraham*. Oxford: Oxford University Press.
Goodman, Nelson. 1955. *Fact, Fiction, & Forecast*. Cambridge, MA: Harvard University Press.
Gregory, Alex. 2013. "The Guise of Reasons." *American Philosophical Quarterly* 50 (1): 63–72.
Grice, Paul. 1968. "Logic and Conversation." In *Studies in the Way of Words*. Cambridge: Cambridge University Press.
Grimm, Stephen R. 2010. "The Goal of Explanation." *Studies in the History and Philosophy of Science* 41 (4): 337–44.
Grimm, Stephen R. 2011. "Understanding." In *The Routledge Companion to Epistemology*, edited by Duncan Pritchard and Sven Bernecker. Abingdon, UK: Routledge.
Gwiazda, Jeremy. 2011. "Worship and Threshold Obligations." *Religious Studies* 47 (4): 521–5.
Hacking, Ian. 1967. "Possibility." *Philosophical Review* 76 (2): 143–68.
Hájek, Alan and Philip Pettit. 2004. "Desire beyond Belief." *Australasian Journal of Philosophy* 82 (1): 77–92.
Hartshorne, Charles. 1984. *Omnipotence and Other Theological Mistakes*. Albany, NY: State University of New York Press.
Hasker, William. 1989. *God, Time and Knowledge*. Ithaca: Cornell University Press.
Hasker, William. 2001. *The Emergent Self*. Ithaca: Cornell University Press.
Hasker, William. 2010. "Objections to Social Trinitarianism." *Religious Studies* 46 (4): 421–39.
Hasker, William. 2011. "Deception and the Trinity: A Rejoinder to Tuggy." *Religious Studies* 47 (1): 117–20.
Hasker, William. 2013. *Providence, Evil and the Openness of God*. London: Routledge.
Hasker, William. 2016. "Philosophical Arminianism: A Breakthrough in the Foreknowledge Controversy?" *Religious Studies* 52 (3): 333–44. http://dx.doi.org/10.1017/S0034412515000372.
Hawthorne, John. 2004. *Knowledge and Lotteries*. Oxford: Oxford University Press.
Heil, John. 2003. *From an Ontological Point of View*. Oxford: Oxford University Press.
Helm, Paul. 2010. *Eternal God: A Study of God without Time*. Oxford: Oxford University Press.
Hempel, Carl G. 1950. "Problems and Changes in the Empiricist Criterion of Meaning." *Revue Internationale de Philosophie* 41 (11): 41–63.
Hewitt, Simon. 2019. "God Is Not a Person." *International Journal for Philosophy of Religion* 85 (3): 281–-96. http://dx.doi.org/10.1007/s11153-018-9678-x.
Heyting, A. 1956. *Intuitionism*. Amsterdam: North-Holland Pub. Co.
Hill, Jr., Thomas E. 1971. "Kant on Imperfect Duty and Supererogation." *Kant-Studien* 62 (1–4): 55–76.
Hintikka, Jaakko. 1962. *Knowledge and Belief*. Ithaca: Cornell University Press.

Hoffman, Joshua and Gary Rosenkrantz. 2017. "Omnipotence." In *The Stanford Encyclopedia of Philosophy*, edited by Edward N. Zalta. Metaphysics Research Lab, Stanford University, winter 2017 edn. Palo Alto, CA.
Howard-Snyder, Daniel, ed. 1996. *The Evidential Argument from Evil*. Bloomington, IN: Indiana University Press.
Huemer, Michael. 2007. "Epistemic Possibility." *Synthese* 156 (1): 119–42.
Humberstone, I. L. 1987. "Wanting as Believing." *Canadian Journal of Philosophy* 17 (March): 49–62.
Humphreys, Paul. 1997a. "How Properties Emerge." *Philosophy of Science* 64 (1): 1–17.
Humphreys, Paul W. 1997b. "Emergence, Not Supervenience." *Philosophy of Science Supplement* 64 (4): 337–45.
Humphreys, Paul. 2017. *Emergence*. New York: Oxford University Press.
Jantzen, Grace. 1984. *God's World, God's Body*. London: Darton, Longman & Todd.
Johnston, Mark. 2009. *Saving God: Religion After Idolatry*. Princeton: Princeton University Press.
Kagan, Shelly. 1989. *The Limits of Morality*. Oxford: Clarendon Press.
Kelp, Christoph. 2015. "Understanding Phenomena." *Synthese* 192 (12): 3799–816.
Kenny, Anthony. 1979. *The God of the Philosophers*. Oxford: Oxford University Press.
Khalifa, Kareem. 2012. "Inaugurating Understanding or Repackaging Explanation?" *Philosophy of Science* 79 (1): 15–37.
Khalifa, Kareem. 2013a. "Is Understanding Explanatory or Objectual?" *Synthese* 190 (6): 1153–71.
Khalifa, Kareem. 2013b. "Understanding, Grasping, and Luck." *Episteme* 10 (1): 1–17.
Kim, Jaegwon. 2005. *Physicalism, or Something Near Enough*. Princeton: Princeton University Press.
Kim, Jaegwon. 2006. "Emergence: Core Ideas and Issues." *Synthese* 151 (3): 547–59.
Kleene, Stephen Cole. 1965. *The Foundations of Intuitionistic Mathematics*. Amsterdam: North-Holland Pub. Co.
Kment, Boris. 2014. *Modality and Explanatory Reasoning*. Oxford: Oxford University Press.
Kosso, Peter. 2007. "Scientific Understanding." *Foundations of Science* 12 (2), 173–88.
Kretzmann, Paul E. 1922. "The 'Angel of the Lord' in the Old Testament." *Theological Monthly* II (2): 33–6.
Kriegel, Uriah. 2015. "Existence, Fundamentality, and the Scope of Ontology." *Argumenta* 1 (1): 97–109.
Kripke, Saul A. 1977. "Speaker's Reference and Semantic Reference." *Midwest Studies in Philosophy* 2: 255–96.
Kripke, Saul. 1980. *Naming and Necessity*. Cambridge, MA: Harvard University Press.
Kvanvig, Jonathan L. 1985. "Traditional and Limited Doctrines of Omniscience." Presentation at the Eastern Division Meetings of the American Philosophical Association.
Kvanvig, Jonathan L. 1986. *The Possibility of an All-Knowing God*. London: MacMillan Press.
Kvanvig, Jonathan L. 1989a. "The Analogy Argument for a Limited Acccount of Omniscience." *International Philosophical Quarterly* 29: 129–38.
Kvanvig, Jonathan L. 1989b. "Conservatism and Its Virtues." *Synthese* 79: 143–163.
Kvanvig, Jonathan L. 1989c. "Unknowable Truths and the Doctrine of Omniscience." *Journal of the American Academy of Religion* 57 (3): 485–507.
Kvanvig, Jonathan L. 2003. *The Value of Knowledge and the Pursuit of Understanding*. Cambridge: Cambridge University Press.
Kvanvig, Jonathan L. 2006. "Epistemic Closure Principles." *Philosophy Compass* 1 (3): 256–67.

Kvanvig, Jonathan L. 2008a. "Closure and Alternative Possibilities." In *Oxford Handbook of Skepticism*, edited by John Greco. 456–84. Oxford: Oxford University Press.
Kvanvig, Jonathan L. 2008b. "Pointless Truth." *Midwest Studies in Philosophy* 32: 199–212.
Kvanvig, Jonathan L. 2009a. "Conservation, Concurrence, and Counterfactuals of Freedom." In *Metaphysics and God*, edited by Kevin Timpe. 112–26. Malden, MA: Blackwell.
Kvanvig, Jonathan L. 2009b. "Knowledge, Assertion, and Lotteries." In *Williamson on Knowledge*, edited by Duncan Pritchard and Patrick Greenough. 140–60. Oxford: Oxford University Press.
Kvanvig, Jonathan L. 2009c. "Precis of *The Value of Knowledge and the Pursuit of Understanding*." In *Epistemic Value*, edited by Duncan Pritchard, Adrian Haddock, and Alan Millar. 309–13. Oxford: Oxford University Press.
Kvanvig, Jonathan L. 2009d. "Responses to Critics." In *Epistemic Value*, edited by Duncan Pritchard, Adrian Haddock, and Alan Millar. 339–53. Oxford: Oxford University Press.
Kvanvig, Jonathan L. 2011a. "Against Pragmatic Encroachment." *Logos & Episteme* 2 (1): 77–85.
Kvanvig, Jonathan L. 2011b. *Destiny and Decision: Essays in Philosophical Theology*. Oxford: Oxford University Press.
Kvanvig, Jonathan L. 2011c. "The Rational Significance of Reflective Ascent." In *Evidentialism and Its Critics*, edited by Trent Dougherty. 34–54. Oxford: Oxford University Press.
Kvanvig, Jonathan L. 2014. *Rationality and Reflection*. Oxford: Oxford University Press.
Kvanvig, Jonathan L. 2017a. "The Cognitive Dimension of Heavenly Bliss." In *Paradise Understood: New Philosophical Essays about Heaven*, edited by T. Ryan Byerly and Eric Silverman. 62–81. Oxford: Oxford University Press.
Kvanvig, Jonathan L. 2017b. "Creation and Conservation." In *The Stanford Encyclopedia of Philosophy*, edited by Edward N. Zalta. Metaphysics Research Lab, Stanford University, fall 2008 edn.
Kvanvig, Jonathan L. 2018. *Faith and Humility*. Oxford: Oxford University Press.
Kvanvig, Jonathan L. 2021a. "Metatheology and the Ontology of Divinity," In *The Divine Nature: Personal and A-Personal Perspectives*, edited by Simon Kittle, (Abingdon: Routledge, forthcoming 2021).
Kvanvig, Jonathan L. 2019b. "Theoretical Unity in Epistemology." In *Knowledge, Skepticism, and Defeat: Themes from Klein*, edited by Cherie Braden, Branden Fitelson, and Rodrigo Borges. pp. 39–56. New York: Springer.
Kvanvig, Jonathan L. 2021. "Theoretical Unity and the Priority of Propositional Justification." In *Doxastic and Propositional Justification*, edited by Luis R. G. Oliveira and Paul Silva. Oxford: Oxford University Press.
Kvanvig, Jonathan L. and Hugh J. McCann. 1988. "Divine Conservation and the Persistence of the World." In *Divine and Human Action: Essays in the Metaphysics of Theism*, edited by Thomas V. Morris. 13–49. Ithaca: Cornell University Press.
Lakoff, George. 1993. "The Contemporary Theory of Metaphor." In *Metaphor and Thought*, edited by Andrew Ortony. 2–202. Cambridge: Cambridge University Press.
Lataster, Raphael. 2014. "The Attractiveness of Panentheism—a Reply to Benedikt Paul Göcke." *Sophia* 53 (3): 389–95.
Lataster, Raphael. 2015. "Theists Misrepresenting Panentheism—Another Reply to Benedikt Paul Göcke." *Sophia* 54 (1): 93–8.
Lauria, Federico and Julien Deonna. 2017a. "Introduction. Reconsidering Some Dogmas About Desire." In *The Nature of Desire*, edited by Federico Lauria and Julien Deonna. New York: Oxford University Press.

Lauria, Federico and Julien Deonna. 2017b. *The Nature of Desire*. New York: Oxford University Press.
Leftow, Brian. 2006. "Divine Simplicity." *Faith and Philosophy* 23: 365–80.
Leftow, Brian. 2016. "Naturalistic Pantheism." In *Alternative Concepts of God*, edited by Andrei Buckareff and Yujin Nagasawa. 64–88. Oxford: Oxford University Press.
Lesher, James H. 1992. *Xenophanes of Colophy: Fragments: A Text and Translation with Commentary*. Toronto: University of Toronto Press.
Levine, Michael. 1994. *Pantheism: A Non-theistic Concept of Deity*. London: Routledge.
Lewis, David. 1979. "Counterfactual Dependence and Time's Arrow." *Noûs* 13: 455–76.
Lewis, David. 1988. "Desire as Belief." *Mind* 97 (418): 323–32.
Lewis, David. 1994. "Humean Supervenience Debugged." *Mind* 103: 473–90.
Lewis, David. 1996. "Desire as Belief II." *Mind* 105 (418): 303–13.
Lewis, David. 2001. "Truthmaking and Difference-Making." *Noûs* 35: 602–15.
Lipman, Martin A. 2016. "Against Fundamentality Based Metaphysics." *Noûs* URL: https://doi.org/10.1111/nous.12179.
Lipner, J. J. 1984. "The World as God's 'Body': In Pursuit of Dialogue with Rāmānuja." *Religious Studies* 20 (1): 145–61.
Loux, Michael J. 1978. *Substance and Attribute a Study in Ontology*. Dordrecht, Holland: D. Reidel.
Ludlow, Peter and Gabriel Segal. 2004. "On a Unitary Semantical Analysis for Definite and Indefinite Descriptions." In *Descriptions and Beyond*, edited by Marga Reimer and Anne Bezuidenhout. 420–37. Oxford: Oxford University Press.
MacFarlane, John. 2011. "Epistemic Modals Are Assessment-Sensitive." In *Epistemic Modality*, edited by Andy Egan and B. Weatherson. Oxford: Oxford University Press.
Mackie, John L. 1977. *Ethics: Inventing Right and Wrong*. New York: Penguin Books.
Mackie, John Leslie. 1982. *The Miracle of Theism*. Oxford: Oxford University Press.
Mander, William J. 2000. "Omniscience and Pantheism." *Heythrop Journal* 41 (2): 199–208.
Marcus, Ruth Barcan. 1961. "Modalities and Intensional Languages." *Synthese* 13 (4): 303–22.
Martin, Christian B. 2007. *The Mind in Nature*. Oxford: Oxford University Press.
Marušić, Berislav and John Schwenkler. forthcoming. "Intending Is Believing: A Defense of Strong Cognitivism." *Analytic Philosophy*.
Mawson, Tim J. 2005. *Belief in God: An Introduction to the Philosophy of Religion*. Oxford: Oxford University Press.
Mawson, Tim. 2006. "God's Body." *Heythrop Journal* 47 (2): 171–81.
McCann, Hugh J. 2012. *Creation and the Sovereignty of God*. Bloomington: Indiana University Press.
McCann, Hugh J. and Jonathan L. Kvanvig. 1991. "The Occasionalist Proselytizer: A Modified Catechism." In *Philosophical Perspectives 5: Philosophy of Religion*, edited by James E. Tomberlin. 587–616. Atascadero, CA: Ridgeview Publishing Co.
Meconi, David Vincent. 1999. "What Has Athens to Do with Jerusalem?" *Review of Metaphysics* 53 (1): 190–91.
Mehta, Neil. 2017. "Can Grounding Characterize Fundamentality?" *Analysis* 77 (1): 74–9.
Meier, Samuel A. 1999. "Angel of Yahweh." In *Dictionary of Deities and Demons in the Bible*, edited by Karel van der Toorn, Bob Becking, and Pieter W. van der Horst. 53–9. Grand Rapids, MI: Eerdmans, 2nd edn.
Menzel, Christopher P. 1986. "A Complete, Type-Free "Second-Order" Logic and Its Philosophical Foundations." Tech. Rep. CSLI-86-40, Center for the Study of Language and Information, Stanford University.

Menzel, Christopher. 2016. "Problems with the Bootstrapping Objection to Theistic Activism." *American Philosophical Quarterly* 53 (1): 55–68.
Menzel, Christopher P. forthcoming. "In Defense of the Possibilism-Actualism Distinction." *Philosophical Studies*.
Merricks, Trenton. 2001. *Objects and Persons*. Oxford: Oxford University Press.
Mill, John Stuart. 1874 [1957]. *Theism*. New York: Liberal Arts Press.
Mizrahi, Moti. 2012. "Idealizations and Scientific Understanding." *Philosophical Studies* 160 (2): 237–52.
Molnar, George. 2003. *Powers: A Study in Metaphysics*. Oxford: Oxford University Press.
Moltmann, Jürgen. 1981. *The Trinity and the Kingdom: The Doctrine of God*. Philadelphia: Fortress Press.
Moore, G. E. 1903a. "The Refutation of Idealism." *Mind* 12 (48): 433–53.
Moore, George Edward. 1903b. *Principia Ethica*. Cambridge: Cambridge University Press.
Moore, George Edward. 1925. "A Defence of Common Sense." In *Contemporary British Philosophy*, edited by J. H. Muirhead. 193–223. London: Allen & Unwin.
Moore, George Edward. 1939. "Proof of an External World." *Proceedings of the British Academy* 25: 273–300.
Morris, Thomas V. 1984. "The God of Abraham, Isaac, and Anselm." *Faith and Philosophy* 1 (2): 177–87.
Morris, Thomas. 1987a. *Anselmian Explorations*. Notre Dame: University of Notre Dame Press.
Morris, Thomas. 1987b. "Perfect Being Theology." *Noûs* 21: 19–30.
Morris, Thomas V. 1991. *Our Idea of God: An Introduction to Philosophical Theology*. Downers Grove: InterVarsity Press.
Morris, Thomas V. and Christopher P. Menzel. 1986. "Absolute Creation." *American Philosophical Quarterly* 23: 353–62.
Moss, Jessica. 2010. "Aristotle's Non-trivial, Non-insane View That Everyone Always Desires Things under the Guise of the Good." In *Desire, Practical Reason, and the Good*, edited by Sergio Tenenbaum. 65–82. Oxford: Oxford University Press.
Mullins, Ryan T. 2016a. "The Difficulty with Demarcating Panentheism." *Sophia* 55 (3): 325–46.
Mullins, Ryan T. 2016b. "Divine Perfection and Creation." *Heythrop Journal* 57 (1): 122–34.
Mullins, Ryan T. 2016c. *The End of the Timeless God*. Oxford: Oxford University Press.
Mullins, Ryan T. 2018. "Why Can't the Impassible God Suffer? Analytic Reflections on Divine Blessedness." *TheoLogica: An International Journal for Philosophy of Religion and Philosophical Theology* 2 (1): 3–22.
Mumford, Stephen. 2004. *Laws in Nature*. Abingdon: Routledge.
Mumford, Stephen and Rani Lill Anjum. 2011. *Getting Causes from Powers*. Oxford: Oxford University Press.
Murphy, Mark C. 2017. *God's Own Ethics: Norms of Divine Agency and the Argument From Evil*. Oxford: Oxford University Press.
Nagasawa, Yujin. 2008. "A New Defense of Anselmian Theism." *Philosophical Quarterly* 58: 577–96.
Nagasawa, Yujin. 2017. *Maximal God: A New Defense of Perfect Being Theism*. Oxford: Oxford University Press.
Nelson, Mark T. 1991. "Utilitarian Eschatology." *American Philosophical Quarterly* 28 (4): 339–47.
O'Connor, Timothy J. 2012. *Theism and Ultimate Explanation: The Necessary Shape of Contingency*. Malden, MA: Blackwell Publishing Ltd.

O'Connor, Timothy and Hong Yu Wong. 2015. "Emergent Properties." In *The Stanford Encyclopedia of Philosophy*, edited by Edward N. Zalta. Metaphysics Research Lab, Stanford University, summer 2015 edn.
Oppy, Graham. 1997. "Pantheism, Quantification and Mereology." *The Monist* 80 (2): 320–36.
Orsi, Francesco. 2015. "The Guise of the Good." *Philosophy Compass* 10 (10): 714–24.
Peacocke, Arthur. 2004. "'The End of All Our Exploring' in Science and Theology." *Zygon* 39 (2): 413–29.
Peters, Ted. 2007. "Models of God." *Philosophia* 35 (3–4): 273–88.
Pfeifer, Karl. 1997. "Pantheism as Panpsychism." *Conceptus: Zeitschrift Für Philosophie* 30 (77): 181–90.
Pfeifer, Karl. 2016. "Pantheism and Panpsychism." In *Alternative Conceptions of God: Essays on the Metaphysics of the Divine*, edited by Andrei Buckareff and Yujin Nagasawa. 41–9. New York: Oxford University Press.
Pinnock, Clark, Richard Rice, John Sanders, William Hasker, and David Basinger. 1994. *The Openness of God: A Biblical Challenge to the Traditional Understanding of God*. Downers Grove: InterVarsity Press.
Plantinga, Alvin. 1974. *The Nature of Necessity*. Oxford: Clarendon Press.
Plantinga, Alvin. 1980. *Does God Have a Nature?* Milwaukee, WI: Marquette University Press.
Polka, Brayton. 2015. "Hebrew Scripture and the Wisdom of Philosophical Reason, or What Has Athens to Do with Jerusalem?" *The European Legacy* 20 (3): 273–83.
Pollock, John. 1974. *Knowledge and Justification*. Ithaca: Cornell University Press.
Pollock, John L. 2001. "Defeasible Reasoning with Variable Degrees of Justification." *Artificial Intelligence* 133: 233–82.
Preston, Aaron. 2005. "The Implications of Recent Work on the History of Analytic Philosophy." *The Bertrand Russell Society Quarterly* 127: 11–30.
Prince, Huw. 1989. "Defending Desire-as-Belief." *Mind* 98 (January): 119–27.
Pritchard, Duncan. 2009. "Knowledge, Understanding, and Epistemic Value." *Royal Institute of Philosophy Supplement* 84: 19–43.
Pritchard, Duncan. 2010. "Knowledge and Understanding." In *The Nature and Value of Knowledge: Three Investigations*, edited by Adrian Haddock, Alan Millar, and Duncan Pritchard. 3–90. Oxford: Oxford University Press.
Quine, W. V. 1950. *Methods of Logic*. Cambridge, MA: Harvard University Press.
Quine, W. V. 1953a. *From a Logical Point of View*. Cambridge, MA: Harvard University Press.
Quine, W. V. 1953b. "Three Grades of Modal Involvment." *Proceedings of the XIth International Congress of Philosophy* 14: 65–81.
Quine, W. V. 1970. *Philosophy of Logic*. Cambridge, MA: Harvard University Press.
Quine, Willard V. O. 1951. "Two Dogmas of Empiricism." *Philosophical Review* 60 (1): 20–43.
Quine, Willard V. O. 1948. "On What There Is." *The Review of Metaphysics* 2 (5): 21–38.
Raven, Michael J. 2016. "Fundamentality without Foundations." *Philosophy and Phenomenological Research* 93 (3): 607–26.
Rawls, John. 1971. *A Theory of Justice*. Cambridge, MA: Harvard University Press.
Raz, Joseph. 2010. "On the Guise of the Good." In *Desire, Practical Reason, and the Good*, edited by Sergio Tenenbaum. 111–38. Oxford: Oxford University Press.
Rehm, David. 1999. "What Has Athens to Do with Jerusalem?" *Ancient Philosophy* 19 (2): 436–40.

Roberts, John. 2010. "Some Laws of Nature Are Metaphysically Contingent." *Australasian Journal of Philosophy* 88 (3): 445–57.
Rogers, Katherin A. 2000. *Perfect Being Theology*. Edinburgh: Edinburgh University Press.
Rohwer, Yasha. 2014. "Lucky Understanding without Knowledge." *Synthese* 191 (5): 1–15.
Rorty, Richard, ed. 1968. *The Linguistic Turn: Recent Essays in Philosophical Method*. Chicago: University of Chicago Press.
Rosen, Gideon. 2006. "The Limits of Contingency." In *Identity and Modality*, edited by Fraser MacBride. 13–39. Oxford: Oxford University Press.
Rosen, Gideon. 2009. "Metaphysical Dependence: Grounding and Reduction." In *Modality: Metaphysics, Logic, and Epistemology*, edited by Bob Hale and Aviv Hoffmann. 109–36. Oxford: Oxford University Press.
Rosen, Gideon. 2017. "Ground by Law." *Philosophical Issues* 27 (1): 279–301.
Ross, W. D. 1930. *The Right and the Good*. Oxford: Oxford University Press.
Russell, Bertrand. 1903. *Principles of Mathematics*. Cambridge: Cambridge University Press.
Russell, Bertrand. 1905. "On Denoting." *Mind* 14 (56): 479–93.
Russell, Bertrand. 1919. *Introduction to Mathematical Philosophy*. London: Allen & Unwin.
Sanders, John. 1997. *The God Who Risks*. Downers Grove: InterVarsity Press.
Sayre-McCord, Geoff. 2014. "Metaethics." In *The Stanford Encyclopedia of Philosophy*, edited by Edward N. Zalta. Metaphysics Research Lab, Stanford University, summer 2014 edn.
Schaffer, Jonathan. 2004. "Quiddistic Knowledge." *Philosophical Studies* 123 (1–2): 1–32.
Schaffer, Jonathan. 2009. "On What Grounds What." In *Metametaphysics: New Essays on the Foundations of Ontology*, edited by David J. Chalmers, Ryan Wasserman, and David Manley. 347–383. New York: Oxford University Press.
Schaffer, Jonathan. 2016. "Grounding in the Image of Causation." *Philosophical Studies* 173 (1): 49–100.
Schaffer, Jonathan. 2017. "Laws for Metaphysical Explanation." *Philosophical Issues* 27 (1): 302–21.
Searle, John. 1990. "Collective Intentions and Actions." In *Intentions in Communication*, edited by Philip R. Cohen, Jerry Morgan, and Martha Pollack. 401–15. MIT Press.
Segerberg, Krister. 1976. "A Neglected Family of Aggregation Problems in Ethics." *Noûs* 10 (2): 221–44.
Sellars, Wilfred. 1956. "Empiricism and the Philosophy of Mind." In *Minnesota Studies in the Philosophy of Science*, edited by H. Feigl and M. Scriven. Vol. 1, 253–39. Minneapolis: University of Minnesota Press.
Setiya, Kieran. 2010. "Sympathy for the Devil." In *Desire, Practical Reason, and the Good*, edited by Sergio Tenenbaum. 82–110. Oxford University Press.
Sidelle, Alan. 2002. "On the Metaphysical Contingency of Laws of Nature." In *Conceivability and Possibility*, edited by John Hawthorne and Tamar Gendler. 309–36. Oxford: Oxford University Press.
Singh, Keshav. forthcoming. "Acting and Believing under the Guise of Normative Reasons." *Philosophy and Phenomenological Research*.
Smart, Ninian. 1972. *The Concept of Worship*. New York: St. Martin's.
Smith, James K. 2013. *Imagining the Kingdom: How Worship Works*. Grand Rapids, MI: Baker Academic.
Smuts, Aaron. 2012. "The Power to Make Others Worship." *Religious Studies* 48 (2): 221–37.
Speaks, Jeff. 2018. *The Greatest Possible Being*. Oxford: Oxford University Press.
Stanley, Jason. 2005. *Knowledge and Practical Interests*. Oxford: Oxford University Press.

Stevenson, Charles Leslie. 1937. "The Emotive Meaning of Ethical Terms." *Mind* 46 (181): 14–31. http://dx.doi.org/10.1093/mind/XLVI.181.14.

Stevenson, Charles Leslie. 1944. *Ethics and Language*. New Haven: Yale University Press.

Strevens, Michael. 2013. "No Understanding without Explanation." *Studies in History and Philosophy of Science Part A* 44 (3): 510–15.

Stump, Eleonore. 2010. *Wandering in Darkness: Narrative and the Problem of Suffering*. Oxford: Oxford University Press.

Stump, Eleonore. 2016. *The God of the Bible and the God of the Philosophers*. Milwaukee: Marquette University Press.

Stump, Eleonore and Norman Kretzmann. 1981. "Eternity." *The Journal of Philosophy* 78: 429–58.

Swinburne, Richard. 1977. *The Coherence of Theism*. Oxford: Oxford University Press.

Swinburne, Richard. 1981. *Faith and Reason*. Oxford: Oxford University Press.

Swoyer, Chris. 1982. "The Nature of Natural Laws." *Australasian Journal of Philosophy* 60 (3): 1982.

Tahko, Tuomas E. 2015. *An Introduction to Metametaphysics*. Cambridge: Cambridge University Press.

Taliaferro, Charles. 1987. "God's World, God's Body." *Faith and Philosophy* 4 (1): 93–8.

Teller, Paul. 1972. "Epistemic Possibility." *Philosophia* 2 (4): 303–20.

Tenenbaum, Sergio. 2013. "Guise of the Good." In *The International Encyclopedia of Ethics*, edited by Hugh LaFollette. Ch. 659. Wiley-Blackwell.

Timpe, Kevin. 2013. "Neo-classical Theism." In *Models of God and Alternative Ultimate Realities*, edited by Jeanine Diller and Asa Kasher. 195–204. New York: Springer.

Turri, John. 2015. "Understanding and the Norm of Explanation." *Philosophia* 43 (4): 1171–5.

Vallentyne, Peter and Shelly Kagan. 1997. "Infinite Value and Finitely Additive Value Theory." *Journal of Philosophy* 94 (1): 5–26.

van Cleve, James. 1994. "Descartes and the Destruction of the Eternal Truths." *Ratio* 7 (1): 58–62.

van Cleve, James. 2018. "Brute necessity." *Philosophy Compass* 13: e12516. http://dx.doi.org/10.1111/phc3.12516.

van Fraassen, Bas. 1996. "Science, Materialism, and False Consciousness." In *Warrant in Contemporary Epistemology: Essays in Honor of Alvin Plantinga's Theory of Knowledge*. 149–82. Rowman Littlefield.

van Inwagen, Peter. 1983. *An Essay on Free Will*. Oxford: Clarendon Press.

van Inwagen, Peter. 2008. "What Does an Omniscient Being Know about the Future?" In *Oxford Studies in Philosophy of Religion*, edited by Jonathan L. Kvanvig. Vol. 1, 216–30. Oxford: Oxford University Press.

van Til, Cornelius. 1976. *The Defense of the Faith*. Philadelphia: Presbyterian and Reformed Publishing Co.

van Til, Cornelius. 1977. *A Christian Theory of Knowledge*. Nutley, NJ: Presbyterian and Reformed Publishing Co.

Velleman, J. David. 1992. "The Guise of the Good." *Noûs* 26 (1): 3–26.

Volf, Miroslav. 1998. *After Our Likeness: The Church as the Image of the Trinity*. Grand Rapids, MI: Eerdmans Publishing.

Wainwright, William J. 1974. "God's Body." *Journal of the American Academy of Religion* 42 (3): 470–81.

Ward, Keith. 1999. "The God of the Philosophers and the God of Abraham, Isaac, and Jacob." *Journal of Jewish Thought and Philosophy* 8 (2): 157–70.

Weintraub, Ruth. 2007. "Desire as Belief, Lewis Notwithstanding." *Analysis* 67 (2): 116–22.
Wierenga, Edward. 1979. "Intrinsic Maxima and Omnibenevolence." *International Journal for Philosophy of Religion* 10 (1): 41–50. http://dx.doi.org/10.1007/BF00143154.
Wierenga, Edward. 1989. *The Nature of God*. Ithaca: Cornell University Press.
Wierenga, Edward. 2011. "Augustinian Perfect Being Theology and the God of Abraham, Isaac, and Jacob." *International Journal for Philosophy of Religion* 69 (2): 139–51.
Wilkenfeld, Daniel A., Dillon Plunkett, and Tania Lombrozo. 2016. "Depth and Deference: When and Why We Attribute Understanding." *Philosophical Studies* 173 (2): 373–93.
Williams, Bernard. 1985. *Ethics and the Limits of Philosophy*. Cambridge, MA: Harvard University Press.
Williamson, Timothy. 1994. *Vagueness*. New York: Routledge.
Williamson, Timothy. 2000. *Knowledge and Its Limits*. Oxford: Oxford University Press.
Williamson, Timothy. 2013. *Modal Logic as Metaphysics*. Oxford: Oxford University Press.
Wilsch, Tobias. 2015. "The Nomological Account of Ground." *Philosophical Studies* 172 (12): 3293–312.
Wilson, Alastair. 2016. "Grounding Entails Counterpossible Non-Triviality." *Philosophy and Phenomenological Research* 92 (3): 716–28.
Wilson, Jessica M. 2013. "Nonlinearity and Metaphysical Emergence." In *Metaphysics and Science*, edited by Stephen Mumford and Matthew Tugby. 201–31. Oxford: Oxford University Press.
Wilson, Jessica. 2014. "No Work for a Theory of Grounding." *Inquiry : An Interdisciplinary Journal of Philosophy* 57 (5–6): 535–79.
Wolff, Johanna. 2013. "Are Conservation Laws Metaphysically Necessary?" *Philosophy of Science* 80 (5): 898–906.
Woltersdorff, Nicholas. 1975. "God Everlasting." In *God and the Good: Essays in Honor of Henry Stob*, edited by Clifton J. Orlebeke and Lewis B. Smedes. 181–203. Grand Rapids, MI: Eerdmans.
Wolterstorff, Nicholas. 1991. "Divine Simplicity." *Philosophical Perpectives* 5: 531–52.
Wong, Hong Yu. 2005. "The Metaphysics of Emergence." *Noûs* 39 (4): 658–78.
Zagzebski, Linda. 2006. "Omnisubjectivity." In *Oxford Studies in Philosophy of Religion, Volume 1*, edited by Jonathan L. Kvanvig. Oxford: Oxford University Press.

# Index

A posteriori 43
A priori 43
Abraham xi, 28
Adams, Marilyn 97
Adams, Robert 120
Agent causation 83
Akrasia 127, 205
Alanen, Lilli 88, 98
Analytic philosophy 6, 214
Anjum, Rani Lill 87
Anscombe, G. E. M. 121
Anselianism 31
Anselm vii, 7, 144, 188
Anselmian 144, 145, 151, 164, 173, 187, 200, 202
Anselmianism 7, 95, 136–7, 145
Anthropomorphism 57, 83, 90
Anti-realism 37
Apophaticism 83
Aquinas 89, 98, 188
Aristotelian 156, 191, 199, 200
Aristotle 5, 15, 77, 200
Armstrong, David 98, 205
Aseity 41, 56
Atemporality 13
Atmanspacher, Harald 190, 205
Attitudinalism 129, 158
Augustine viii, 87, 97, 172, 188, 205
Augustinian 172
Ayer, A. J. 6, 158, 205

Baillie, James 76, 205
Baker, Derek 125, 205
Barth, Karl 44
Barth, Karl 44, 191, 205
Basic actions 88
Bauer, William 87, 205
Baumberger, Christoph 85, 205
Bayne, Timothy 31, 120, 149, 150, 175, 177, 205
Bennett, Jonathan 88, 98, 205
Bennett, Karen 31, 206
Bernstein, Sara 31, 206

Biernacki, Loriliai 190, 206
Bigelow, John 14, 206
Bird, Alexander 84, 87, 206
Bivalence 102, 127, 193
Blackburn, Simon 158, 206
Boethius viii
Boethius viii, 188
Bohn, Einar Duenger 11, 206
Bradley, F. H. 6, 206
Bradley, Richard 135, 206
Brahma 18
Brahman 66
Brand, Myles 135, 206
Bratman, Michael 135, 206
Brentano, Franz 6
Broad, C. D. 146, 156, 206
Brookes, Frances 22, 206
Brouwer, L. E. J. 39, 127, 206
Buckareff, Andrei 62–63, 206

Calvin, John 163–171, 206
Camp, Wesley Van 85, 206
Campbell, Douglas 135, 206
Cantorian 59–60
Carnap, Rudolf 6, 206
Cartesian 62, 76
Cartesian voluntarism 88, 98
Causation 90
Cebes 65
Chisholm, Roderick 6, 121, 207
Christian 23
Classical Theism 10, 87, 188, 189, 190, 191, 195, 197
Clayton, Philip 156, 190, 207
Cognitivism 157
Coleman, Sam 90, 207
Collins, John 135, 207
Conceivability 6
Conee, Earl 43, 207
Confirmation ix, 6
Constitution 149, 154–157
Corruptibility 65–68
Cosmological arguments viii, 10

Counterfactuals 5
Craig, William Lane 178, 189, 191, 207
Cray, Wesley D. 31, 207
Cross, Charles 135, 207
Culp, John 190, 207
Curley, Edward 88, 98, 207
Cyprian 29

Dasgupta, Surendranath 65–66
Daskal, Steven 135, 207
Davies, Brian 89, 207
Davies, Paul 156, 207
Davison, Scott 178, 207
De dicto 113
De re 113
De te 114
Demiurge 57–58
Deonna, Julien 135, 207
DeRose, Keith 141, 207
DeRosset, Louis 104, 207
Descriptive 31, 35, 121
Designer 9
Divine conceptualism 15, 16
Divine Foundationalism 11
Donnellan, Keith 77, 208
Drewery, Alice 84, 208
Dualism 64
Dummett, Michael 6, 39, 127, 208

Eilan, Naomi 114, 208
Emergentism 156–157
Emotivism 158
Epistemic v, 9
Epistemological 10
Epistemological project 11
Epistemology 6
Eternality 185, 188, 189, 195
Ethical monotheism 123, 127
Ethical naturalism 129, 130
Ethical Theory vi, 38, 39
Ethics vii
Eusebius 29
Evaluative 31, 35, 121, 157
Event causation 83
Excluded middle 102, 127, 193
Expressivism 129, 158

Faithfulness 185
Fallibilism 199
Fantl, Jeremy 124, 208

Fatalism 14
Fetzer, James 141, 208
Findlay, J. N. 165–166, 168, 208
Fine, Kit 31, 99, 208
First cause 9
Flint, Thomas 128, 132, 194, 208
Florio, Ciro 76, 208
Foundationalism 11
Frankfurt, Harry 88, 98, 208
Freddoso, Alfred 132, 208
Freedom 185
Freedom/foreknowledge problem 128
Frege, Gottlob 6, 39, 208
Frigerio, Aldo 76, 208
Fundamentality viii, 31, 165

Garcia, Jorge 135, 208
Gardiner, Georgi 85, 208
Garrett, Susan R. 29, 208
Gaunilo 145
Geach, Peter 173, 193, 194, 208
Geisler, Norman 200, 208
Gentzen, Gerhard 39, 209
Gibbard, Allan 158, 209
Gibbs, Jr., Raymond W. 22, 209
Glazier, Martin 85, 209
Gocke, Benedikt 189, 190, 209
Goodman, Lenn 162, 209
Goodman, Nelson 6, 209
Goodness, metaphysical 56, 122
Goodness, moral 123
Grace 185, 195
Gregory, Alex 125, 209
Grice, H. P. 21, 77, 113, 209
Gricean 113
Grimm, Stephen 85, 209
Grounding 31, 85, 165, 175
Guise of the good thesis 124
Gwaizda, Jeremy 31, 209

Habermas, Gary 191
Hacking, Ian 141, 209
Hagar 28
Hagen, Jason 76, 209
Hajek, Alan 135, 209
Hartshorne, Charles 190, 209
Hasker, William 75, 78, 96, 128, 156, 173, 190, 209
Hawthorne, John 124, 209
Heil, John 87, 209

Helm, Paul  188, 209
Hempel, Carl  54, 209
Hewitt, Simon  90, 209
Heyting, Arend  39, 209
Hill, Tom  30, 209
Hinduism  xi, 18
Hintikka, Jaakko  141, 210
Hoffman, Joshua  131, 210
Holiness  185, 195
Howard-Snyder, Daniel  87, 210
Huemer, Michael  141, 210
Humberstone, Lloyd  135, 210
Hume, David  121
Humean  36, 85, 121, 157
Humeanism  158
Humphreys, Paul  156, 210

Imaginability  6
Immanence  185
Immutability  41, 56, 185, 188, 189, 195
Impassability  41, 56, 188, 189, 195
Incommensurability  146
Ineffability  48
Intuitionism  39
Irenaeus  29
Isaac  28
Isaiah  24

Jantzen, Grace  61, 210
Jesus  21, 23, 26, 28
Johnston, Mark  50, 52, 53, 58–9, 61, 210
Justice  185, 195
Justin Martyr  29

Kagan, Shelly  60, 210
Kant, Immanuel  200
Karma  66
Kelp, Christoph  85, 210
Kenny, Anthony  162, 210
Khalifa, Kareem  85, 210
Kim, Jaegwon  62, 210
Kleene, Stephen  39, 210
Kment, Boris  85, 210
Kosso, Peter  85, 210
Kretzmann, Norman  189, 210
Kretzmann, Paul E.  29, 210
Kriegel, Uriah  31, 210
Kripke, Saul  vii, 6, 77, 200, 210

Lakoff, George  22, 211
Lataster, Raphael  190, 211
Lauria, Federico  135, 211
Laws of nature  84–89
Leftow, Brian  20–7, 59, 80, 112, 119, 212
Lesher, James  81, 212
Lewis, David  5, 14, 135, 154, 212
Libertarianism  128
Lipman, Martin  31, 212
Lipner, J. J.  61, 212
List, Christian  135, 212
Literal  22, 23
Logic  39
Logical Empiricism  6, 36, 200
Logical Positivism  6, 36
Lombard, Peter  188
Loux, Michael  15, 212
Love  195
Ludlow, Peter  77, 212

MacFarlane, John  141, 212
Mackie, J. L.  36, 86, 212
Marcus, Ruth Barcan  6, 212
Martin, Christian  87, 212
Marusic, Berislav  135, 212
Mawson, Tim  61, 188, 212
McCann, Hugh  53, 120, 170, 188, 211, 212
McDowell, Josh  191
McGrath, Matthew  124, 208
Meconi, David  162, 212
Mehta, Neil  31, 212
Meier, Samuel A.  29, 212
Meinongianism  14
Menzel, Christopher  14, 64, 98, 100, 104, 107, 178, 185, 212, 213
Mercy  185, 195
Merricks, Trenton  156, 213
Metaethics  vi, 35, 37, 38, 129
Metaphorical  22
Metaphysical  10
Metaphysical necessity  68, 85, 130
Metaphysical project  11
Metatheology  v, vi, 4, 6, 37–42, 46, 54, 55, 93, 119, 185, 191, 192, 195, 197
Mill, John Stuart  9, 10, 133, 135, 136, 213
Millian  133
Mizrahi, Moti  85, 213
Models  5
Molinism  128, 133

Molnar, George 87, 213
Moltmann, Jurgen 75, 78, 96, 213
Monism 14
Monotheism 56, 61, 73, 75, 78, 96, 110, 111, 128, 150, 185
Monotonicity ix
Moore, G. E. 6, 36, 121, 213
Moorean 90
Moral agency 55
Morris, Thomas V. 9, 10, 43, 98, 107, 136–8, 146–9, 167–72, 178, 189, 213
Moses vii, 157
Moss, Jessica 125, 213
Mullins, Ryan 189, 190, 213
Mumford, Stephen 87, 213
Murphy, Mark 5, 31, 145, 150, 151, 152, 153, 159, 213

Nagasawa, Yujin 31, 101, 120, 138–50, 166–77, 199, 202, 205, 213
Names for God 48–50
Naturalistic fallacy 36
Necessary existence 11
Necessitarianism 14, 64, 91
Necessity, accidental 98
Necessity, nomological 98
Nelson, Mark 60, 213
Neo-classical theism 188, 189, 195, 196, 197
Nominalism 15
Non-cognitivism 37
Non-literal 23
Normative 31, 35, 121, 157

O'Connor, Timothy 156, 189, 213, 214
Omnibenevolence 83, 134, 143, 168
Omnipotence 76, 109, 110, 134, 143
Omnipresence 109
Omniscience 82, 134, 143
Ontological argument 11, 82, 99, 100, 145
Ontology 14, 15, 16
Open Question argument 36
Orsi, Francesco 135, 214

Pairing problem 63
Palsgraff v. Long Island Railroad Co. 17
Panentheism 89, 190, 195
Pantheism 56, 87, 89, 190
Paul, St. 22, 28

Peacocke, Arthur 190, 214
Per impossibile reasoning 13, 17, 76, 86, 149
Peters, Ted 190, 214
Pettit, Phillip 135, 214
Pfiefer, Karl 87, 214
Phaedo 65
Philosophical theology 186, 195, 197
Pinnock, Clark 190, 214
Plantinga, Alvin 11, 19, 88, 98, 99, 138, 145, 189, 194, 214
Plato viii, 65, 77, 78, 79
Platonic 27, 123
Platonism 15, 16, 155
Polka, Brayton 162, 214
Polytheism 57, 96, 110, 112
Possibility, logical 6
Possibility, metaphysical 6
Pragmatic 9
Pragmatics 22
Preston, Aaron 6, 214
Price, Huw 135, 214
Pritchard, Duncan 85, 214
Pro tanto ix, x, 121, 152
Problem of the Pantheon 57, 78–9, 110
Process theology 190
Properties, accidental 5
Properties, essential 5, 19, 47
Properties, great-making 11
Protagoras 123

Quantification, restricted 16, 74
Quantification, unrestricted 16
Quine, W. V. O. 6, 15, 16, 19, 39, 214

Ramanuja 66
Ramsey, Frank 60, 214
Raven, Michael 31, 214
Rawls, John 46, 46, 214
Raz, Joseph 124, 125, 214
Realism 11, 15
Reference-dubbing 48
Reflective equilibrium 46–47
Rehm, David 162, 214
Revelation, general 42
Revelation, special 42
Righteousness 185, 195
Ritschl, Albrecht 38, 215

Roberts, John 84, 215
Rogers, Katherin 7, 8, 188, 215
Rohwer, Yasha 85, 215
Rorty, Richard 53, 215
Rosen, Gideon 31, 85, 215
Rosenkrantz, Gary 131, 215
Royce, Josiah 38
Russell, Bertrand 6, 39, 64, 73, 76, 77, 215
Russellianism 77–78
Ryle, Gilbert 6, 215

Sanders, John 190, 215
Sass, Hartmut 190, 215
Satan 28, 127
Sayre-McCord, Geoff vi, 215
Schaffer, Jonathan x, 13, 31, 84, 85, 156, 215
Schwenkler, John 135, 215
Scope fallacy 19
Searle, John 75, 215
Segal, Gabriel 78, 215
Segerberg, Krister 60, 215
Sellars, Wilfrid 6, 215
Semantic 10
Semantics 22
Setya, Kieran 125, 215
Shiva 18
Sidelle, Alan 84, 215
Sider, Ted 43, 215
Simplicity, divine 41, 56, 185, 188, 189, 195
Singh, Keshav 125, 215
Skepticism 3, 6, 43, 44, 121
Smart, Ninian 19, 21, 31, 215
Smith, James K. 23, 215
Smuts, Aaron 31, 214
Social trinitarianism 75, 79, 96
Socrates 77, 79, 123, 124, 125
Speaks, Jeff 48, 49, 52, 215
Stanley, Jason 124, 215
Stefansson, H. Orri 135, 216
Stevenson, Charles 158, 216
Stoics viii
Strevens, Michael 85, 216
Strobel, Lee 191
Stump, Eleonore 79, 114, 162, 189, 216

Submission vii, 25, 26, 80, 112–4, 120–1, 129, 153, 159, 170, 171, 176, 202
Subservience 25, 79, 112, 113
Supervenience 32, 33, 121, 122, 148, 149, 153, 154, 167
Surrender 25, 79, 112, 113
Swinburne, Richard 120, 173, 190, 193, 216
Swoyer, Christopher 84, 216
Synoptics 23

Tahko, Tuomas 31, 216
Taliaferro, Charles 61, 216
Teleological arguments viii, 10
Teller, Paul 141, 216
Tenenbaum, Sergio 125, 216
Tertullian 29
Theology vii, 3, 38, 40, 41, 42, 46
Theology, philosophical 6, 8, 14
Theory of obligation 36, 157
Theory of value 36, 157
Thomism 38, 41, 190, 191, 192
Timelessness 189
Timpe, Kevin 189, 216
Transcendence 41, 48, 56, 185
Transcendental argument 85
Trinitarianism 29, 75
Truthfulness 185, 195
Turri, John 85, 216

Vallentyne, Peter 60, 216
Value incommensurability 81, 147
van Cleve, James 88, 98, 89, 216
van Inwagen, Peter 107, 128, 173, 216
van Til, Cornelius 191, 216
Vedas xi
Velleman, David 125, 216
Vishnu 18
Volf, Miroslav 75, 78, 96, 216

Wainwright, William 61, 92, 163, 216
Ward, Keith 162, 216
Weakness of will 125
Weintraub, Ruth 135, 216
Westminster Catechism 196
Wierenga, Edward 82, 163–4, 166, 168, 217
Wilkenfeld, Daniel 85, 217

Williams, Bernard 33, 217
Williamson, Timothy 14, 31, 64, 91, 104, 157, 194, 217
Wilsch, Tobias 85, 217
Wilson, Jessica 31, 86, 217
Wisdom 185, 195
Wittgenstein, Ludwig 6
Wolff, Johanna 84, 217

Woltersdorff, Nicholas 189, 217
Wong, Hong Yu 156, 214

Xenophanes 80–81
Xenophanian 83

Zacharias, Ravi 191
Zagzebski, Linda 189, 217